The Cossacks fle.. .. ... furniture and emptying closets and cupboards.

"I want my daughter back," Dovid repeated, pretending he was not the one who rescued her.

"Are you a gambling man?" Aleksandrov smiled.

"I'll make you a wager." Dovid sized up Aleksandrov. "We arm wrestle, and if I win, you back off, and I get my daughter back." He stood resolute as though unaware that he was outnumbered and outgunned.

"And if I win, what do I get?" Aleksandrov's nostrils flared, and he smiled with amusement.

"My other daughter." Dovid stood eyeball to eyeball with Aleksandrov. Neither backed down.

The dragoon gathered around the table, and broken glass screeched beneath their boots. Aleksandrov removed his saber and his tunic. Hairy as a bear, he stepped close to the table with his right foot forward and placed his elbow on the table.

Dovid removed his wool coat and rolled up the sleeves of his white shirt. While physical strength mattered, he knew this was as much about positioning as strength. He placed his elbow on the table, tightened his core muscles, and opposed Aleksandrov. The two men gripped each other's hand. The goal was to pin the other's arm onto the surface of the table, the winner's arm over the loser's.

Mikola slammed his palm on the table, and the wrestling began. In an instant, merriment filled the room, and the Cossacks began their howls of encouragement and support for their commandant.

Anna's Promise

by

D.G. Schulman

Anna's Promise

Cover Art by *Rae Monet, Inc.*

The Wild Rose Press, Inc.
PO Box 708
Adams Basin, NY 14410-0708
Visit us at www.thewildrosepress.com

Publishing History
First Edition, 2023
Trade Paperback ISBN 978-1-5092-4701-1
Digital ISBN 978-1-5092-4702-8

Published in the United States of America

Dedication

For the boy next door, who gave me a Royal electric typewriter when I turned sweet sixteen and has never stopped believing in me. Stew, I love you forever.

Acknowledgments

Thanks to my husband, Stewart Schulman, for putting up with me retreating to my office for hours every night for years, and for providing encouragement when I needed it most. Thanks to my mother, Anne Klempner (of blessed memory), for filling my childhood with rich stories of her youth and the life of her family in Siedlce, Poland, including details so vivid that those who passed before I was born are part of who I am today. I'm indebted to my daughters, Rachel and Chava, who walked that fine line of constructive criticism and support and provided deep insights into all aspects of character and story.

I'm grateful to my dear friend and writing companion, Helen Hedger, for her endless optimism, inspiration, and willingness to read, edit, and reread, and to my trusted readers; you know who you are.

And finally, sincere thanks to Rhonda Penders, President/Editor-in-Chief, The Wild Rose Press, who remembers what it feels like to be an unpublished author and was always responsive and respectful. I'm forever indebted to Josette Arthur, my editor, who was kind, patient, and usually right. Thank you, Jo, for your attention to detail and for signing up to make *Anna's Promise* the best it could be.

Chapter One—Far Out

Southwood, Michigan
January 1975

Ben Friedman hated large parties, especially when they required a tie. He dreaded the thought of small talk and already felt uneasy as he moved with the crowd under rows of grand chandeliers that cast a glow over him. The doors to the ballroom swung open, displaying an elegant room set with white tablecloths, exotic centerpieces with birds of paradise soaring, and banquet tables spread with enough food to feed a small country.

This was the year he and his friends would celebrate their rite of passage into adulthood. It was five thirty p.m. Saturday night, January 11, 1975, and Ben's extended family joined over two hundred of the Steins' closest family, friends, and acquaintances in celebrating Alan's bar mitzvah. Ben and Alan had been best friends since kindergarten. Ben would do his best to be sociable.

The Raleigh House was, hands down, the most elegant and popular venue around. Even so, Ben thought, this was way over the top. His friends looked up to him, literally as he towered over them with his broad swimmer's shoulders. They whistled to him from inside the ballroom where they gathered. Like Ben, all the boys were dressed in electric polyester suits, and many wore eyeglasses the size of cocktail coasters. The girls from his class hovered awkwardly over the boys in their platform shoes, but none were taller than him. It seemed to him they all wore braces and maxi dresses and had enormous hair in different colors. Every hand held a mocktail—all with colorful paper cocktail parasols.

Ben serpentined through the crowd, dodging Ellen, who could talk more about nothing than anyone he knew. She had been trying to catch up with him since the service at the temple that morning. He smiled, relishing the memory of sitting in the back row of the temple, making wisecracks with Howard and Ricky while Alan delivered his coming-of-age speech on the burning bush. Ellen was enrolled in his grandma's dance classes and was always offering to partner with him. He knew she'd had a crush on him since the third grade.

"Hey." Howard sidled up alongside Ben and took a long swig of the mock screwdriver he held.

"I don't think I'll ever get used to these over-the-top celebrations," Ben said. Of course the Steins would take it up a notch, but he didn't get the point. After this momentous "rite of passage," nothing would change except the Bar Mitzvah Club would be over and Hebrew school would be a thing of the past. All the hoopla reminded him of a going-out-of-business sale.

Ben looked right and left and was relieved to find Ellen had changed course and met up with the rest of the girls in their class.

"This party is far out." Howard scanned the crowd and then focused on Ben. "You seem totally stressed."

"This just isn't my scene."

"Take a chill pill, dude. Your bar mitzvah is still months away."

Ben was comforted that he didn't need to elaborate.

Howard got him. He liked that they had each other's back.

James Taylor's "How Sweet It Is" blared from the orchestra. Colored lights reflected off a large mirrored disco ball suspended from the ceiling above the dance floor. The music stopped, and the master of ceremonies asked everyone to find their tables.

"Ladies and gentlemen, please put your hands together and welcome our bar mitzvah boy, Alan Stein!"

Applause exploded, and the overhead lights went dark. The red and blue lights on the disco stage flashed. The Bee Gees' "You Should be Dancing" began to play. Alan strutted onto the stage in white bell-bottoms, a black nylon disco shirt open at the neck, and a white vest and jacket. He gyrated across the floor, rolled his shoulders, and planted one hand on his hip while he pointed into the crowd and rotated to cover the room. His classmates screamed. They stood on their seats, clapped, and kept the beat.

Alan mesmerized the room. Ben rolled his eyes in disbelief. Only Alan could pull this off. The music and his energy transformed him into another being. The practiced signature disco moves took over. His hips swayed, and he covered the length of the dance floor strutting, did his box shuffle, and then shifted to the classic hip-and-point move. Next, he slid onto the floor in splits and crossed the stage in knee drops.

"How did he do that?" Howard exclaimed.

When the music stopped, Alan was surrounded by a crowd of friends and family. The MC announced, "Ladies and gentlemen, please join us on the dance floor now. As Van McCoy says, let's 'Do the Hustle'!"

Ben searched for Grandpa Mo and Grandma Ann in

the crowd and found them entering the ballroom together just in time. With a sassy salt-and-pepper pixie haircut, Grandma was dressed to the nines in a black diamond mink over an apricot sequin cocktail dress. No one had a grandmother like he did, Ben thought. At seventy-four, she still had the lithe body and energy of a dancer. As the first grandchild, he always felt that he was their favorite.

"I was worried you weren't coming. Is everything okay?" Ben met them in front of the dance floor.

"Fine, honey, we just needed to wait until sunset." Grandma gave Ben a quick hug and handed her coat off to Grandpa.

"Why?" Ben frowned, perplexed.

"We don't drive until Sabbath ends. It's probably time we talked about that." Grandpa shook Ben's hand, pulled him in, and gave him a couple of quick slaps on the back.

Ben nodded, took his grandma's hand, and walked her to the dance floor. That made sense and explained why they always had Friday night dinner at Grandma and Grandpa's house. Ricky and Howard hooted, and Howard punched Ben in the arm. Ben rubbed his arm and refocused his attention to the moment. The orchestra started, and Grandma swung her arms and clapped with every major beat.

"It's four/four time," she said softly to Ben below her breath. "One, two, three, and…"

Ben copied her moves, right, left, right, tap.

"Keep your hands moving." Grandma nodded and pumped her hands in circles like a bicycle, smiling all the while at Ben. "Twirl to the right, clap. Twirl to the left, clap."

Howard pulled Ricky, a member of their Bar

Mitzvah Club, and some other friends into the line next to Ben and his grandma. A line formed behind them, and in synchronization, they all pointed up-down four times with their right pointer finger. Grandma called out the moves, and they followed her into the chicken dance.

"Roll hands, wings right, wings left, right, left, turn, and close."

They started again in a new direction.

In no time, both the old and young guests were lined up to do the hustle, some learning for the first time. Ben was awed at how his grandma moved gracefully, flowing through the moves with a deliberate definition that allowed the others to copy. Seeing her one with the music, enjoying herself, made him happy. When the orchestra ended the extended dance, he got out of the way, making room for the many guests crowded around his grandma wanting to learn more about her dance classes.

Sweaty and breathless, the boys fled the dance floor. "Let's get a drink." Ben wrapped his arms around Howard and Ricky's shoulders and led them toward the bar. The girls gravitated to the photo booths where they grabbed a pair of glitter peace glasses, a mustache, guitar, or sign reading *Can you Dig it*, *Far Out*, or *Groovy*. They struck a pose in groups.

"Let's raid the shrimp bar." Alan's energy was like a wave that pushed the group in another direction. "Mountains of shrimp on ice." He raised his arms, bowed theatrically, and gestured toward an enormous table of ice strewn with mounds of pink shrimp, lemons, and bowls of classic cocktail sauce.

Ben had never seen anything like it before. Alan dipped a shrimp in cocktail sauce and ceremoniously fed it to his girlfriend, Shari.

"Ben, try some," Alan urged. The photographer turned to the group of friends, covering them with bursts of bright light.

"I've never had shrimp." Ben eyed the shrimp cautiously.

"Then you haven't lived. I once ate thirty-eight shrimp." Alan let out a delighted chuckle and filled a plate for Ben.

Rubbery. But he liked the cocktail sauce with a kick of horseradish.

"Let's see who can eat the most shrimp." Alan doled out generous servings that didn't even make a dent in the bar.

They each scarfed down a half dozen in less than thirty seconds.

"This sauce is hot." His lips tingled.

"It's not that hot." Alan baited Ben to continue the contest.

The band played "YMCA," and the girls screamed and ran from the photo booth to the dance floor. They lined up and danced in synchronized moves, forming the letters with their bodies.

Ben watched, amused. His lips and tongue itched. *Too much cocktail sauce.* His new suit was suddenly uncomfortable, and he tugged at the tie. He went to the bar to get a ginger ale. Howard followed and stood behind him in line. Ben waited and scratched his chest.

Howard inhaled another half dozen shrimp. "Far-out party, eh?"

"Yeah, right on." Ben scratched his arms.

"Are you okay?" Howard stepped closer to Ben. "You've got some kind of rash. Hey, buddy, you look like the Pillsbury Doughboy. What's going on?" Howard's eyes widened, and his mouth gaped open.

Ben dropped his plate and grasped at his collar, which was tightening around his throat. He slumped to the red floral carpet, struggling to breathe. The sound became distorted, and he seemed to be looking at the room through a narrow tube. He felt like his six-year-old self, thrashing underwater in Lake Erie, unable to get air.

"*Help*," Howard yelled, over the blaring speakers. "Ben's in trouble!" He ran to the bartender and pulled him to Ben. "He's going to die. Do something!"

Instantaneously, a crowd formed around him. Murmuring and whispering swept through the hall. Vibration from the floor infused Ben's body, like a stampede of elephants running through the ballroom. He trembled and heard distorted voices shouting from all directions.

"It's Ben Friedman," someone exclaimed. "He's collapsed!"

The room went eerily quiet. The music stopped.

"Call 911!" His father, Steven, hollered and touched his shoulder.

"Ben, it's Mom." His mother, Aliza, knelt beside him, ripped off his tie, and opened his shirt. Suddenly, she yelled, "His face is turning blue. He can't breathe!"

The squeezing pressure on his chest was unbearable. Pain ran through his arms, neck, and back. He felt a hot flush across his face and neck. Intense dizziness consumed him, and he fell into a dark tunnel.

Chapter Two—Names

Southwood, Michigan
January 1975

Ben lay unconscious in the hospital bed on a ventilator, providing life-sustaining oxygen. He was drifting in and out, between worlds. He looked down from an aerial view. Tension rose from his family and the medical team huddling around him, and their whispers reached him past the hiss of the ventilator.

Grandpa tapped lightly at the hospital room door and entered in a camel cashmere overcoat, marching like a soldier. He had a full head of silver hair. A tall man who presented as all ankles and wrists with a long square beard followed him. Unlike Rabbi Greene at the family's Reformed Temple, who dressed like a regular guy, this rabbi wore a black fedora-type hat, and everything he wore was black or white. Ben had never seen him before. His suit was black, and his shirt was white. Grandpa gave Mom a quick hug and introduced Rabbi Silverstein to his father and the team of doctors.

Grandpa sat beside Ben on the bed and took his hand, the one without the IV, and held it to his lips. Grandpa's shallow breaths matched the hissing rhythm of the ventilator. The "hospital smell" laden with alcohol, drugs, and disinfectants was overpowering.

"Has he awoken?" Grandpa asked.

The team of somber doctors shook their heads. "Ben is in a coma caused by anaphylaxis."

"So, what are you doing?"

"We've done all we can. We need to give him time."

Rabbi Silverstein sat beside Ben, recited some psalms, and Mom broke down sobbing. *The way they are acting, you'd think I was going to die.*

"What is *he* doing here?" Dad asked Grandpa in a hushed tone, nodding toward the rabbi.

"Rabbi Silverstein is a long-time friend and my rabbi. He wanted to see Ben before making a recommendation."

"He has a recommendation?" Dad scoffed. "The doctors are telling me my son may not make it." His voice cracked.

They can't be serious. Ben was incredulous and looked down at himself on the ventilator for the first time. It was weird, and he could not believe what he saw.

Rabbi Silverstein stepped into the circle of family and doctors. The rhythmic sound of the breathing machine was like white noise containing all frequencies across the spectrum of audible sound.

"The idea that changing one's name can change one's life is part of Jewish life. The practice comes from the Talmud. The world was created with words, and the letters of the Hebrew alphabet have powerful spiritual energy. When someone is dangerously sick, the names Chaim, Hebrew for life, or Rafael, God has healed, are traditionally added to help them heal," Rabbi Silverstein explained.

"This is ridiculous." Dad snorted.

"Do it." Mom choked. "Add life to his name." She reached for Grandpa's hand.

"We'll do it first thing in the morning at the prayer service during the Torah reading," Rabbi Silverstein said. "Your father will be called up, and we'll add Chaim to Ben's name and say the blessing for him to have a complete healing."

Now you're talking! Ben liked this rabbi and was glad to see someone thinking outside the box. He could always count on Grandpa to bring in the big guns at the last minute. Ben seemed to be the only one in the room who felt that everything would be okay.

His earliest memories were with Grandpa and Grandma and filled him with joy. They'd often spent Sundays in the summer on Grandpa's thirty-eight-foot cabin cruiser, *Sunchaser*. His sister, Estie, would stretch out on a red cabana-stripe beach towel, tanning herself with baby oil on the front deck with a stack of teen magazines. He'd sit up high on the flying bridge with Grandpa who would explain the navigation system and the controls. Grandpa wore a navy captain's hat perched on top of his thick salt-and-pepper hair. His hands were large, rough, and bronzed. Ben wore a matching child-sized navy captain's hat, and sometimes Grandpa let him take the helm and drive the boat through the azure water of Lake Erie when the weather was good. The long lazy days allowed him the chance to ask Grandpa what it was like when he was growing up in Siedlce, and sometimes Grandpa would tell him stories about his mom and his uncle Ira when they were kids just four years apart.

Now a memory filtered through of one Sunday, the summer before Joel was born, when Uncle Ira and Aunt Nanci were engaged, and they'd all gone together out to Strawberry Island, a sand bar and swimming shoal. Grandma stood in the shallow water at the side of the boat, zinc oxide on her nose, preparing lunch. The rocking of the boat while anchored made her seasick.

His parents, uncle, and aunt played Frisbee like carefree young couples in Lake Erie, and the sun glistened on the water like nothing could dispel the gaiety of the afternoon. His mom and Aunt Nanci laughed and waded in the sand bar. Mom was buoyant and pregnant. The cold mud squished between his toes. Aunt Nanci's face was fresh with a sunburnt nose and cheekbones, golden highlights in her auburn whorl of curls. They got distracted, wandered away from the Frisbee toss, and shared confidences as women do. Both were on the precipice of a new exciting stage of life. Mom was expecting another baby, and Aunt Nanci was planning her and Uncle Ira's wedding. They'd clicked from the beginning, more like sisters than sisters-in-law, sharing every intimate detail. He would never forget that day for a couple of reasons. It was a time when anything was possible, and the bonds of his family seemed unbreakable.

Chapter Three—"The Blue Danube"

Siedlce, Poland
December 31, 1914

"Wake up, Chana." Mama touched Chana lightly on the shoulder.

Chana Weisman pulled the wool blanket over her head and groaned.

"It's five o'clock, and the water carrier hasn't come. There isn't a drop of water in the barrel. You must go to the pump and bring water."

Chana thrust the blanket off and glared at her sister Sora, willing her awake. She watched her sleep and could see her breath. Sora was sixteen, almost two years her senior. For as long as Chana could remember, Sora was the pretty and popular one. And Chana was the smart one who knew how to get things done.

Soundlessly, Chana rolled off the horsehair mattress and pulled on her leggings and skirt, which she held together around her slender waist with a safety pin since the button had fallen off and been lost. She drew in a deep breath as if she could make herself small enough to avoid contact with the gray scratchy wool sweater she slipped over her head. She irritably lifted the top of the water barrel from which they would fill the samovar and found the wooden barrel empty. Her stomach growled like a tiger. The mantel clock sounded a full strike and counted five hours.

Startled, Chana dropped the lid. The wobbling wood clattered, and the sound exploded throughout the room. Raizel cried out, half awake, and Chana ran to soothe the baby back to sleep. She then put on the hand-me-down black wool coat (grateful to have it) and ankle-high button shoes, picked up the wooden pail, and slipped silently into the frozen dawn, closing the battered apartment door behind her.

Their white two-story apartment house on Piekna Strasse had been one of the loveliest in the Jewish quarter. The windows were adorned with shutters, and balconies decorated with flower boxes on the second floor overlooked the steady stream of horse-drawn carriages that traveled the wide and busy street. The Weisman family occupied one of four street-level apartments. The Prusses owned the building and had occupied the entire second story until a cannonball was shot through the outside wall of the second story in September 1914 during the occupation. The Pruss family had fled, abandoning most of their belongings, but the black scorched gaping hole remained. Each time Chana entered or left the building, the blackened wall reminded her of the night of endless explosions culminating in the terrifying blasts through the apartment wall.

A crow flew overhead, and the snow crunched beneath her shoes. The bitter wind stung as it whipped across her face. Chana thought winter in Siedlce had never felt so cold and brutal. Since August 1st, when Germany declared war on Russia, nothing had been normal. In November, the Russians attempted to take Warsaw. Then the Germans attacked the Russians at Lodz, forcing their withdrawal. German or Russian soldiers occupied every city, and Cossacks had made Siedlce their home. There was little food to be had, provisions were scarce, and the Cossacks took what there was for themselves.

Chana thought all of Europe had gone mad. She stopped to rewrap the scarf tightly around her raven hair and slender neck and then ran to the well. Breathless, she pumped repeatedly to no avail. Her hands were numb from the cold.

From nowhere a group of drunken Cossacks appeared and formed a ring around her like a cage while making crude remarks in Russian. It was 5:20 a.m. on Thursday, December 31, 1914, in Siedlce, Poland, and the New Year's drinking had already begun. Chana steeled herself and pretended not to understand their filthy minds. One tall Cossack brandishing his saber stepped forward and looked Chana brazenly in the eye.

"The cold makes you pretty."

Chana didn't believe him. The Cossacks roared with laughter at her helplessness. The tall one pushed Chana aside and pumped the well firmly with his free hand. Momentarily, water burst forth and overflowed the wooden pail. Chana snatched the pail and broke through the cage of laughter. As she ran, the icy water splashed about her feet like bayonets.

Chana slammed the solid door on the blustery wind and set down the wooden pail. She hugged herself to stop the shivering and welcomed the warmth of the fire from the stove. Her ten-year-old brother, Yitzchak, and four-year-old sister Reva played on the floor, stacking cups into tall towers. Mama was in the kitchen forming loaves of bread and spooning applesauce into baby Raizel's open mouth.

"That water's not from the bath house, I hope," Mama said. "You know there's been another outbreak of cholera?"

Sora waltzed across the room humming, spun gracefully, and embraced Chana. "You're a jewel to get water on this frigid morning." She put her right hand on Chana's waist and placed Chana's left hand on her right shoulder. Chana clasped her sister's hand at shoulder height as Sora began to hum the repetitive famous movement of Strauss' "The Blue Danube." "Dun-dun-dun-dun-dun, dink-dink, dink-dink."

Sora led Chana in a waltz around the apartment from the small kitchen into the large dining and living room. They turned while making a classic box on the mottled wooden floor. Chana was transported to the mesmerizing performance of Strauss' waltz at the Warsaw Philharmonic last summer, before it was destroyed by Russian bombers. That night was a dream now as though from another life.

As they glided around the wooden floor, Sora stumbled upon a spoon and a pot that she guessed Raizel had been banging together and then abandoned. The sisters rolled to the floor laughing and split apart.

Sora exclaimed, "How did you get that stubborn pump to work?" She filled the samovar with water and turned up the fire on the brass urn to boil.

"I had help from a few strong men." Chana squatted in front of the hulking cast-iron behemoth wood stove to warm her numb hands and feet. She inhaled the aroma of baking bread. Yitzchak and Reva huddled around, knocked her off-balance, and climbed into her lap.

"Those miserable Cossacks, I suspect." Mama snuck a quick look at Chana as she mopped up the applesauce from Raizel's face. She then slid more loaves into the oven.

"They didn't bother me, Mama. It's always the same, each one trying to outdo the other." Chana unwrapped the scarf, and her dark hair cascaded over her shoulders.

Reva snatched up the scarf and put it over her head to hide her blond hair.

"Did they touch you?" Mama demanded.

"No, they're all talk and bravado." Chana hung her coat on the mahogany coatrack and umbrella stand by the door. "Sora, I suspect Aaron will be at the upshern celebration tonight?" She changed the subject to assuage her mother's fears.

"He may be." Sora turned away. "It's all the same to me."

"That dreamy dancing bespeaks otherwise." Chana spread butter on a hot roll and giggled. "He seeks you out like a thirsty man in search of water."

"I'm going to Masha, the dressmaker," Sora fired back and slipped into her coat.

"Picking up a new dress for tonight?" Chana teased as she tore off pieces of the hot bread.

"It happens that Masha can no longer pay me to write letters to her relatives in America, so we're exchanging services," Sora snapped and turned to leave.

"Sora," Mama called before Sora escaped, "please drop Yitzchak at cheder and stop by the meat market to help Tatty so he can close early and join us at the upshern."

Sora nodded in agreement, helped Yitzchak into his coat, and slammed the heavy door behind them. The family photos on the wall trembled. Chana didn't remember her father ever working such long hours. Since the war began, he was out late at night, seeking capital to be returned when meat was sold and traveling to rural villages to buy cattle.

Mama shook her head at Chana and clicked her tongue. "Tsk, tsk, tsk… Chana, you're set on mortifying your sister with impertinent comments."

Chana laughed with amusement and put on an apron. "What can I do to help, Mama?" She kissed baby Raizel's blond head. "Please, tell me again, Mama, what will it be like when we go to America?"

Chapter Four—The Mission

Southwood, Michigan
January 1975

"Hey, there! Good to have you back. Thirsty?" Mom handed Ben a Styrofoam cup with a straw now that the ventilator and IV had been removed.

He blinked his mother into focus. She was still in the turquoise taffeta ball gown she'd worn to the bar mitzvah Saturday night. She must not have left the hospital.

"My lips and tongue feel thick." He was having trouble getting his mouth working again. He sipped ice water through a straw.

"You gave us quite a scare." Mom's mascara streaked down her face, a sign of the drama he'd caused.

"Sorry I ruined the party. What time is it?"

"Almost nine p.m. on Monday. It's been a few days we'll never forget. Dad, Joel, and Estie should be here soon."

"A few days?" Ben was agitated. "I've been unconscious for a few days?" He bolted up in bed.

"We're just glad to have you back. What's the last thing you remember?"

"Not being able to breathe and then a sensation of floating." He felt like he'd been run over by a truck.

"Everyone was so worried and just wanted you to be okay. But I think we'll pass on the shrimp at your bar mitzvah." Mom smiled tenderly and winked at Ben.

"I feel so stupid. I'm sure everyone knows what happened." Ben was mortified as he remembered the crowds around him while he nearly suffocated in the ballroom of the Raleigh House.

"Well, there's nothing for you to feel stupid about."

"So, exactly what happened?" Ben shuddered as an image of the disco ball flashed before his eyes, and the anxiety returned.

"Honey, you had a severe allergic reaction to the shrimp. Your whole body reacted. Your throat swelled, and you couldn't breathe. When your blood pressure dropped dramatically, you went into a coma."

"I can't believe I almost suffocated in a room full of air." He couldn't shake the feeling.

"The doctor says you're out of the woods now."

"I only remember images and pieces. Is there anything I should know?" Ben held his breath.

"We're going to have to make some changes. Even trace amounts of shellfish can trigger a serious reaction now. The doctor advised us to avoid eating in restaurants completely."

"I don't get it. I've eaten in restaurants all my life without any problems."

"Seems that shellfish allergies typically emerge during teenage or adult years."

"Knock, knock." Dad pushed open the door to Ben's hospital room, and Estie and Joel followed him in. Estie carried a large floral arrangement with a bird of paradise that looked like one of the centerpieces from the bar mitzvah.

"Is this a good time to visit?" Grandma peeked in and smiled at Ben. When he grinned back, she went to him and planted a kiss on his head. "Grandpa's waiting on valet parking. He'll be right up. How are you feeling?"

Ben coughed. The bouquet of lilies and roses surrounding the exotic bird of paradise was overwhelming in the small hospital room.

"Those flowers are irritating Ben." The words leaped to Grandma's lips. With concern creasing her forehead, she graciously took the centerpiece from Estie and carried it out of the room.

"You're looking better, son." Dad loosened his tie and sat down at the foot of the bed. While Joel climbed up and onto Ben, Estie clung to her father.

"Breathing again." Ben grinned sheepishly and looked down at the hospital gown to ensure he wasn't exposed. His little brother had found the electric controls and was now raising and lowering the height of the bed like they were at an amusement park. He was glad to see his near death hadn't spoiled Joel's playful spirit.

"Stop that, Joel!" Dad's dangling feet were unable to reach the floor, and he wrestled the hand control from Joel. Estie started to bawl.

The night nurse followed Grandma back into the room and was visibly disturbed by the commotion. "Visiting hours are over for today." She took the remote control and lowered the bed to its proper position. She gripped Ben's wrist and took his pulse, which was rapid. "All visitors out." Her directive was nonnegotiable.

Grandma squeezed Ben's free hand and gave him a quick hug before the nurse began herding the family out. "Grandpa so wanted to see you. Well, we'll get back to our scheduled classes next week."

"Ready to boogie." Ben smiled at his grandma as

she backed out of the room, rolling her hands in circles like she was in the middle of the hustle.

Mom sat at the edge of the vinyl chair, and Estie and Joel flew into her arms for good-bye hugs. She wrapped her right arm around Estie and her left arm around Joel in a tight group hug. "Missed me, huh?" Mom kissed the tops of their heads, and Dad placed his hands on Mom's shoulders, from behind, and kissed the top of her glossy chestnut hair.

"I'll walk you down to the lobby." Mom stood and directed the group toward the door while the night nurse scowled. "Maybe we'll catch up with Dad."

"Do you need anything, son?"

"I'm okay." Ben smiled. He felt the strong connection of his family and didn't want them to go. They smothered him in hugs and kisses before they left, escorted out by the nurse.

A sudden knock at the door startled Ben, and his grandpa peered in. "Are you up for a visitor?" he said, a meaningful look in his eyes.

"Grandpa! I'm so glad to see you. The nurse just booted everybody out. They must have been going down one elevator while you were coming up in another."

"Well, that worked out." Grandpa surveyed the small hospital room. They were alone. A smile curled the corners of his mouth. "I brought you a few things to keep you occupied." He handed Ben a brown bag.

"I think I remember you being here with someone I'd never seen before." Ben caught his grandpa's eye before he reached in the bag and pulled out a deck of cards, a few sci-fi paperback books, and a colorful cube. "What's this?" He held up the cube, each side sporting nine squares of yellow, red, blue, orange, white, and green.

"It's a 3-D puzzle called Rubik's Cube. It was invented last year by a friend of mine, a Hungarian sculptor and professor of architecture. To solve the puzzle, twist the cube until each side is a solid color." Grandpa's green eyes sparkled, and he sat on the bed beside Ben.

"Very cool." Ben started twisting.

"Just keep in mind it took the inventor thirty days to solve it." Grandpa winked.

"So, you *were* here, weren't you? Some of it really happened, and some of it was just memories. The recollections of Sundays we spent on *Sunchaser* when I was growing up were so vivid. They felt so real. We were talking about things. I was wondering about Poland; were there boats in Siedlce?" Ben focused intently on his grandpa.

"Not cabin cruisers like *Sunchaser*. There were row boats that we sometimes took out on the river. Siedlce lies between two small rivers, the Muchawka and the Helenka. The Helenka was the most scenic, but that was before the war. One of the reasons I liked settling in Michigan was because there are so many lakes and so much water. When I saw all the water, I had to have a boat."

"Did it turn out the way you hoped it would, I mean, coming to America?" Ben had heard stories about Grandpa Mo and Grandma Ann getting married in 1915 when they were just seventeen and fifteen years old, in the throes of WWI. Grandma had told him how they traveled by wagon to Holland and took a steamship to New York.

"That's a big question, Ben. For now, I'd say I

imagined some things would be different, but I shouldn't complain. Life has been good, and we are blessed."

"What did you hope would be different?"

"I guess I'd hoped I'd be able to hang on to and give over more of the good and rich pieces of our old life, but they didn't fit in America, and no one was interested."

"I'm interested. Share them with me. You know, I'm good at puzzles. I can make the pieces fit."

"I'll bet you can." Grandpa laughed. His eyes shone, and he pulled Ben close to him in a hug and kissed his neck. "Do you remember coming into Emerald City Marina that day when the flags were extended straight out on their poles and the sky was greenish?"

"Sure, that is one of my most vivid memories. I was in position on the deck, spring line secured through the boat cleat, rope in hand." He looked up to his grandpa as he had that day high on the flying bridge, waiting for direction.

"It wasn't easy in those winds. I was counting on you to dock that cruiser." Grandpa took off his cap and ran his hand through his thick silver hair.

Ben recalled the roar of the engines had quieted as they entered the *no-wake* zone of the marina. The boat reeled at the slower speed.

"Drop a fender over the side to cushion contact," his grandpa directed. "Get ready with that spring line. She's pushing us strong from the northwest."

Once they turned into the well, Ben jumped from the boat deck to the dock and leaned in to hold the boat. The ropes burned through his hands as he affixed them in a cleat. Grandpa had thrown the engines into idle, and Ben had secured ropes on the stern side.

"That's my boy." Grandpa winked and grinned.

"Even in those winds, you made a smooth landing. I couldn't have done it without you. I'm counting on you, Ben. Without you, we'll all be adrift. It's up to you now." He shifted, about to stand, preparing to leave.

Ben reached for Grandpa's hand. "Wait, I need you, Grandpa." He detained him for another moment.

"Don't be frightened, Ben. Nothing can stop you. I can see that you're ready to take on the world. You're guided by a light from within. I've done all I can. Now this mission is yours, but I'll be with you. You'll be well soon. You've got this."

"I don't know what you mean." Ben was upset by his grandpa's words. "What mission is mine?"

Grandpa put an arm around Ben's shoulders, and Ben felt his grandpa's strength imbue him. Suddenly sleepy from the medication, he rested his head on Grandpa's chest and fell into a restless sleep.

The wind picked up, and the color of the water changed from azure to smoldering gray. Grandpa called the couples in from the water using the megaphone. As they swam back to the boat and pulled themselves onto the swim deck, the weather changed. Mom was the first to remove her sunglasses. It had grown dark. Shivering with goose bumps, she wrapped herself in a blue oversized striped beach towel. She handed rolled striped towels of orange, mint, and taupe to Aunt Nancy, Uncle Ira, and Dad.

Bad weather was moving in. The boat rocked from side to side. Grandma hung over the side, and Mom grabbed the rail to keep from losing her balance, especially challenging given her shifting center of gravity. They pulled up the anchor, turned over the twin inboard engines, and Ben pushed the throttles forward.

He was on the bridge, wearing the captain's hat. The smell of diesel fuel wafted over the deck. Hearing above the roar of the engines was now impossible. The rough waters and wind thrust the bow high out of the water and propelled the cruiser toward shore. His heart raced. Handling the boat on his own in those winds with that tide would be nearly impossible. If they crashed or capsized, they would take on water and sink in the destructive power of the massive storm.

Ben awoke from an agitated sleep to a commotion in the hospital room. He took a moment to remember where he was. His tongue and lips still felt thick, and he was in the bed with the electric pendant that controlled the head and foot motors. The walls of the small white private room were covered with monitors. He felt his grandpa's presence. He bolted up and saw nurses trying to awaken his mother, who was asleep in the vinyl chair. The clock read 3:05 a.m.

"It's Grandpa," Ben blurted.

Mom startled awake and jumped to her feet. In a moment she sat on the bed, enveloped Ben in her embrace, and rocked with him as he shifted and sobbed.

"Grandpa died," he said as a wave of grief washed over him. He broke down and trembled, gasping to catch his breath.

"It was just a bad dream." Mom stroked his thick disheveled hair and quivered. "Grandpa is home asleep with Grandma."

"Mrs. Friedman," the nurse gently interrupted. "There's an urgent call for you at the nurses' station. They're transferring it here."

"It's too soon for him." Ben began the wheezing that preceded an asthma attack. He couldn't breathe.

"He needs an inhaler." Mom panicked.

"I'll take care of him," the nurse intervened, and he quieted.

The phone on the nightstand lit up and rang. His mother picked up the receiver. "Mom? Why are you up in the middle of the night?"

Ben heard his grandma's voice and envisioned her reclined on the brown velvet chaise lounge in her bedroom, wrapped in her rose-colored chenille robe, and Grandpa on the bed in his blue plaid pajamas.

"He wasn't sleeping well." She was crying.

He visualized her wiping the tears that streamed down her face with her sleeve.

"He kept getting up and said he had heartburn. And when I woke to go to the bathroom, I didn't hear him breathing."

"Mom, we need to call 911." Ben's mother turned away from him and lowered her voice.

"They'll be here. There's the doorbell now. It must be Steven."

"Mom, please put Steven on."

Waiting the thirty seconds to hear Dad's voice amid the shuffling of the phone felt like an eternity. Finally, Ben heard his father's strong voice come through.

"Aliza, the paramedics should be here any minute. Dad is unresponsive."

"I know." Aliza looked over her shoulder at Ben.

"What do you mean, *you know*?"

"It's hard to explain."

His penetrating gaze was on his mother. Ben eavesdropping on family conversations since he was old enough to understand was no secret.

"Ben told me, but I thought it was a bad dream from

26

the medication and everything that has happened. Listen, Ben needs an inhaler or something. He's having difficulty breathing. Please take care of Mom and call me back when you have more information."

Chapter Five—Unpacking

Southwood, Michigan
January 1975

Nanci Rosen dragged the collapsed moving boxes to the second floor of their craftsman-style home. Midway, she stopped on the landing, repositioned her load, and collected her wild auburn hair into a ponytail. Her face warmed beneath the flawless makeup. She wore carefully selected fitness wear, leggings and a tank that were well suited for packing. She was thin but rarely exercised and fought back the suspicion that her life was coming apart.

Throughout four years of medical school and three years of residency, the third bedroom had been Ira's office. It smelled of Marlboro cigarettes and was exactly as he'd left it—his gym bag spilling its contents onto the wooden floor, the bookshelf overloaded with medical textbooks and journals, the desk strewn with business cards and prescription notepads. A border of family photos seemed to contain it all, but not really. She didn't know where to start and fell into her husband's high-back ergonomic office chair, which swiveled from side to side and glided effortlessly across the gleaming wooden floor.

She constructed some boxes, securing them with tape. When the photos on the desk caught her attention, she reached out to touch the picture of the three of them taken when Rubie was only fifteen months old—throwing her blond head back and laughing. Nanci stared at Ira's receding hairline and studied his warm chocolate eyes. It was as though a machine were whirring inside him. His hunger was one of the things that attracted her to him. He couldn't get enough of her.

Nanci stepped over the barbells and heard herself counting repetitions as Ira sweated and pumped iron. She recalled his inner stillness, which surfaced only when he was in motion. She slid the white doctor coats off their hangers. She smelled him, a bit of musk and spice, and intense longing swept over her. They had mapped out their life. They'd carefully planned the timing of their marriage, their pregnancy, their first home, but single parenting wasn't part of the plan.

She touched the scar above her upper lip, won in an ice-skating competition when she was twelve, as she read the words on the school of medicine diploma before taking it down. She'd never forget the tireless hours invested in that medical degree and Ira's elation on graduation day. Carefully, she wrapped the mahogany frame in the white doctor coats with the red embroidered pockets reading *Dr. Ira Rosen*. She packed away their dreams.

They were so close. Ira only had one more year to finish his orthopedic residency. Moonlighting at the clinics was supposed to relieve the financial pressure. Plus, it gave Ira the extra money he needed to buy Nanci the things he said she deserved, like diamond earrings for her twenty-ninth birthday. She twirled the earring in her right ear.

They'd marked the date she would go off birth

control and they would give Rubie a brother or sister. But that was before he was fired from his orthopedic surgery residency. Before he was convicted on sixty-six counts of drug trafficking and 258 counts of writing illegal prescriptions. She knew all the charges and then the sentence of twenty months.

Nanci threw herself on the desktop and swept the prescription notepads into the box. She didn't understand how all this happened. Ira just said he had been in the wrong place at the wrong time.

She had never been to Minnesota, but in just three days their lives, which were being packed neatly into boxes, were to be relocated. The plan had made sense when she and Ira discussed it with Sydney Blackwell. He was an expert on preparing families for the trauma of incarceration. From the outset he focused on how to keep the family together and not fall apart. By moving, Nanci and Rubie could take advantage of visitation often, maybe even conjugal visits.

Nanci counted seven steps and a landing and then seven more steps, hearing Rubie's singsong voice in her head. She cut herself a plate of brownies for breakfast and sat on a box. One at a time she removed and inspected the family photographs from their respective shelves. Dressed to the nines in coordinating shades of lavender and purple, everyone beamed in the family wedding portrait taken six years ago. The next photograph was Rubie wearing a red wool coat and white knit hat, sitting in a pile of golden leaves with more leaves raining down upon her. Her arms were stretched above her head, like helicopter propellers, after throwing the leaves into the air. Her blue eyes were squeezed shut, and her mouth was wide open, squealing with delight.

The third photo was a close up of just the two of them radiantly smiling at one another, fresh and young, unstoppable. For the first time she focused on Ira's classic white collar protruding above the tuxedo jacket. She'd never thought about white-collar crime before.

Nanci was startled when the phone rang. Sydney Blackwell's number displayed across the screen. She picked it up.

"What's wrong? It's the middle of the night in California." She confirmed the time on the kitchen clock. It was 6:06 a.m. Eastern Standard Time.

"Everything's okay. I didn't mean to scare you. I just got some important information. They're moving Ira." Sydney had made a career of working with families of first-time offenders of white-collar crime, and he was tuned in to prevent triggering events.

"Moving him to where?" She touched the scar above her upper lip and traced the outline of her lips.

"Loretto—seventy miles east of Pittsburgh. This is a win. Loretto is also low security. Not the minimum security we were hoping for, but it's half a day's drive."

"What about Minnesota?" She surveyed the towers of boxes.

"That's why I'm calling you in the wee hours of the morning, Nanci. We talked about this possibility. That's the thing; once you're in the federal system, we don't have any control. They can move Ira at any time. We lobbied for him to be within the standard five hundred miles of home, and Loretto is closer to you than Sandstone, Minnesota. To boot, Loretto has a minimum-security satellite on the grounds. I'm going to work on getting Ira in there."

"What do I do?" Nanci stood and shivered.

"Unpack and plan a visit. I'll be in touch." Sydney's voice was warm and relaxed.

Nanci nearly jumped out of her skin when someone appeared, knocking on the kitchen door. She recognized her brother-in-law, Steven, and fumbled with the door lock and dead bolt to let him in.

"Hey, sister." Steven gave Nanci a quick hug. "I'm afraid I have some bad news."

"Is there any other kind?" She was still looking at the towers of boxes and getting her head around the idea of unpacking what she'd just packed and not moving to Minnesota.

"It's Pa—I just came from there." Steven's conversations with Nanci were historically brief, to the point, and centered around details of family life. "I don't know how to say this, other than to just say it. Pa passed away during the night."

Nanci crumbled onto the kitchen floor in a fit of weeping.

Chapter Six—Moving

Sandstone, Minnesota
January 1975

The tennis courts and golf courses were a myth. It was six a.m., and the lights were blinding, especially bright on the top bunk. The lower bunks were taken by those with seniority. Ira rested his muscular arm across his eyes as he forced himself awake. He felt hungover. Not because he wasn't used to getting up early; he was normally making rounds by six a.m. But now there was no such thing as a good night's sleep. He was awakened at midnight, three a.m., and five a.m. for inmate counts. The guards were required to verify that every inmate was there, in the flesh.

He swung himself over the side, landed softly on the cold linoleum floor, and did his best to make the bed. It was a rule. Ira hadn't made a bed in years. When he used to leave for the hospital, Nanci would still be snuggled in, sleeping deeply, hugging her pillow. Before leaving, he would lean down and kiss her serene face surrounded by a whorl of curly auburn hair.

"I'm not sharing a john with a Jew!" Hecter, the obtuse occupant of the lower bunk, bellowed, and a tattooed arm hurled a boot at Ira while he sat on the toilet.

Ira missed the ordinary things: bathroom doors, a belt, car keys in his pocket, and a cigarette whenever he wanted. He missed driving and deciding what he wanted to eat. He missed calling Nanci in the middle of the day. Most of all he missed Rubie. He had ninety minutes from lights on to shower, dress, and eat breakfast until he clocked in for his job, which at the moment was laundry. Not that he knew anything about laundry.

He entered the stark concrete shower. A rat scampered across the floor and squeezed into the drain grate. The smell and feel of wet concrete suddenly reminded him of the open poolside showers of Edgewood Swim Club where he had spent the best summers of his life.

"Marco," a twelve-year-old version of himself called out, and he felt himself gliding through the deep-blue waters with his arms waving beneath the satin surface. He wasn't afraid to jump off the high dive, as others were. Edgewood was one of the few pools with a high dive back then. He liked competitive diving for pennies, dimes, and nickels. Quarters were in the twelve-foot deep end and were the ultimate prize.

Ira hadn't thought of Edgewood for two decades. Every summer day he and fifty other kids from Southwood Gardens had congregated and spent their days at Edgewood. They ate hot dogs or hamburgers and played ping-pong when it rained. Father-son sleepovers, with the fathers playing cards all night, were unsurpassed. His dad was an outstanding poker player and taught him Texas Hold'em. The stakes weren't big back then, but his dad was known for pulling the royal flush.

The snack shop served "suicide" drinks, a mixture of all the sodas. Sleeping bags lined the parquet floor of the great room. No one complained that the floor was hard. A piano flanked one wall, and the room was big enough for parties—even bar mitzvahs. The back wall was all sliding glass doors overlooking the pool and grounds where they played volleyball and shuffleboard.

Summers were a collage of night swims, movie nights, limbo contests, and neighborhood barbecues. His dad, Mo Rosen, was one of the community organizers who brought everyone together. Ira had so many friends. Had they read about him in the *Free Press*? Would they learn where he was, and would they visit? Or write?

How great a pool would be now. He smiled when he remembered the twin girl lifeguards at Edgewood whose names he couldn't remember. One of them had webbed toes. When that loud speaker announced, "Adult swim," all the kids had climbed out of the pool at ten minutes to the hour and piled onto the rubber chaise recliners and baked in the sun for what seemed like an eternity. Ira didn't like to wait. He'd go off and play Donkey Kong or Frogger. Labor Day Picnic was the best day of the year. They'd eat all the ice cream left in the freezers.

"Ira Rosen, report." The speaker crackled and jarred him back to the present. He dried himself with the small thin towel and dressed quickly in the issued khakis.

At the office the warden looked up from his paperwork briefly. "Rosen, you're moving. Pack your things."

Ira was shocked. "What?"

"You're moving," the warden repeated with urgency.

"When?" Ira absorbed the meaning of his words.

The warden opened an envelope that was handed to him. "After breakfast." He paused, unfolded a letter, and read it. "Oh, and your father died."

Chapter Seven—Fresh Meat

Siedlce, Poland
January 1915

At ten a.m., the shop bell rang, and the narrow wooden door on Piekna Strasse banged closed behind Mrs. Bialystock, wrapped in a woolen shawl wet with snow. She seemed to walk from side to side rather than forward, schlepping herself to the counter. She hadn't bought on credit until the pogrom of 1906.

Dovid wiped the meat cleaver on his long white butcher's apron, leaving a bloodstain, and hung the cleaver on his belt. He adjusted the bill of his tweed cap and greeted Zalman's wife with the warmth of a friend.

"Mrs. Bialystock, I have your pickled tongue ready for you." Dovid fished the beef from the brine in the barrel. "It's been curing for fourteen days." He wrapped the beef tongue in brown paper and tied the package with string. "It's just how Zalman liked it."

He instantly regretted mentioning Zalman. The pain was still palpable, and he turned the conversation to happier subjects. "How is Ita Miriam and the children?"

"Baruch is turning three, and we're having the upshernish tonight. You'll come to the beit midrash and cut his hair?" Her face lit up when she spoke of Baruch.

"I'm no barber, but I'll take a snip." Dovid winked and smoothed his mustache. After two daughters he remembered when his son, Yitzchak, finally reached his third birthday and the community celebrated the age-old custom of cutting his hair after allowing it to grow untouched from birth. He remembered that his Yitzchak suddenly seemed taller with the snipping of the golden curls. From that day he wore a kippah on his head and tzitzit, the four-cornered fringed garment.

"Esther and the children will be there too. I have something special from the smokehouse for the celebration. Wait just a minute." Dovid rushed to the smokehouse and returned with another hefty brown paper parcel wrapped in string, which he slid across the wooden counter.

He resisted the longing to ask about Ita Miriam's husband, Jakow.

"Reb Weisman, you are too kind, but we both know I can't pay for this." She always addressed him with the respectful title of "Reb" but shook her head to reject the package.

"You're right about that. Esther would be furious with me if I let you pay. It's for the celebration."

He emerged from behind the counter, surprised that she seemed smaller than he remembered. He walked her to her wagon, carrying the package, as he inquired into the rest of Mrs. Bialystock's grandchildren. She didn't argue as Dovid helped her up onto the seat and set the smoked meat beside her. He untied the horse, lovingly known as Shayna, who whinnied and struggled to move the wagon forward. The wagon remained at a standstill, and Shayna strained until she collapsed on her side. Mrs. Bialystock gasped and covered her mouth with her hands.

Shayna scrambled, but like a turtle on its back, she

had fallen into a hollow in the street and was unable to get her feet beneath her to stand. Dovid ran to Shayna, steam rising from her black-and-white spotted torso. He put his hand on her chest and felt the pounding of her heart. Unable to regain her feet, she panicked, and her hooves flailed in the air. He stroked her hot coat and whispered to her, "You're all right, girl. You're all right."

He unhitched her from the wagon and patted her chest until she was calm. He slung two circles of rope around the legs under her and then leaned in with his wide back and shoulders and pulled evenly until Shayna rolled over and scrambled to her feet.

"She needs water." Dovid tied her bridle to a post. Shortly, he returned with a wooden bucket of water. When Shayna refused to drink, he dropped a piece of carrot into the bucket, and she drank greedily until the five-gallon bucket was nearly empty.

Mrs. Bialystock rhythmically repeated, "Good girl, Shayna, good girl."

He re-hitched Shayna and surveyed the wagon. He discovered the right rear wheel was sunk deep into the wet snow and mud. He leaned in and lifted the wagon wheel until it started to roll forward.

"Thank you, Reb Weisman," she called back. "See you at the beit midrash, at three p.m." She waved, and Shayna clopped down Piekna Strasse.

A crowd had gathered outside the meat market, something Dovid tried to avoid. He looked unassuming in his tweed cap and white butcher apron, but with years of manual labor, he had developed a brawny body of iron muscles. He quickly slipped back inside, followed by Noach Stein, a neighboring tobacco shopkeeper with a wild black beard who routinely bartered cigarettes for meat.

Noach haggled with Dovid at the chopping block while he prepared stew beef from a foreshank. The shop bell rang again at 10:40 a.m., and the door banged closed, this time behind three Cossacks in tall black fur hats, knee-high boots, and long coats belted at the waist. They wielded sabers and rifles. In one brutal motion, they grabbed Noach by the arms and threw him into the street.

"How is it, Weisman, that you have meat when there is none?" Commandant Aleksandrov smiled broadly and eyed the beef with the soft, cream-colored fat on the butcher block. He pressed a filthy finger into the red meat, and the hole quickly disappeared, regaining its original shape. "And it's so fresh," he added as his black eyes glistened with hunger.

The smell of fresh meat permeated the shop, not a bad smell, but distinct and especially unmistakable when meat was scarce. The butcher shop was narrow but deep and occupied a short run of street front at the commercial end of Piekna Strasse that generally saw less foot traffic. The black-and-white sign that hung over the door said simply *Weisman's Meat*, and in Hebrew below were the words *kosher* and *shochet*, someone trained in ritual slaughter according to Jewish law.

But Commandant Aleksandrov was unduly intimate with the modest butcher shop. He'd stationed Comrades Vladimir and Mikola at the door and now motioned for them to stride across the scarred floor, leaving a trail of mud. They positioned themselves at the chopping block and stood erect with rifles at their sides.

"You'll wrap those beef cubes and the brisket that goes with them. And don't forget the liver, tongue, and sweetbreads. We're a large and hungry unit." Aleksandrov chortled, his hot breath visible in the cool air. He strutted behind the counter and prodded at cold beef and lamb hanging from wooden pegs in the wall. "Comrades Vladimir and Mikola," he directed them, "load this meat in the wagon."

Dovid was stock-still as the Cossacks cleared the meat from the wall and carried it out the door. When Vladimir and Mikola were outside loading the wagon, Dovid broke the silence. "Commandant, if you take the meat week after week, you'll find one week there's none even for you. Leave enough for me to feed my family, and I won't complain."

"And who will you complain to?" Aleksandrov hissed in Dovid's face. His breath smelled of alcohol and tobacco. His coat carried the scent of sweat and gunpowder.

"This is the third time this month." Dovid spoke matter-of-factly. "I borrowed to buy cattle, and if this meat isn't sold, there will be no more."

"You're a gambling man," Aleksandrov jeered.

Dovid went silent when Vladimir and Mikola returned for the rest of the beef and lamb.

Aleksandrov peered into the hallways and scanned the empty store. "Where's my little bird?" he taunted and then jabbed Dovid in the stomach with the butt of his rifle.

Dovid doubled over.

"Wrap the meat!" Aleksandrov shouted. "I don't want to hear your petty problems." The commandant then moved closer and whispered in Dovid's face, "And don't think you can hide meat. We'll come to your house if our stomachs are empty." He snatched the packaged beef from Dovid's hand and cleared out with his comrades.

Dovid was bent over the counter when the shop bell rang again.

Noach Stein rushed in. "Reb Weisman, are you hurt?"

"Noach, I'm fine." Dovid straightened up. "They just knocked the wind out of me."

"But look at your store. They took everything." Noach stared at the empty pegs where meat had hung.

"There's always something for you." He felt his apron pocket and retrieved a handful of beef cubes. He wrapped them in brown paper and tied the small parcel with string. "This will make a nice soup."

"Reb Weisman, I'll appeal to the Siedlce Fellowship for funds to replace your stolen stock. This pilfering and tormenting must end." Noach waved his arms like he did when he spoke to groups in the park.

"If we've lost money, we've lost nothing. If we've lost hope, we've lost everything. We have a celebration at the beit midrash to attend. I'll take one of your excellent cigarettes now." He removed his apron, noted it was noon, and locked the shop door. He walked home with Noach, smoking and listening, while Noach recapped the minutes of the most recent meeting of the Siedlce Zionists.

Chapter Eight—A Secret

Southwood, Michigan
January 1975

"What happened to your face?" Howard asked Ben as he sat down next to him on the edge of his twin bed and looked closer.

"You're looking well too!" Ben smiled a lopsided grin, closed a sci-fi book he was reading, and adjusted his blue plaid pajamas.

"Sorry—I just didn't expect to still find you like this at home."

"Seems like I'm allergic to shrimp and latex. They said the itchy, scaly rash and small blisters should go away in a couple of days. It's not so bad now. Is that my homework?"

"Yeah, where should I put it?"

"On the desk, if you don't mind."

"Everyone misses you and wants to know when you're coming back to school."

"Not until after my grandpa's funeral." Ben picked up the Rubik's Cube on the bed beside him and absentmindedly twisted the puzzle, trying to get all nine yellow squares on one side.

"What's that you've got there?" Howard flipped around the desk chair, sat, and leaned toward Ben.

"A puzzle my grandpa gave me. It's really hard."

"Let me try." Howard held out his hand, and Ben placed the cube in his palm. He started twisting.

"Hey, don't mess up what I've already got."

"How do you do it?"

"I'm just figuring it out. Each color is repeated nine times. There are fifty-four squares, and to solve the puzzle each of the six sides needs all nine squares to be the same color. It's like a math problem."

"Totally not for me." Howard tossed the cube back to Ben. "That rash looks nasty. You doing okay?"

"Not bad taking everything into account." Ben grinned and shook his left arm, and the stainless-steel chain-linked bracelet fell below his pajama sleeve. He flipped over the engraved plate customized with his name, allergies, treatment, and phone number.

"Lots of people have allergies. My cousin is allergic to bee stings and wears one of those bracelets. She nearly died when she stepped on a bee in the clover at our backyard pool. You won't even notice it after a while."

"I suppose you're right." Ben spun the bracelet on his wrist.

"You don't seem like yourself."

"Yeah, I kind of don't feel like myself. It's like I'm watching someone else, or like I lost part of myself. I guess it doesn't feel real. My grandpa was the kindest man I ever knew. I never once heard him raise his voice. He believed in me. They said he had a heart attack, but I think he died because he just wanted to disappear." Ben suddenly jumped up and opened his bedroom door.

Joel ran off dribbling a soccer ball down the hallway.

"Can you do that someplace else?"

"What are you saying?" Howard moved to the edge

43

of his seat.

"Can you keep a secret?" Ben lowered his voice, sat across from Howard, and leaned closer. His heart pounded in his chest.

"Yeah, what's going on?"

"No one's supposed to know, even though it was in all the newspapers. My uncle Ira is in prison." Ben got up and looked out the window at the stark, naked maple tree.

"Really? I haven't heard about it." Howard stood next to Ben at the window.

"He was working in some clinics, distributing illegal scripts for narcotics. They don't want to talk about it, but I think my grandpa died from keeping it all trapped inside."

"Ben, I'm really sorry. I'm here for you, man. What can I do to help?" He put an arm around Ben's shoulders.

"I think you might have already saved my life once." Ben smiled at Howard. "So, how about you just support me and be my friend." He picked up a trophy from the bookshelf he'd won at last year's Midwest regional swim meet.

"Sure—support you how?"

"This bar mitzvah thing, I don't want to do it."

"Are you kidding? You must have that post-traumatic stress thing. Hell, they're going to pay you to party!" Howard stepped smoothly into the hustle moves he'd been learning from Ben's grandma, but soon got still. "Really, though, just because you nearly died at Alan's bar mitzvah party doesn't mean the same thing will happen at yours."

"My grandpa visited me in the hospital, the night he died. He said it's up to me. He wants me to do something.

I just need to figure out what." He wondered if he had the courage his grandpa thought he had.

"He didn't tell you?" Howard raised his eyebrows.

"Not exactly, he talked about the day I helped him dock *Sunchaser* in high winds. Then he said he'd done all he could and now the mission is mine. I fell asleep on him, and I had this dream that I was the captain of the boat in the midst of a massive storm. When I woke up, it was the middle of the night. He was gone, and I knew he had died. It was like a vision or a premonition inside a dream, but it was real." Remembering that night, he almost started to cry, and the words stuck in his throat.

"Well, then, you can't just do nothing."

"That's what I thought. He was the most honest person I knew. He always did the right thing, even when it was hard, but he felt like he failed when his own son wound up in prison."

"I just don't understand what this has to do with your bar mitzvah party." Howard rolled his hands and shrugged his shoulders.

"I can't explain it, but I have this feeling. My family is really messed up right now. We have nothing to celebrate. The celebration would be hollow." He replaced the trophy on the shelf and picked up the Rubik's Cube.

"So how is this going to fix it?"

"I don't know yet, but I'll figure it out, okay? Last week, I nearly died in the ballroom at the Raleigh House, and my grandpa died in his sleep, but not before coming to me with a mission. Does this sound normal to you?" He twisted the cube and suddenly had all nine yellow squares on one side.

"I don't think you should tell anyone else about

this."

"I don't know what to do, but I've got to do something."

Chapter Nine—The Velvet Bag

Southwood, Michigan
January 1975

Ben flipped pancakes from the griddle onto a plate.
It was eight a.m., and he was ravenous. On a normal day
he would have already swum three thousand yards and
been pumped with endorphins. But not today. It was
winter break, and Grandpa had died. Grandma sipped tea
at the glass breakfast table and dialed her sister, Aunt
Sara, in Boston. Photos of Sara at sixteen with shiny
chestnut hair, taken just before she left Siedlce, hung on
the flocked wallpaper on the dining room walls. He
always visualized Aunt Sara as she looked in those
photographs, frozen in time, and he believed his grandma
did the same.

"Sara, it's me," Grandma whispered into the phone.

"What is it, Anna, what's happened?"

"I'm sorry to call so early. It's just that Mo…"
Grandma took a deep breath before croaking out the
words, "He died this morning." Then she burst out
crying.

"Oh, Anna," the voice wailed from Boston through
the phone. "How did it happen?"

"Quietly during the night, like plucking a hair from
milk." Grandma wiped the tears dripping from her chin.
"The stress was too much on his heart. He couldn't bear

it. I just wanted to tell you." She sobbed into the phone.

Aunt Sara's choking cries of grief echoed from the phone into the small kitchen. "I'm so sorry. I wish I could be there."

Ben's throat tightened, and he couldn't hold back tears.

"I know, Sara, I know you would be here if you could. How are you recovering from the surgery? Are you walking yet?"

"Yes, they get you up right away, but I have a long way to go until I can travel. Do you know when the funeral will be?"

"Not yet. The rabbi will come later this morning."

"Anna, you'll have a proper kosher burial?"

"Yes, Sara, I promised Mo. It will all be according to Jewish law." Grandma flinched and blew her nose.

Ben sat across the glass table from Grandma and poured maple syrup on his pancakes. He didn't know why, but that question upset her. What did Aunt Sara mean by a kosher burial?

"Where are you now?" Sara changed the subject.

"At home, with Ben. He's right here, making pancakes." Grandma searched for him and looked at him adoringly.

He slid the maple syrup across the table to go with his grandma's stack of pancakes.

"God bless him, he's such a good boy. Won't he soon be bar mitzvah?" Aunt Sara asked.

"Yes, less than three months away—March 22nd. He already towers over me." Grandma poured on the syrup.

"We'll mark our calendar and plan to be there. Please call me when you have the details for the funeral.

I'll notify the family. I love you, Anna. I'm so very sorry. *Baruch dayan ha'emet.*"

When Grandma hung up the receiver, she murmured the translation of the Hebrew words from long ago, *blessed is the True Judge.*

After breakfast, Ben followed Grandma into the small bedroom, known as the TV room, where she watered the tree beside the couch. Unlike the sofa in the living room, this couch wasn't covered in plastic. This was where Grandpa had read the newspaper and watched continuous sports, mostly baseball and golf. Ben missed him.

The TV news ran endlessly. The broadcast recapped highlights of the past year as the world remembered the Watergate scandal, the oil crisis, President Nixon's resignation, Patricia Hearst's kidnapping, and Hank Aaron of the Atlanta Braves breaking Babe Ruth's home-run record. And then pundits made predictions about 1975.

Grandma turned down the TV volume and sat on the edge of the worn brown plaid couch. She ran her thin bony fingers along the ridges of the corduroy fabric on the throw pillow. The TV room was steeped in his grandpa's spirit. The residue of his energy hung in the air. His reading glasses were on the coffee table next to a neat stack of boating and golf magazines. The faint scent of Old Spice lingered.

"It's comforting here in his space, with his things. I'm expecting him to walk in any time now." Grandma rose, stepped over to a Formica wall unit, and opened a storage cupboard. Inside was a blue velvet bag embroidered with a six-pointed Star of David in silver-and-gold thread. "Grandpa wanted you to have these."

49

She handed the velvet bag to Ben.

"It's beautiful." He stroked the plush velvet. "What is it?"

The doorbell rang.

"That will be the rabbi." She hurried to let him in.

A tall man with a long square beard followed Grandma into the TV room. She introduced him to Ben as Rabbi Silverstein. His eyes twinkled with a warm smile, and he extended a large hand to shake Ben's. Ben had a flash of recognition. Did he know this rabbi? He stood, awkwardly set the velvet bag on the coffee table, and shook the rabbi's hand. He had never spoken to a rabbi who looked like this.

"Your grandma tells me you're a swimmer." The rabbi sat in the armchair across from the couch.

"Yes, I'm on the swim team." Ben was thrown off by the arrival of the Chassidic rabbi. His mind reeled. If he was close to his grandparents, why had he never met him? And why was the rabbi here now?

"The Talmud says a father is obligated to teach his son to swim." Rabbi Silverstein smiled. "When do you practice?"

"Every morning at six a.m., but not today." Ben kept wondering how this rabbi was connected to his grandma and grandpa. Was he a friend of Grandpa's?

"You must be a morning person." The rabbi paused as though it were a question.

"Not really. I have a love-hate relationship with those early morning workouts." Ben looked down, embarrassed he'd said that. "I'm sorry, but how did you say you knew my grandpa?"

"We met long ago when I was a young man. I would visit his jewelry store on Friday afternoon, and we would talk. Then we began to learn together here. For twenty-five years I've come by on Thursday nights, and we learned together."

"Learned what together?" Ben pried.

"Mostly Jewish mysticism. Your grandpa had a love for chassidus, which is the study of the Torah's innermost secrets." Rabbi Silverstein seemed lost in recollection and stroked his beard.

"Could you teach me chassidus?" If his grandpa loved chassidus, Ben wanted to know those secrets too. His heart pounded as he waited for an answer.

"You would need some background to learn chassidus, Ben." The rabbi looked at him with his piercing blue eyes.

"The thing is, I learn really fast." He held his breath.

"Rabbi," Grandma interjected. "Perhaps we keep our Thursday night class, and you can learn with Ben?" She looked sorry she'd made the suggestion the moment the words were out, as though they had escaped without her consent and before she could fully consider what she was saying. She smoothed her skirt. "I know you never learned with Aliza or Ira, but don't you think that's what Mo would want?"

"I do," Rabbi Silverstein answered, his eyes twinkling.

"I will never forget the day I met Mo almost fifty-three years ago. I'd had a particularly terrible day at the millinery shop. My sister Sora had married Aaron and gone to America the previous spring. So I was exhausted from picking up the work she'd done in addition to keeping up with my own. It was cold and gloomy, and I'd been feeling sorry for myself, wallowing in self-pity, hurrying home to help Mama with the children. And there he was, standing tall and handsome, dressed like a gentleman on the street outside our apartment on Piekna Strasse." She paused to blow her nose.

The rabbi listened intently with compassion and took notes.

"He was looking for Sora to write a letter to a relative in America. She had become known for the beautiful letters she composed. There weren't many in our community who were fluent in English and could naturally move between Yiddish, Polish, German, and English. When he learned Sora wasn't there, he appealed to me, and I was unable to resist him from the start. But I felt like a child with my hair in braids, wearing my shabbiest clothes, and I set a time for the following evening for him to come back, determined to meet him as a proper young lady." She laughed at herself and continued to weep. For the better part of an hour, Grandma talked about Grandpa.

The rabbi wrote down the name of the hospital to which Mordechai Rosen had been transported and explained, "The body will not be left alone. It will be properly prepared and guarded while psalms are recited all night. We'll plan the memorial service for the chapel on Sunday or Monday, depending on arrival of any out-of-town family, and the internment will follow at the Memorial Park Cemetery where you've purchased your burial plots."

It was all planned long ago. Rabbi Silverstein assured Grandma he would carry out Grandpa's wishes.

Just when Ben thought the rabbi was going to leave, his gaze rested on the blue velvet bag, and he looked at Ben. "Your tefillin?"

"My what?" He didn't know what he meant.

"In the velvet bag." The rabbi pointed to the coffee table.

"I don't really know. Just before you got here, my grandma gave it to me. She said Grandpa wanted me to have them." Ben reached over and picked up the bag again.

"May I see them?" The rabbi sat still, and Ben brought the plush velvet bag to him. He unzipped it and removed two black boxes in protective cases with long black leather straps wound around them. He examined them carefully. "Mordy used these?"

"Every day, except the Sabbath." Grandma nodded.

"Are you bar mitzvah yet?" The rabbi looked to Ben.

"Not until March." Ben watched the rabbi who paused and seemed to be thinking. He wondered what he was figuring.

"Would you like to put on your grandfather's tefillin?"

"I don't know how," Ben stammered. "I don't even know what they are."

"I can show you." The rabbi unwound the leather straps, removed the boxes from their cases, and kissed them. "I think it will make your grandpa proud and very happy."

Ben was paying attention.

"These boxes contain handwritten scrolls with verses from the Torah about the importance of keeping the commandments and loving God. The boxes are marked—one is strapped to the head and one to the arm while you pray. You're right-handed?"

Rabbi Silverstein had already pushed up Ben's sleeve and positioned the black box on Ben's bicep. He adeptly wrapped the leather strap around Ben's bicep, forearm, palm, and middle finger. He then placed the second box between Ben's eyes, above his forehead and just above his hairline, secured by the leather straps. After adjusting the knot in the back of Ben's head, Rabbi Silverstein placed the yarmulke from the velvet bag on Ben's head. Ben was trembling.

"Close your eyes, Ben. You can think about your grandpa for a moment. Visualize your grandpa surrounded by light. Visualize your family, each one of them surrounded by light. Ask God to bless them."

Ben started crying. He felt as though the leather straps were electric cables and current pulsated through him. In a rush, he felt his grandpa's love wash over him like he had never felt before.

Rabbi Silverstein placed the prayer book in Ben's hands. He opened his eyes and saw the book was open to the Shema and recited the words he knew from the time he was a small boy. His earliest memories were with his mother repeating the words of the Shema before he went to sleep. His tears fell onto the pages of ancient text. His heart pounded, and he couldn't catch his breath. He felt like he had just swum 200 meters.

****

The doorbell rang. "That will be your mother and father now." Grandma stood, preparing to answer the door.

Ben counted the hours as the grandfather clock in the living room chimed. It was already ten o'clock.

Rabbi Silverstein raised a quizzical eyebrow.

"Please stay, Rabbi, if you don't have another commitment. My daughter, Aliza, and her husband, Steven, wanted to speak with you about the funeral arrangements."

"Of course." Rabbi Silverstein nodded and rose, awaiting Grandma to return with Ben's parents. "I'm Rabbi Silverstein. I wish we were meeting on a happier occasion." The rabbi stretched out a hand to shake Dad's as he came in, followed by Mom.

"Steven Friedman and my wife, Aliza, Mordy's daughter." Dad curtly handled the introductions, his eyes circumspect.

Ben fidgeted near the doorway, and Mom shuffled across the TV room and sat next to Grandma on the corduroy couch. He saw his mother assess the Chassidic rabbi, perhaps also wondering why he was her father's choice.

"Do you want to sit down?" the rabbi inquired and studied his father with bright, curious eyes. "Didn't we meet at the hospital?"

"I'd rather stand," Dad said with a somber expression on his face.

Dad paced in the short open space, and his demeanor changed from somber to combative. "I don't know what's involved in an orthodox burial or why this is appropriate, but there are a couple things to clarify in regard to the funeral arrangements."

A wave of hot embarrassment rushed through Ben at his father's disrespect to the rabbi.

"Why don't we start with logistics," Mom, always practical, interjected and rubbed her forehead. "You know, when and where?" She took a small notepad and a pen out of her boho fringe bag.

"These are logistics," Dad cut her off. "After the service, Ira and I feel strongly that Dad would have wanted his body donated to science."

"What?" Mom winced and touched her hand to her heart.

"You know Dad would want to make a difference for others. I don't see why you find that so surprising." A muscle in Dad's jaw twitched as the electricity in the air became palpable.

"This is an important point you make," Rabbi Silverstein agreed. "Jewish law permits that which is necessary to save a life. However, the life must be literally in front of you. No one expects a first-year medical student dissecting a body to actually 'save a life.' "

"Mo never said he wanted to donate his body to science." Grandma's spine stiffened.

"Then even if it were ruled that donating the body to science would further scientific research, this would be prohibited as it wasn't his wish," Rabbi Silverstein declared. "It would be considered a desecration of the dead."

"I don't understand your obsession with the body." Dad huffed.

"Only the body dies." The rabbi fixed his gaze on Dad. "The soul lives forever. We believe in an afterlife and in a future resurrection of the dead. We believe that one's body must be buried complete to be resurrected."

"Well, this is the first I've heard about a resurrection. I must have been out that day," Dad declared with a hint of mockery.

Mom pushed her fingers through her hair and massaged her temples. Grandma drew a deep audible breath and took hold of Mom's hand. Mom sank deeper into herself as Dad's storm progressed from disturbance to depression and then to full-fledged cyclone. Mom was shrinking before his eyes.

Dad continued, "We just want Dad to have a beautiful casket and a dignified burial. We want him to look natural in the casket, the way we remember him. I told Ira that we would go to the funeral home, speak to the director, and pick out something handsome." His voice cracked as he spoke these words.

The rabbi leaned back in his chair and interlaced his fingers. "I see that you care very deeply for your father-in-law and you want to honor him. The Talmud directs that all aspects of the funeral and burial should be kept simple and inexpensive. Some say the caskets were to be simple to keep the poor from being shamed."

"Everyone who knew and loved Dad will be at the funeral to pay their last respects. He shouldn't be viewed in a poor man's casket." Dad's face reddened.

"Before the funeral, your family may have private time to pay their final respects with the casket open. During the funeral, there will be no viewing of the body and no open casket." The rabbi leaned forward and added, "There are a number of problems with an open casket."

"Every Jewish funeral I've been to has had an open casket." Dad gritted his teeth.

"Unfortunately, many people are unaware of Jewish law and the reason behind it and have come to imitate non-Jewish customs."

"What problems are you talking about?" Dad fumed.

"Some are related to the dignity of the deceased, such as gazing at the dead. Preparing the body for viewing also presents very serious halachic problems. Tampering with and manipulating the dead to make them look attractive and presentable is prohibited. Providing a proper burial is the last kindness we can do for our loved ones. And it should be done as quickly as possible. The Zohar describes the soul in a state of anxiety and anguish until the body is buried." The rabbi looked at Dad with an appeal in his eyes.

"Then schedule the funeral for God's sake!" Father blew out his cheeks and thrust an impatient hand through his hair. "And with all due respect, Dad *will* be buried in a beautiful casket."

"Ira needs to be here," Grandma cried, protest and tears in her eyes.

"Where is he now?" the rabbi asked, a thoughtful frown drawing his eyebrows together.

"We think he's been moved from Sandstone, Minnesota, to a federal correctional institution in Loretto, Pennsylvania," Mom replied slowly, her eyes evading his.

"FCI Loretto?" Recognition flickered in the rabbi's eyes. "I know someone there. I'll see what I can do."

Ben couldn't shake the thought that Grandpa was in a state of anxiety and anguish. Yet the rabbi told him that putting on Grandpa's tefillin made Grandpa very proud and happy. There must be more that he could do.

Chapter Ten—Grief

Southwood, Michigan
January 1975

Aliza wandered through the house as though lost in her most familiar setting, a storm of emotion brewing. Shock and utter grief had thrown her off her center, and even simple decisions seemed overwhelming. Black tears streamed down her cheeks. She yearned for another baby to name for her father. The loss left her numb and afraid. She had no time to say good-bye.

She couldn't understand where Ira came up with his crazy ideas, like trying to convince Mom to "donate Dad's body to science." But Mom had agreed they had no right to use Dad's body like that, and the rabbi had said it was against Jewish law. She was tired of arguing and grateful there was a law. She wanted this to be a time of peace and unity for the family.

Having won the battle over donating Dad's body to science, she hoped the funeral planning would follow smoothly and without further incident. She didn't have the energy to keep arguing but shuddered when Steven alluded to Dad's body laid out and presented to relatives and friends for viewing. She knew well enough from dental school the nearly immediate effects of death on the body. The jaw would need to be wired closed to keep it from falling open. Fighting the decomposition that began within minutes must be the underpinnings of the funeral industry economy. This was where the real artistry came in as the body was restored to a look of exemplary health and placed in a respectable, "comfortable-looking" casket. She shivered at the thought of people staring at Dad's lifeless body and was grateful Rabbi Silverstein had vetoed that idea too. There would not be an open casket.

Knowing her Dad, she wasn't surprised by Mom's unbending commitment to ensure that he would have a kosher burial. While she couldn't articulate why this made sense, it did, and she was grateful that she didn't need to explain it to Ira or Steven or anyone else.

The emptiness inside overwhelmed her. The person who loved her most was gone. Dad was the one who accepted her decision not to practice dentistry and embraced her when she shared that she was pregnant and just wanted to be a mom. Dad convinced Mom that as long as she kept up her license, she would always have a means to support herself if necessary. Aliza wanted to remember Dad looking healthy and happy.

She searched for a photo for the funeral director and found a family picture from the July Fourth reunion last summer. Dad was tanned and smiling. He stood on the shore of Lake Erie. One of his arms was around Ira, and the other was around Mom. The rest of the family huddled close. Dad was at his happiest. It was the last time they were together before Ira's arrest.

Chapter Eleven—A Surprise

Siedlce, Poland

Sora took Yitzchak by the hand and skipped alongside him. The morning was bright and cold, but her palms were sweaty. A rush of current propelled her, and for once she didn't try to hold Yitzchak back and ran with him, matching his ten-year-old, unbridled energy. She ushered him into the courtyard behind the Siedlce Jewish Community Center where he joined his classmates playing before school commenced. She stood for an extra moment and watched the boys as they ran like a herd with the fringed tassels of their tzitzit flying, while they kicked a ball across the gated courtyard. Then she quickly cut through Aleksandria Park to make her nine a.m. appointment with Masha. When she arrived, warm and breathless, the dressmaker was bent over the burgundy woolen cloth, stitching the hollow pleats in the Edwardian dress.

"Sora, I can't wait for you to try this on! You won't need a corset or any petticoats." Masha tied off and cut the thread and then turned the natural-waist dress right side out and shook it to straighten the fabric.

"It's exquisite." Sora held the dress to her body and twirled.

"I still need to attach the collar and sleeves and sew on the buttons, but I can do that while you take my letter to Shmuley."

Finally, at one o'clock, with the finished Edwardian dress draped over her arm, Sora sailed to her father's meat market with a song on her lips. She was prepared to help with the usual Thursday afternoon pre-Sabbath line wrapped around the store and stopped abruptly when she found the door locked and the store dark. Confused and worried for a moment, she concluded that Tatty closed early to allow time to freshen up at home and arrive punctually at the upshernish with the family. Finding herself with time on her hands, she headed to the synagogue to change into her new dress and help the Bialystocks set up for their celebration.

The synagogue, known as the beit midrash, was a magnificent structure near the horse market on Zydowska Street. Sora skipped past the Jewish cemetery lined with snow-dusted linden trees. Lost in thought about tonight's event, she followed the tall brick wall that guarded the gravestones.

"Guess who?" Warm hands covered her eyes from behind.

Sora jumped and shrieked, then burst into laughter when she recognized Aaron.

"This is no place for a pretty girl to be walking alone." He circled around in front of her and walked backward, facing Sora. The visor of his tweed wool cap and navy wool jacket collected snowflakes. His long legs were slender and his waist too narrow for his broad upper body. Although he was only nineteen, his dark full beard made him look older than he was. His hazel eyes flickered with excitement as he said, "Tonight, after the upshernish, will you meet me? I have a surprise!"

Sora's skin warmed, and her heart fluttered wildly.

When she arrived at the beit midrash, Chana was already slicing marble cake and preparing for the celebration. Mama had laid the tables with smoked meat, herring, and cakes.

"I can't wait to see the dress Masha made for you!" Chana touched the fine fabric. "Put it on now so we can see this freer bodice and deep pleating. Is it too bold to wear such a red dress?"

"Masha says this is burgundy, quite different from red. Don't you think?" Sora held the dress up to the light.

"Yes, I see now. We've never had such a gay dress."

"Well, it's not for a funeral, after all." Sora waltzed, making full use of the deep pleating. "I could do anything in this dress!" She glided across the floor.

"Do anything most beautifully," Chana swooned.

At four o'clock Baruch sat beaming in an elevated chair in the social hall and put a kopek in the charity box. Dark curls were scattered on the scarred floor around him. Tatty held the ornate scissors and carefully snipped from a long curl in the back while the proud parents, Ita Miriam and Jakow, huddled close and gave Baruch a piece of candy. Mama went next, handed Raizel off to Tatty, and snipped another curl. The children snatched cake from the table, and since the parents sat back, not scolding and supervising as they normally did, Sora let them enjoy too many sweets. She avoided looking at Aaron but detected his gaze on her from across the room. Warmth stole into her cheeks.

The beit midrash was packed with the community. The line to snip Baruch's hair was long, but everyone waited patiently, most eager to greet Jakow and wish him mazal tov! No one had seen Jakow since the night of the raid, eight years ago, the night the Cossacks beat him with the butt of a rifle. Sora remembered that terrible time, and her lips quivered. Days after the chief of police was assassinated by a man dressed as a Jew, Zalman was killed when the soldiers opened fire in the street. While no one spoke of it, everyone remembered. Sora finally reached the front of the line. She snipped Baruch's hair with the ornate scissors and handed them to Chana in line behind her. Tatty embraced Jakow and drank to his health.

The women with young children were the first to leave. Mama took the little ones home to bed. The men lingered and noshed on what remained of the smoked meat and cakes while they talked politics, war, and news of the draft. Tatty joined the men in the library for the Talmud class. Sora stayed busy cleaning up from the crowd until Chana knowingly took over and shooed Sora out to join Aaron, inconspicuously standing by.

Once outside in the cold crisp air, Aaron grasped Sora's hand and pulled her with him, and they ran past the cemetery and the great synagogue in the glow of the moon.

They stopped, breathless and panting, beside the long black wooden stable behind the horse market. Aaron unlatched and opened the stable door. The sweet smell of hay wafted over them. Rows of stalls housing dozens of horses stretched out to their left and to their right.

"Micah, we're here," Aaron called out and pulled the creaky stable door closed.

"Aaron, my friend." A lanky redhead wearing layers of scarves and sweaters came forth from one of the stalls. With a shovel in hand, he greeted Aaron with a hearty slap on the back. "Come this way. Everything's ready."

Micah led them to the rear of the stable and pushed the back doors open wide onto a snow-covered wooded landscape. Two Friesian stallions whinnied and restlessly stepped in place. Their black feathery tails stretched to the snow, and their wavy manes wrapped around their chests like silk scarves with the whip of the wind. They were hitched to a curved wooden sleigh with a red leather upholstered seat. Her heart skipped a beat at the sight of the scenic landscape, and her flesh trembled with sparks of electricity.

"One hour, Aaron, you must have them back in one hour." Micah shook the crop for emphasis.

"We'll be back within the hour." Aaron winked at Micah and lifted Sora into the sleigh before she knew what was happening. Aaron clambered up into the seat beside her and spread a plaid wool blanket over her lap. "Giddyup!" he called out.

"Yah!" Micah yelled and swatted the Friesians' hinds with the crop. Strong and sure-footed, the Friesians pulled the sleigh gracefully onto the snowy trail into the forest.

Sora brushed the snowflakes from her eyelashes and wrapped a scarf over her wavy chestnut hair, but her cheeks were warm. Stunned at finding herself in such a situation so unexpectedly, she was speechless. The leather seat was wide enough for the two of them, but not without touching. She could feel the heat of his body beside her.

"Surprised?" He beamed and glanced at her as he managed the reins.

"Astonished, I'd say." She relaxed.

"Sometimes I forget there's a beautiful world out here. I come here to be reminded. I know I've been too forward, but I need you to see it too." He looked up beyond the canopy of evergreens to the star-filled sky.

"I can't believe we're still in Siedlce. The snow, the towering trees, the rising moon, all so undisturbed and serene." She felt like she was wrapped in a cocoon.

"We don't have to stay in Siedlce. Come to America with me." He stopped the horses, and the sleigh glided to stillness.

She breathed in the cold air. "How can I leave my family?"

"We'll make a life in America and send for them. Someone has to start. If you agree, I'll speak to your father. Just say you'll think about it, won't you?" He took her hands in his.

Silently and involuntarily, she felt herself nodding. She felt a stillness inside. The fear and struggle stopped. A dizzying wave of euphoria swept over her. Neither of them spoke as they looked up and took in the vast star systems overhead. The immensity of the universe made anything seem possible. After a while, Aaron turned the sleigh back toward the stable, and Sora rested her head on his shoulder.

When they reached the stable, it was dark. Aaron secured the horses, and Sora put her arms around him as he lifted her down from the sleigh. She kept her arms wrapped around his neck for an extra moment. When her feet were firmly on the ground, she said, "I'll talk to my tatty."

He skipped across the landscape and did cartwheels in the snow. She laughed her consent with her entire body, looked into the sky, extended her arms, and twirled.

"Micah." Aaron hitched the reins to a post and

patted the Friesian's head. He snatched his hat from the snow and called into the stable. "We've returned!"

When there was no answer, he opened the stable doors and came face-to-face with Micah slouched, beaten, and restrained by two men from Aleksandrov's dragoon. The commandant signaled to his men. They hurled Micah to the dirt floor and advanced toward Aaron. But Aleksandrov looked beyond Aaron with open pleasure and cooed to Sora, "Come to me, my little bird."

"Run, Sora!" Aaron yelled before the rifle butt struck him in the ribs. Then he collapsed in pain.

Micah charged the men and struck one in the head with a shovel. Aleksandrov fired on Micah. He stumbled, holding his bleeding gut, and dropped to the ground. Aaron doubled over. Sora's flesh crawled with dread as she awaited the next shot. Blinded by fear for Aaron's life, she ran to the beit midrash where she prayed she'd find her father.

Chapter Twelve—Together

Southwood, Michigan
January 1975

"I finally have everything packed, and it's six a.m. Friday when Sydney Blackwell calls from California. Please pass the lox."

Ben handed the platter of smoked salmon to Aunt Nanci, and she paused her story to pile lox on a bagel. Sunday morning brunch at home, one of the necessary *changes* to avoid exposing him to trace amounts of shellfish that could trigger another severe allergic reaction, would be an adjustment. He helped Mom by slicing bagels and making platters so everyone could serve themselves. *Note to self—next week set up a buffet.*

Estie clomped down the stairs, stormed in, and dropped herself into an open chair at the dining table next to Grandma Libby. Grandma Libby and Grandma Ann were machatunim, that was, their children were married to one another, and they shared three grandchildren, Ben, nearly thirteen, Estie, ten, and Joel, who had just turned five. Ben didn't know any other machatunim who were also best friends. For as long as he could remember, his grandmas did everything together.

"Pass the bagels, please." Estie surveyed the spread on the table. "Not exactly the Gandy Dancer," she muttered.

Mom's face fell, and he wished his sister wasn't always such a downer. While he knew the happiness meter in the house wasn't exactly at an all-time high, his sister always seemed to have a knack for making every bad situation worse. And lately, more so than usual.

"And he says, 'They're moving Ira,' and I say, 'Moving him to where?' And Sydney says, 'Loretto, seventy miles east of Pittsburgh.' " Aunt Nanci swept her curly auburn hair into a messy bun and secured it with a scrunchy she wore on her wrist. Curls broke loose and framed her fresh face. Despite a full layer of makeup, she looked completely natural.

"Loretto is much closer." Mom poured freshly brewed coffee.

Suddenly, Grandma Ann entranced the atrium with a rush of cold air and snow flying from the shoulders of her fur coat. Grandma Libby's hand flew up, and Grandma Ann caught her eye right away and waved. She took a seat at the open place beside Grandma Libby and slipped her arms out of the red fox jacket.

Mom poured Grandma a cup of hot coffee while Aunt Nanci continued without coming up for air.

"And there's a minimum-security satellite. Sydney will try to get Ira in. So the plan has changed again. I canceled the apartment in Minnesota and the moving van. The realtor wanted to do an open house next week, and I canceled that too." She sat back in her chair and drew a breathless sigh.

"Ira will be home soon!" A smile took possession of her lips as Grandma Ann sprang the news.

"I don't think so." Steven raised an eyebrow with hesitation. "We applied for furlough so Ira can come home for Dad's funeral, but they were moving Ira and couldn't get us an answer. The timing is unfortunate. Regardless, we've got to schedule Dad's funeral."

"The reason I'm late is I was with Rabbi Silverstein working out the details. He confirmed with Loretto this morning. Ira will be arriving DTW at 6:50 this evening, accompanied by an officer from the justice department. The graveside service will be at two tomorrow afternoon at Beth El Memorial Park."

"Oh, my goodness!" Aunt Nanci shrieked and jumped up from the table.

"*That's* what I'm talking about! Mom, you're the best!" Mom and Aunt Nanci threw their arms around Grandma. Rubie squirmed from the table and pushed her way into the group hug, always ready for a squeeze.

"We have Rabbi Silverstein to thank. As it turns out, he's personal friends with the chaplain at Loretto." The ghost of a smile touched her mouth.

How cool is that? Ben thought to himself.

Aunt Nanci broke loose from the group hug and pulled Rubie alone into her arms. "Daddy is coming home to visit." She knelt down and spoke slowly, making certain that Rubie understood. "Daddy is coming home to see you."

Rubie's face lit up, and she squealed, "Daddeeeee," with the final syllable rising an octave and the shrill peal trumpeting to every corner and crevice.

Estie clasped her hands over her ears. When Rubie's squeal subsided, Estie blurted out, "Is it always going to be like this?"

"Everything will be all right." A flicker of irritation and then sadness showed in Mom's eyes, and she went to Estie, placing her hands on Estie's shoulders. Estie squirmed away, and Mom announced, "First come, first served for made-to-order omelets in the kitchen."

Joel and Rubie made a beeline to the kitchen galley, and Ben followed. Mom fixed her gaze on Estie, who seemed to grow increasingly moody and sullen with every passing day, building an impenetrable wall around herself.

Bowls of ingredients Ben prepped that morning were laid out on the butcher-block island beside a large pitcher of raw scrambled eggs. He'd thought the omelet bar was a terrible idea and voted for make-ahead quiche and casseroles. In a heartbeat Mom was pouring raw eggs into a hot oiled skillet, and she looked happy.

"I want to make my own omelet!" Joel excitedly snatched handfuls of cheese and tomatoes from the bowls on the counter. Then he climbed onto a stool to be a part of the omelet-making operation.

Ben had suggested disposable plates, paper cups, and plastic cutlery, and Mom vetoed. In fact, every idea he had to get her out of the kitchen and makes things easier, she refused. Mom *wanted* to be busy. Since Grandpa died, she hadn't been herself. She'd been agitated. Or maybe it started with his anaphylactic reaction. He went back to the atrium.

Ben sat by his grandmas who were engaged in intimate conversation. He was used to the way they read each other based on something as subtle as the look in the other's eyes.

"At the Stein bar mitzvah, Loretta Marx was huddled with her group by the bar, pointing at me. They all turned and stared, like I didn't know what they were talking about. You know her. She always needs some fresh gossip to share." Grandma Ann brought Grandma Libby up to speed.

"Who needs 'em." Grandma Libby flicked her hand like she was swatting away a fly.

"Ira is really coming this evening?" A frown creased Dad's forehead as he gently touched Grandma Ann's wrist.

"Yes, tomorrow we'll be together to bury Dad." She choked, her eyes filling with tears.

Chapter Thirteen—Furlough

Southwood, Michigan
January 1975

Ira rolled over on the pillow-top mattress and cool Egyptian cotton linens. He didn't remember the last time he'd slept so well. He flipped open the gold cigarette case on the nightstand and lit a Marlboro. The hammered gold case had been his father's until he quit smoking. Ira inspected the case as he recalled the pact he'd made with him. When he continued smoking, despite the health risks being discovered, his father gave him the beautiful gold case if he promised to cut down to one pack a day. Which he did, and he carried the case in his coat pocket over his heart ever since. He thought he missed the ordinary things—bathroom doors, a belt, car keys in his pocket, and deciding what he wanted to eat—but he missed his family. He'd become numb to the crippling pain of being separated from Nanci.

Before the move to Loretto, he counted the days for Nanci and Rubie to move close by. In Minnesota, he'd convinced himself that he'd get through this if Nanci and Rubie were near. The sentence would be doable if he could see them. He closed his eyes, inhaled deeply, and smelled Nanci on his skin. A panic rose up within him as he stubbed out the cigarette and calculated how far off it would be until he was with her again.

D.G. Schulman

With Nanci in the shower, Ira dressed and went down the hall to his office and fell back into his ergonomic chair. He swiveled from side to side and trailed his hands across the surface of his desk. None of the familiar photographs were on his desk. The walls were bare of his diplomas. Everything was packed as though it were going to Minnesota. Again, he thought, the wrong place at the wrong time.

The free weights were on the floor in front of the closet. Ira guessed Nanci didn't know how to pack them, and now she didn't need to. He glided the chair across the high-gloss oakwood floor and reached down to retrieve the dumbbells. From a seated position he did five sets of ten bicep curls, alternating arms. He heard Nanci counting repetitions in his head as he sweated. The panic dissipated, and he found his inner stillness.

"Daddy!" Rubie called and ran down the hall toward the office.

"In here, sweetie." Ira put down the weights and hugged Rubie.

"You're sticky." She wiggled away.

"You're right." He swept her up into his arms.

"Did Papa go back to be with God?" She got serious.

"Yes, my darling." His heart gave a twist in his chest. He was taken aback by her question and reminded that Rubie was always a precocious child. Ira brushed the curls off Rubie's face, and his warm fingers stroked her cheek.

Nanci appeared in the doorway, smelling fresh. Ira released Rubie and let her run to Nanci. Then he rose and wrapped his arms around them both. "You smell wonderful," he said to Nanci as he buried his face in her damp rose-fragrant hair.

"How does pancakes for breakfast sound to everyone?" Nanci put a hand on her belly, her face showing a short-lived sign of uneasiness, before a smile flickered across her face.

Ira saw she was feeling the stress too.

"Pancakes for breakfast would be terrific. We'll all help."

He lifted Rubie onto his shoulders and carried her down the stairs.

****

Anna was glad that Ben spent the night in the guest bedroom across the hall. The house was quiet without the sports and news broadcasting from Mo's TV room. It was altogether too roomy without Mo. She watched the clock, awaiting Ben's return from swim practice. Mo's presence lingered, and she felt a chill that reached to the very bottom of her spine. She sat on the brown corduroy couch, and a shiver ran like a ghostly touch over her skin.

She couldn't bear the thought of burying her Mo in the frozen earth. She started to imagine people at the funeral offering condolences, and it all seemed surreal. They would approach Ira and want to know where he'd been and how things were. Was life going well? She and Mo hadn't told anyone outside the family that Ira was incarcerated. Of course, a few people read the articles in *The Detroit News* and the *Free Press*. She sensed who they were by the way they looked at her and their probing questions. She was afraid they would judge him for one mistake and even after he'd served his time, he would be labeled. They would all be labeled. So she pretended that everything was okay when beneath her gracious smile there were days she could barely breathe.

In early August 1965, as Aliza started her second

year of dental school, they'd packed the town car to move Ira into the freshman dorm. Ira was one of fifty high school students, out of five hundred applicants, accepted to a seven-year BA/MD Honors Program in Medical Education. But it wasn't effortless. It took years of discipline and hard work. Six days a week, including Sunday mornings, from the age of ten, Anna drilled Ira with stacks of index cards covering topics such as vocabulary, prime numbers, and the periodic table of elements. It was what they did. The program she'd created for Aliza was refined and expanded. When he mastered the name, symbol, and atomic number of all one hundred elements, he was rewarded with a ski trip. Anna knew from the moment she set foot in America that education was the ticket to survival, safety, and success. She set high expectations and never accepted excuses. There was no limit to the lengths she would go to make sure her children had every advantage.

The August day she dropped Ira off on campus, they had lunch at a trendy restaurant on Main Street before parking in front of the dorm and then carrying boxes and suitcases up the steamy flights of stairs to third-floor Hayden. The atmosphere was electric. Ira was derailed and made friends before they even passed through the common rooms and started up the stairs. His roommate and he became inseparable, and their dorm room was the cool place to be. It was always like that. People gravitated to Ira, and he seemed not to notice.

Anna had cried on the lonely ride home, but they'd been tears of joy and satisfaction. She'd done her best to raise her son to be disciplined and hard-working, committed to family, and to have grit. At the end of the day, how was it possible that he wasn't a mensch? What had she missed? How had they failed?

It was the last thing her tatty had told her. "Promise me, Chana, raise your children in the ways of Torah. Raise your son to be a mensch."

At first she had tried to show her children the beauty of a Torah life, but so many more exciting and enticing diversions captured their imaginations and connected them to their friends. Her half-hearted efforts were met with indifference. Somehow it all appeared irrelevant. She didn't know how to compete when it seemed she offered only a list of things they couldn't do. In Siedlce, Torah was integrated into community and into life. America was different. At some point she stopped trying. How had she given up so easily? What was she thinking?

Ben came in smelling of chlorine and joined his grandma Ann on the couch and brought her back to the present. "The men from the funeral home are here to drop off prayer books, folding chairs, and a coatrack. Is it okay if they put them in the living room?"

"Except for the coatrack. Have them put that in the foyer," Anna murmured, her head bowed slightly. *And so it begins*.

Chapter Fourteen—Storm the Stable

Siedlce, Poland

"Tatty!" Sora cried out, and her gaze darted from one bearded man to the next, searching for her father in the social hall. She was breathless and flushed from running in the cold. Remnants of the upshernish remained, and the men gathered in heated political debate, nibbling the final scraps of smoked meat and herring while the samovar whined as the water continued to boil.

Sora found her father in the library. She rushed to him, weeping and trembling. In a heartbeat, he excused himself from the rabbi's class and was with her in the social hall. His penetrating gaze ran over her from head to toe, and his eyes held a worried expression.

"Sora, where have you been?" Tatty led her away from the crowd and into the coat room.

Chana was inside, bundling up and getting ready to go, when they slipped in.

"We were at the horse market, Tatty. Something terrible has happened. They shot Micah, and I don't know what they've done to Aaron. We need to help him." Sora wailed, clutching her father's arm.

Chana darted close to Sora. She went rigid, and her face had gone as white as the wall behind her.

"How many are there?" Tatty took hold of Sora's

hands.

"I don't know…that awful Cossack commandant and at least two of his soldiers. But Micah knocked one of them unconscious with a shovel. Tatty, we've got to hurry." Sora gripped his coat sleeve.

"And where's Aaron?"

"He was in the back of the stable with Micah. He told me to run. Then that commandant hit him with his rifle." Sora clung to her father.

"You stay here with your sister." Tatty put on his coat.

"They might have shot him," Sora whimpered.

"Pray, they haven't." Her father handed her a book of psalms.

"What if they come here looking for me?" The words half died in her throat, and she felt as if drops of ice were running down her spine.

Her father drew a concealed Colt 1911 semiautomatic pistol from his shoulder holster. She backed away as nausea gripped the muscles of her stomach. He re-holstered the pistol, turned to her sister, Chana, and held her firmly by the shoulders. He looked directly into her eyes, and she became still and focused.

Tatty drew the pistol from the holster again, slowly this time, and displayed the weapon in his large hands before Chana.

Her eyes were fixed upon him.

"Listen carefully to what I tell you now and don't get distracted by what's happened. You must always treat a gun as if it's loaded. You must never point a gun at anything you don't wish to destroy. You must never put your finger on the trigger unless you're ready to fire, and you must always be aware of what's in front of and behind your target. Do you understand?"

Chana bobbed her head, her eyes unblinking.

"Repeat what I said." He snapped his fingers.

"Always expect a gun to be loaded. Never point it at anyone…" she stammered.

"Wrong—never point at anything you don't wish to destroy. Repeat what I said again." Tatty snapped his fingers twice, communicating urgency, and they went back and forth like that until Chana repeated every rule correctly.

"This gun is loaded and ready to fire. It's cocked and locked, which means it has a bullet in the chamber and the safety is on. It will not fire until you choose to fire, and that will require you to grip it in your hand and manually turn off the safety, which is this bar on the left rear of the frame."

He demonstrated, pushing the safety down and then up again with his thumb. "Now you show me how to turn the safety off and on again."

Chana jerked her thumb forward and clicked the steel bar down and up.

"Now let me show you how to grip it." He stood beside Chana and placed the weapon in her delicate hand, wrapping her left support fingers over her right for stability. The index finger of her firing hand was positioned straight on the frame.

"How will I know if I should pull the trigger?" Uncertainty flickered in her eyes. She raised her chin and looked through the iron sights, with her hands quivering.

"If you fear for your life, pull the trigger."

"Do I shoot to kill?" Chana lowered the weapon, checked that the safety was on, and put the pistol in her coat pocket.

"Shoot to stop the threat." Tatty drew both his daughters into his arms and kissed the tops of their heads.

His touch had a calming effect. Sora always believed she was the older, stronger sister, the protector. But now she knew she lacked the indomitable spirit in Chana, a spirit her father saw. A spirit that would endure long after their father was gone.

Within minutes, Tatty enlisted Noach, proprietor of the cigarette shop, and Dan, the blacksmith, to join him in an attempt to rescue Aaron. Sora's heart seemed to turn over. With tears in her eyes, she opened the book of psalms and beseeched the heavens above.

****

Dovid took the backwoods as the shortest route to the horse market, but the snow was deep, and the sky was black. An owl hooted, the wind whistled, and the snow crunched beneath his feet. He was comforted to know that Noach carried the standard military-issue 1911 semiautomatic pistol in .45 caliber. When they approached the stable, it appeared to be deserted. Dovid listened at the door for any movement inside but heard nothing. He signaled to Noach and Dan directions to infiltrate the stable.

Noach held the pistol at his chest, flung the door open, and hugged the wall while he cut the angles and cleared the front of the stable one section at a time. The stable seemed empty. Noach went to the left, and Dovid and Dan fanned out to the right, each taking a shovel and a pitchfork as weapons. They inspected the long row of stalls, peering into each one. Dovid was afraid of what they would find. Many stalls were empty, and it seemed the horse thieves were gone.

Dovid discerned the metallic smell of blood beneath

the sweet smell of hay. It was a smell he knew well. He stepped from stall to stall until he discovered the red-soaked hay at his feet. He unlatched the wooden half door and swung it open. Two bodies lay face down in the hay and dirt. Dread rolled through the pit of his stomach. Dovid knelt beside the redheaded boy and rolled him over. He put his head to Micah's chest, and his throat contracted with emotion. Micah was dead. Beside him lay a Cossack soldier in uniform who was pierced through the heart with a saber.

"Over here," Dovid called to Dan.

Dan knelt over Micah's lifeless body. "He's cared for these horses since he was a boy. He didn't deserve this." He pinpointed three gunshots to Micah's stomach and wrapped his limp body in a horse blanket.

"I think he gave them more of a fight than they expected." Dovid pulled the saber from the dead Cossack and tried to envision the fatal struggle.

"Soon this place will be swarming with Cossacks looking for their comrade. We need to get out of here." Dan surveyed the stable with apprehension.

"We need to find Aaron." A savage fury flared up within Dovid, and he hurled open the stall doors as he ran the length of the long stable. The few remaining horses were uneasy; they snorted and squealed a high-pitched, ear-piercing scream. Then he heard a grunt and a long groan. Dovid followed the vibration to the back stall and flung open the door. Aaron lay trampled in the hay. His face was bruised and bleeding, and his eye was swollen shut. A Cossack stood over Aaron, kicking him senseless.

"You're in time to watch your young heroic friend leave this world." The Cossack sneered as he swung his rifle and pointed it at Aaron's head. A piercing shot exploded, and the Cossack faltered and fell backward.

Noach bolted into the stall with the Colt pistol still pointed on the writhing Cossack. He put a second round in the Cossack's head.

Dovid fell to his knees. What would he tell his daughter? A sudden chill swept through his body. He tilted Aaron's head and met his eyes. They were blank, and his face was dark and distant. He let his gaze wander slowly down Aaron's broken body. He checked him for injuries and found he was badly beaten with some broken bones but not shot. His heart beat faster from a combination of fear and excitement—Aaron was alive.

"You're going to be okay. We're getting you to a doctor." Dovid spoke softly to Aaron who was slipping in and out of consciousness. "Dan, hitch the horses to a wagon so we can take our men home." He spoke bravely, though unspeakable pain gripped his heart.

Within minutes the wagon was ready. Aaron moaned when Dovid lifted him onto the bed of pale straw. A moment later, Micah's body, wrapped in horse blankets, was laid beside him.

As coachman, Dovid eased the horses into the night. It was darker. He knew there would be retaliation. The violence only escalated in a cyclical pattern of retribution and revenge. The tension built, and violence was unleashed. The Cossacks attempted to regain power and control through more abuse and terror. He needed to prepare his family and warn the community for what was coming next.

Chapter Fifteen—At the Edge

Southwood, Michigan

At 5:58 a.m., like every other morning, Ben's toes were at the edge of the pool. He adjusted his goggles and took the plunge. He dove with his arms stretched like arrows into the pool, cutting the water elegantly with his goggles secured by a silicone cap. He angled upward to keep from scraping the bottom and transitioned smoothly into a butterfly stroke, maintaining the momentum of the dive. He turned for his second lap before his teammates were halfway across the pool. Underwater, his senses were sharp, and he heard his teammates' voices echoing in the natatorium.

His father sat in his usual place on the bleachers, drinking his coffee, reading legal briefs, and watching Ben. A deep and pleasurable satisfaction swept across his father's face. Ben could see his father was proud of him, his discipline, and knowing the importance of sacrifice to succeed. These were qualities his father believed would make Ben a fine partner one day.

Ben had his own reasons for throwing off the covers at five fifteen a.m. when the rest of the world was rolling over and deep in slumber for at least a couple more hours. At first it was physical. After nearly drowning as a small child in Lake Erie, he had a fierce drive to learn to swim at an early age. The doctor recommended swimming for his asthma, and over time his capacity to hold his breath and breathe deeply increased. He refused to succumb to a weak constitution. Now it was about the rush. His body sliced through the water, and he focused on his stroke. The rhythm pulsed through him. He'd crank out six thousand yards before his first class—butterfly, backstroke, breaststroke, and freestyle. On most days, the endorphins made him feel invincible and happy. He swam all four strokes of the medley relay equally well.

He practiced good turns, adhering to Coach Walker's yelling, which reverberated even under water. He swam another lap. And another and judged his distance from the wall as he approached the end of his lane. Swiftly, he somersaulted underwater and pushed off the wall for speed. Again and again, unaware he was now the only one left in the pool.

"Friedman!" Coach Walker bellowed through the megaphone. "Out of the pool. Move and you can still make the first-hour bell."

The coach threw a towel at Ben as he pulled himself from the water. He snatched the towel in midair, draped it around his neck, and peeled off his goggles. The endorphin rush kicked in.

Coach Walker slapped Ben on the back. "Morning swims like that make champions. See you on Saturday."

Chris Boyce and Andy Fox were packing up their swim gear when Ben came into the locker room.

"Hey, Ben." Chris slapped Ben's back. "We're gonna qualify at the prelims and kill the medley relay at the state meet this year! Andy's times are awesome on the backstroke. Tom Peters can take breaststroke, I've got the butterfly, and you'll bring it home with your record-setting freestyle."

"Right on, our team is way better than last year." Ben rubbed the towel over his wet hair. He screwed up his face. "Ugh, we were bad."

"That we were! I gotta book it. Catch you later."

The first-hour bell rang, but today Ben wasn't in a hurry. He was excused from classes for his grandpa's funeral. He thought it would be good for him to make the swim team practice. Not just because a state qualifying meet was coming up, but because he needed a break, a time when he would stop thinking and feeling entirely. He dressed quickly and met up with his father back at the bleachers.

Hot air finally began to blow from the vents in the emerald Lincoln town car. Ben's hair was still wet, and he shivered on the cold leather seats.

"Damn, this boat is terrible in the winter." His father let up on the gas as the town car started sliding sideways on the icy street.

"Dad, did you mean it when you told the rabbi that you'd get Grandpa a beautiful casket?" Ben looked out the window, and his skin tightened with goose bumps.

"While I'm still alive, your grandpa won't be buried in a poor man's box. You never knew my father, but you were named after him. He would have been crazy for you, Ben. He was hit by a car crossing the street and died when I was your age. It was during the recession of 1949. Unemployment was peaking with all the GIs back in the job market. My dad was a smart and proud man and somehow always found work, sometimes menial work that paid little. He had the kind of mind that he could have been an engineer, but he never acted like a job was beneath him. I wanted him to be buried with the dignity of a king, but he was laid to rest in that poor man's box."

His father turned up the speed of the windshield wipers against the melting snowflakes. "But things are different now."

"Did you have a bar mitzvah?" Ben adjusted the angle of the hot air blasting on him.

"Not hardly." His father looked a bit embarrassed. "But I did get a job as a stock boy at the local grocery store, Lucky's Market, where my father was working at the time of the accident. I worked there until I went to college, and that helped pay the bills."

"You said I was named after him?"

"Yes, his name was Benjamin. Grandma Libby called him Benji." He parked the car in the freshly plowed driveway in front of Grandma Ann's sprawling ranch home. He leaned back and rested his hands on the steering wheel.

"You don't talk about him much."

"He wasn't here long. Your grandpa Mo became a father to me when your mother and I started dating. He put me through law school. Now they're both gone." His father's eyes flickered with affection, and his voice cracked.

Ben's throat tightened, and he nodded, confounded by this new information.

****

When Uncle Ira threw the first shovel of dirt onto Grandpa's casket, it made Ben's skin quiver. He had never been to a funeral before and didn't know what to expect. No one talked about it. The thud of dirt on the casket even made Uncle Ira flinch. Yesterday, he'd been in FCI Loretto, and today he shoveled earth into Grandpa's grave. He buried his hands in his coat pockets, drifted back to the group, and mumbled, "I'm sorry I disappointed you, Dad. Forgive me for all the pain I caused you."

Aunt Nanci stuck close by Uncle Ira. The family huddled around the exterior of the temporary red tent, which was constructed for the service, and stood on the green Astroturf laid out on the snow around the grave. Uncle Ira's accompanying officer from the justice department respectfully positioned himself at the gated cemetery entrance. One by one the family and community stepped forward to pay their respects and say their good-byes. A heavy blanket of snow continued to fall, and the landscape was blinding white. The bitter wind beat the canvas of the tent, and it snapped and cracked like a whip.

Ben took the shovel next and dropped a shovelful of earth onto the casket. *I know you're counting on me, Grandpa. I can feel you're with me, and I won't let you down.*

Grandma Ann stepped up next to Ben and struggled to pull the shovel from the frozen mound of dirt, which was now snow covered. She managed to scoop a small bit of earth into the grave when her purse swung out and caused her to lose her footing. Ben imagined her going into the grave with Grandpa and grabbed her by the arm. Uncle Ira rushed over and took his mother's other arm. He tried to lead her to the car, but she refused and clutched her fur coat collar close around her neck, fending off the cold.

"I need to stay until the grave is completely covered."

Uncle Ira and Grandma Libby stayed close by her side.

Next, Mom took the shovel, picked up a load of earth, and spilled it into the grave. She paused and whispered, "Dad, you always said there was nothing I couldn't accomplish, but things are a mess. I need your help."

Mom sobbed and pushed the shovel into the dirt. Dad wrapped his arms around Mom like a bear, as though he were protecting her. Suddenly, a crack reverberated in the frozen air. Not the wind whipping the canvas—more like an explosion or fireworks. Uncle Ira screamed and broke away, clutching himself and dropping to his knees. His face was contorted in pain. Dad dragged Uncle Ira into the tent. Blood stained the snow. Grandma Ann's head snapped right and left, and she scanned the cemetery. Another round of fire exploded, and the flash pinpointed the attacker. He was leaning across the hood of a black Cadillac in the circular drive, looking down the barrel of a semiautomatic rifle aimed directly at them.

Ben's heart seemed to plummet to the pit of his stomach. He dropped to the ground and tried to pull Grandma down with him, but she twisted away. Another round of fire exploded, and the group scattered in all directions. Some ran to their cars, and others sprawled flat on the snow.

Grandma Ann went white. Incredulous, Ben watched his grandma step behind the Rosen family's tall, granite monument, he assumed for cover. He could see her from his position, but he didn't recognize her face, hardened and shadowed. She unzipped her purse, narrowed her eyes, and pulled out a gun. What the hell! Ben didn't know she had a gun. She pushed down the thumb safety, aimed at the man reaching across the

Cadillac, and pressed the trigger. The explosion rang in his ears. She pressed again and again until the attacker fell to the pavement. Ben couldn't hear a thing, temporarily deafened by the ringing in his ears. Did she even know how many shots she had fired? She was frozen like a statue. He was grateful when Rabbi Silverstein rushed to Grandma's side and lowered her weapon so the muzzle of the gun covered the ground.

Grandma shouted, "Have we stopped the threat?" She pressed a hand to her throat, staring at the blood on the snow.

"Someone call 911!" Dad yelled. "Tell them there's been a shooting. We need the police and an ambulance."

Chapter Sixteen—Hey, Little Apple

Siedlce, Poland

The sun began to sink in the west, and Esther completed the last-minute preparations in the kitchen for the Sabbath.

"It's almost Shabbos in the world," the shamash from the shul passed by, calling in the street. "Jews, ready yourselves for the Sabbath."

She was more than ready. With the Cossacks pilfering the meat market again on Thursday, and the tragic incident at the horse market after the upshernish Thursday night, the peace of Shabbos was all she wanted.

Her daughters each did their part and didn't need to be asked. Sora tidied the house and put out the brass candlesticks with candles. Chana set the table and put out Tatty's silver cup to bless the wine. Esther provided two loaves of braided challah bread that Chana arranged in front of Tatty's place, covered with a fine cloth Esther had embroidered with Hebrew letters spelling *Shabbat Shalom*. The aroma of roasted chicken and sweet rugelach, fresh from the oven, permeated the apartment.

She'd bathed herself and the three youngest children, and their faces shone. Dressed in their best garments, they were ready to welcome the Sabbath Queen. At that magical moment, despite the terrible events of the week, she felt blessed. Her loving husband, Dovid, stretched out a beckoning hand, drawing her toward him. His complexion was ruddy against his freshly laundered white shirt. She met his adoring gaze, and her chest ached with love for him. Together they had endured another week.

Her husband kissed the children. Then he blessed each one, working from oldest to youngest in succession, as he did every Friday night before going to synagogue. First, he blessed Sora and Chana, then his son Yitzchak, and the younger ones, Reva and Raizel. Tonight, he seemed to say the words more slowly. "May God bless you and guard you. May God show you favor and be gracious to you. May God show you kindness and grant you peace."

Sora brought her father his gold pocket watch as he prepared to leave for the synagogue. "Tatty, the doctor said that Aaron has some cracked ribs and bruises, but with rest he'll be fine."

"Thank God, Sorale." Dovid drew her close and embraced her with his strong arms.

"We want to go to America," Sora said almost in a whisper. She blushed and looked away.

"We?" Dovid tilted his head forward and scratched the back of his neck. His gaze turned to Esther.

"Aaron said we can make a new life in America and send money for all of you to come," Sora stammered. "He was going to speak to you himself… He wants to marry me." Her face was now bright red.

Esther clasped her hand to her throat. Her cheeks grew hot at the thought of Sora marrying. *Sora is just a child.* She tried to catch Dovid's gaze, silently appealing to him to put a stop to this.

Dovid ran a knuckle down Sora's cheek. "Sorale, do you want to marry him?"

"Yes, I do, Tatty." Sora smiled, and her eyes and nose crinkled.

Dovid kissed the top of her head. "We can talk more about this after Shabbos." He looked at Esther, his eyes misted with tears, and checked his pocket watch before sliding it into his vest pocket. "I'll be late for the service." Swiftly, he left for the synagogue.

****

Esther was resting on the sofa when the heavy wooden door burst open, and a cold wind invaded the house with a crowd of Cossacks. They stamped their muddy boots in a rhythmic stride across the scrubbed wooden plank floor, with their sabers at their waists. She bolted upright, flanked by Sora and Chana, and surveyed the group, recognizing the heavily mustached Cossack who appeared to be the commandant.

He stood erect and stared her down with steel-black eyes and raised eyebrows that brushed against the fur of his hat. He looked Chana up and down and then did the same to Sora, slowly with open appreciation. His gaze followed every curve of Sora's shapely form. Her daughters were barely two years apart, but the difference between fourteen and sixteen was like a bud and a rose in full bloom.

"What do you want?" Esther demanded.

"We are thirsty," Aleksandrov said. The commandant's expression suddenly changed, and he smiled agreeably.

Esther looked to Chana. "The men would like a drink before they are on their way."

Chana retrieved a bottle of vodka from the

sideboard. Aleksandrov snatched it from her hand and drank greedily straight from the bottle.

Esther held her breath, waiting and hoping they would take the vodka and leave. The commandant passed the bottle around. Then as though by a telegraphed signal, the brutish men in their baggy trousers and loose-fitting tunics roared with laughter and settled into the sofa with their legs spread wide. Some gathered at the dining table, which was set for the Sabbath, and pulled up their socks. The commandant retrieved the bottle and took the seat at the head of the table. He smoothed his coat, admired the silver cup, and filled it with vodka. Laughing brazenly, he chugged it in a single motion. He eyed the brass candlesticks in the center of the table and fingered the white lace tablecloth. Then he leaned back, closed his eyes, and inhaled.

Esther glanced toward the bedroom where the younger children slept. *Please God*, she prayed, *let them leave peacefully.* The ticking clock on the mantel struck the hour, and five consecutive chimes sounded. She looked to the entry door, expecting her Dovid to return from synagogue any moment.

She remembered the Siedlce pogrom in September 1906. From Friday night to Monday, the Cossacks set fire to houses, stores, and stalls using kerosene. Her brother Meir escaped the fire with burns, but they finished him off with their rifle butts. Gunfire lasted all day. They robbed, murdered, and raped. She stopped the horrors clawing at her mind and brought back her focus.

"We need to uplift the mood." The commandant drank and passed the vodka to the others. He stood on a chair and began singing a popular Russian folk song, "Hey, Little Apple!" in a deep and rich voice.

"Hey, little apple, but where are you rolling to? You will get in my mouth—and will never come out!"

The Cossacks joined the ditty, stamping their feet and clapping. They drank with gusto. Two soldiers at the dining table paired up in an arm-wrestling competition. They locked arms, veins bulging in their necks, sweating, grimacing, and turning red while struggling to see who was the strongest.

One Cossack and then another took the stage in a contest with each other. Hooting and hollering, they sought to outperform and demonstrate their strength, speed, and manliness. Throwing the empty bottle to the floor, they demanded another and spun and jumped with fervor. They danced spontaneously, squatting and alternately kicking with arms crossed over their chests. Continuously passing vodka, they jumped high above the plank floor and touched their fingertips to their toes while suspended in air.

Dovid finally returned from synagogue. He slowly closed the door behind him and entered the chaotic scene. Esther locked desperate eyes with her husband.

He mouthed the question, "Where are the children?"

She nodded toward the bedroom.

Abruptly, the dancing and arm wrestling stopped.

Dovid didn't miss a beat. "So you visit my home." He addressed Aleksandrov who was in his seat at the head of the dining table. "You must be hungry."

She couldn't take her eyes from his face.

Dovid squeezed her arm as he brushed past her and whispered to Sora and Chana in Yiddish, "Go check on the children."

On cue, Esther brought out challah, and Dovid offered the bread to the commandant, who ripped off a hunk and threw the rest to the men on the couch. In short order, Esther brought roasted chicken followed by carrots and potatoes. They pulled the chickens apart, sucked the meat from the bones, and devoured every scrap of the seasoned greasy skin.

Suddenly, the commandant looked around. "Where are your daughters?"

Esther pretended to smile and brought out the babka. "They'll be right back. They just went to check on the children."

She sliced and passed out the cinnamon-sugar babka laced with nuts and seeds, sticky with streusel topping. She kept passing until there was nothing left.

The men on the couch were sinking into a satiated stupor. The commandant stood and yanked the tablecloth from the table, sending dishes flying and breaking. The Cossacks sprang to their feet. The commandant snuffed out the Shabbos candles with his boot. Selectively, he stooped to pick up the brass candlesticks and the silver cup, rolled them in the tablecloth, and put them inside his tunic.

"Where are your daughters?" he bellowed.

"They should be coming now." Esther stiffened and locked eyes with her husband. Dovid held her elbow as they walked together toward the bedroom and opened the door.

The children slept, and Chana and Sora leaped from the straw mattress into their tatty's arms.

"Are they gone?" Chana implored, clutching her father's muscular arm.

"Not yet. They're asking for you." Tatty stroked his daughter's silken hair.

"You stay, Chana," Sora directed her sister. "It's me

they want." She smoothed her dress, and before they could argue or hold her back, Sora stood before the commandant.

He raised a bushy eyebrow, his lips parted, and an expression of pleasure washed across his face as he scanned Sora's body, stopping at her breasts and hips. "My little bird...now we go!" The commandant motioned with his hand, and the men instantly encircled Sora and dragged her from the house.

Esther cried out like an animal howling and crumbled into her husband's arms. Dovid carried her to the couch. Esther restrained him with all her might.

"Where are you going?" Esther implored.

He broke from his wife's hold and slipped into his coat. He slung Sora's coat over his arm. "To get our daughter."

"Then I'll lose both of you," Esther wailed. Intense pain radiated from her chest as though her heart were ripped out, and tears stung her cheeks.

Chapter Seventeen—Mirrors

Southwood, Michigan

Anna stepped into the foyer and suddenly felt confined in the airless hallway. Sheets hung over the long wall of mirrored bifold doors, signaling it was a time to concentrate on one's inner self, not outward appearances. She put one foot in front of the other, feeling numb and adrift as though she were not quite in her body.

When the police questioned her, she'd simply said, "I feared for my life and my family."

Her purse was lighter now. The police had taken the 1911 pistol and the testimony of witnesses. After Steven presented a preponderance of evidence for a case of self-defense and justifiable homicide, they let her go.

Heavy winter coats tightly packed a pair of steel clothing racks on casters. Dirty snow had melted from boots and pooled on the white tile. Anna's home was crowded with friends, neighbors, and relatives awaiting the family's return from the cemetery. The phone was ringing off the hook, and the din of conversation filled every corner. With Ira's trip to the emergency room and Anna's visit to the police station, it had been hours since they left Memorial Park. Some of the people seated at the dining room table with hot coffee hadn't even been at the cemetery, and Anna had no idea who they were. Libby was in the kitchen, brewing another pot of coffee, and answered the speaker phone.

"Anna Rosen?" said a woman breathlessly as if she were running. "This is Andrea Bashaw of *The Detroit News*, and I'd like to interview you about your heroic action at Memorial Park Cemetery this afternoon."

"This isn't Anna Rosen," Libby managed to break in. "And Anna is mourning the loss of her husband. This isn't a good time."

"Are you a relative? Did you witness the shooting? Don't talk to anyone else. I'll be right over. Remember, Andrea Bashaw of *The Detroit News*." She hung up.

Steven helped Anna slip out of her fur coat, and a chill passed over her, as though from an open window on the back of her neck, and she shivered, feeling Mo's presence for a brief moment. Mo hadn't liked that Anna carried a gun, but Anna knew that today he saw things differently.

The phone kept ringing, and voices came from outside. Rabbi Silverstein, Ira, Nanci, and Rubie arrived, along with the officer from the justice department, who followed at a respectful distance. Ira wore his coat as a cape over his right shoulder where his arm was in a sling. He looked pale and haggard. The men shook the snow from their coats and hung them.

Anna breathed a quiet sigh of relief at the sight of Ira and hugged him tightly, carefully navigating the sling.

"We're going to start calling you Annie Oakley, Mom." Ira dropped a kiss on his mother's cheek, and the group burst out in laughter and applause. The next thing Anna knew, the whole crowd in the house was on their feet applauding. She barely heard the hand clapping through the ringing in her ears, but she felt a wave of heat run through her heart.

Aliza and Ira hooked their arms in their mother's, and Anna tightened her hold on them as they walked with her to the dining room where a white memorial candle that would burn for seven days awaited on the credenza to be kindled. Whispers and murmurs traveled from person to person.

Anna stepped up to the table, and a hush fell over the room. Aliza, Steven, Ben, Estie, Joel, Nanci, Ira, Rubie, and Libby gathered around her. She struck a match, touched the flame to the wick, and was transported to the sacred space marked by the lighting of a candle. Aliza and Ira wrapped their arms around their mother's waist.

Ben stood behind with his hands on his grandma's shoulders, wearing his bar mitzvah suit, which was now his funeral suit. Estie and Joel hovered near their father. For a quiet moment no one spoke or argued. Shared grief bonded her family together. The flame danced and flickered, reaching up and bringing light.

A neighbor handed a box of tissues to Anna, and she blew her nose loudly. She couldn't contain the despair and stress of the day. Her mouth twisted, forming inarticulate sounds. She stood in the bosom of her family, taking slow, deep breaths until the sense of impending doom subsided.

Friends and neighbors milled around baskets of bagels and catered platters and filled their plates. They speculated about what had happened at the cemetery, who was shooting at Ira, and why.

Anna sought out the low mourners' stool beside the sofa, and Libby brought her a plate of lentils, a hard-boiled egg, and a cup of hot coffee.

Anna shook her head. "How can I eat when my husband lies dead in the cold ground?"

Libby sat on the ottoman next to Anna and handed her the egg. "I know you don't want to eat, but it is the shiva meal, a meal of condolence. At least eat an egg, as a reminder of the circle of life."

Anna nodded and took a small bite.

"Just so you aren't surprised, reporters from the newspaper and probably the TV are coming soon. Seems you've become a local hero." Libby gave a mirthless laugh.

"I can't talk to anyone today." Anna realized the phone continued ringing.

"I'll handle them. They're just doing their job, looking for news of interest in our humdrum suburban life—and this is definitely colorful."

"How did they find out so quickly?" Anna sat straight and for the first time looked around the entire living room.

"They have people who get paid to listen to the live police scanner in pursuit of the next story."

"I think I'd rather be in the kitchen with the kids." Anna handed Ben her plate and followed the sound of Aliza's voice into the breakfast nook where she also found Ira, Nanci, and Rubie tucked away at the dinette table. Ben put his grandma's plate on the kitchen counter and kept his distance from the group, occupying himself with the Rubik's Cube.

Anna sensed Ben's sudden withdrawal and fixed on untangling the complex web of emotions brewing within him, rested her eyes and attention on him. She had an inkling it had something to do with Ira based on the way he glanced at him with reproving eyes.

"Ira, I thought we'd lost you too. What happened out there?" Aliza handed Rubie a plate of bakery cookies with rainbow sprinkles.

Ira reached into his breast pocket and pulled out the pounded gold cigarette case, which now had a significant dent in the front. He held it up and smiled. "Dad was looking out for me, even now. The first shot went right through my jacket into the case, and the second grazed my left arm. Just a flesh wound." He poked his finger through the hole in his suit jacket, grinned, and hugged Rubie with his good arm.

Anna reached out for her husband's gold cigarette case and opened it to see the engraved inscription inside, *Always and forever, Anna*. She hadn't seen the case for at least a decade but remembered gifting it to Mo on Valentine's Day, entirely unaware it would one day save their son's life.

"You still haven't quit? You're the only one I know who can say smoking saved your life." Aliza inspected the dent in the cigarette case and passed it back to Ira.

"Without that case in my inside pocket, the bullet would have hit me directly in the heart, and I wouldn't have been here now to tell the story." Ira returned the gold case to his breast pocket.

"So how did you get here? We've been trying, with no success, to push through your furlough for days." Aliza swept her hair out of her eyes, and her face flashed dumbfounded joy.

"Best I can tell, it was that prison chaplain that greeted me in Loretto. He seemed to know I was coming before I even got there." Ira ate a piece of cake. "You have no idea how good this food is."

"You mean a clergyman? Like a pastor?"

"Actually, a rabbi. The real deal, long beard, black hat, and those strings hanging." Ira took a second piece of cake from the tray on the counter. "Like him. He looked just like him." He laughed and pointed.

At that moment, Rabbi Silverstein entered the kitchen and smiled warmly at Anna. She rose and motioned for him to join them.

"You must be Dr. Rosen." He extended a hand to shake Ira's good arm.

"Do you have something to do with my being here? I mean the furlough and all?" Ira stood and gave the rabbi a heartfelt handshake.

"I just made a call to a friend in Pittsburgh. We were in yeshiva together. I don't know how many years ago. He's the chaplain at Loretto now. I trust he was there for you? After today, we need to *bench gomel*."

Anna nodded and smiled. She suddenly remembered her father benching gomel in synagogue. Ira raised an eyebrow with a quizzical look.

"It's a tradition to say a blessing after surviving a life-threatening situation." Rabbi Silverstein tenderly knelt down beside Rubie. "And you must be very happy to see your daddy."

Rubie smiled shyly, slid off her chair, and clung to Ira's leg, burying her face and golden curls in his pants.

Rabbi Silverstein turned to Anna. "I'm so sorry for your loss." Then the rabbi addressed them all. "Next time we meet, may it be for a happy occasion." He nodded knowingly. "A bar mitzvah is coming soon. Mordy will be proud."

"I only wish I could be there," Ira said and draped an arm around Ben's shoulders.

"Don't touch me!" Ben exploded with rage and shoved Ira. "You bring trouble everywhere you go. This is all your fault." Ben bared his teeth like a wild dog. "You caused the stress and the heartache that killed him. If it weren't for you, he would still be alive!" His eyes blazed with bitterness.

Ira staggered into a chair and knocked it over. Rubie started to cry.

"Ben, what are you saying? Stop it, stop it, now." Aliza scooped up Rubie and folded her arms around the child's trembling body. "You apologize to your uncle, this minute." Her eyes shone angrily now.

Ben broke down crying. Rabbi Silverstein took Ben gently by the arm and quickly led him out of the kitchen. Anna followed. At that moment she regretted that Rabbi Silverstein hadn't been part of their family up until now. She longed for Mo to be there beside her and not in the cold earth. She wished the children were little again and that she could start over.

Ben collapsed on the corduroy couch in the den, crying and blowing his nose. Anna handed him a box of tissues.

"I'm sorry," he sobbed.

"It's okay to cry. Those tears are healing tears." Anna hugged him and stroked his back, soothing him.

"I should never have said those things." Ben pulled away and held his head in his hands.

"There will be an opportunity to apologize to your uncle," the rabbi assured him.

Anna stayed closed by his side. It was now Ben's turn to take slow, deep-belly breaths.

"Your grandpa died because it was his time. There is no such thing as 'before his time.' We live in the world of one percent, Ben. Like a glacier, we see only the tip above the water's surface, and the rest is hidden. Your grandpa never abandoned his Judaism. He immersed himself in chassidus. He had faith, and he was at peace. You need to learn."

Ben nodded and sat up straight. "I just need a minute."

The rabbi patted his shoulder before he left.

She was quiet and allowed him time to calm down and regain control of himself.

"What are these?" Ben picked up one of the books piled in front of him on the large square coffee table.

"Grandpa's reading material," she said.

He picked up the one on top, *The Laws of Shabbos, Vol 1*. Below it was volume two. He turned the pages and scanned. "This looks readable, practical, and most importantly in English. Only the footnotes are in Hebrew. At Alan's bar mitzvah, Grandpa said, 'We don't drive until Sabbath ends. It's probably time we talked about that.' "

"I remember." She leaned back into the corduroy cushions.

"I think Grandpa left these books just for me." Ben's eyes shifted nervously to his grandma. "You won't mind if I borrow these volumes?"

"Not at all. Consider them your inheritance."

****

"Mrs. Rosen, I'm Andrea Bashaw with the *News*. You said you would speak to me first. Why were you carrying a gun at your husband's funeral?"

Camera lights blazed across the living room as the reporters searched for Anna and called out their questions.

"I'm Katie Flood from CBS television to interview Dr. Ira Rosen and Anna Rosen about the shooting at Memorial Park Cemetery this afternoon. This is Jack Smith, my cameraman. We'll need only a few minutes of your time." Katie pushed her way to the front of the crowd. "At CBS our viewers would like to know who taught you to shoot like that."

"Was this shooting connected to Dr. Rosen's incarceration last year?" a *Free Press* reporter called out from the back.

Libby raised her arms and shouted over the tumult. "Mrs. Rosen is mourning her husband and isn't prepared to answer any questions at this time."

Steven and the officer from the justice department formed a wall on either side of Libby, and together they walked the reporters back. When they'd forced them over the threshold and onto the porch, Libby closed and locked the door.

Anna sighed and lowered herself onto the mourners' stool while Steven and Libby sat next to her on the plastic-covered couch. From that angle, the plastic-covered furniture struck her as a symbol of her American family life. Protecting the furniture against spills and stains had been the main objective.

The rabbi pointed with his index finger and counted men for the minyan. "We could use you for the tenth in the prayer service." He spoke to Steven. "Reciting the mourners' kaddish is something you can do for your father-in-law now," he urged.

"I'll pass. I'm not feeling that God is especially great at this moment," Steven responded coolly.

Just before seven p.m., friends and relatives streamed into the house for the evening prayer service.

A flood of emotions rushed through her. People she hadn't seen for years embraced her, and longtime friends of Mo joined the minyan.

Ira accepted a prayer book from the rabbi and said, "I want to thank you for whatever strings you pulled to get me here."

"It wouldn't be right for you to be deprived of attending your father's funeral."

"No one else saw it that way." Ira shrugged.

"Torah does not support incarceration." The rabbi set a basket of yarmulkes on an end table and handed one to Ira.

"What does the Torah support?" Ira placed the yarmulke on his head.

"Atonement and correction." The rabbi looked him directly in the eye and smiled. "Then you can get back to fulfilling your purpose."

"Rabbi, I'm not sure how much you know about what happened, but I was in the wrong place at the wrong time." Color ebbed into his cheeks.

Anna recognized a man in a gray suit who was striding across the living room in a knit yarmulke. He shook Rabbi Silverstein's hand while his free hand remained in his pocket. "I'm Rabbi Greene, a friend and rabbi to the Rosen family for many years."

Suddenly, the officer from the justice department stood and motioned to his watch, notifying Ira it was time to go. Anna could not bear the sight of her son being escorted back to prison.

Chapter Eighteen—Plea Bargain

Loretto, Pennsylvania

The blinding fluorescent lights flashed on at the same moment the loudspeakers blared, "The compound is now open."

Ira lowered himself from the top rack of the military-style bunk and stood for the five a.m. count. A cold shiver ran all the way down his spine. He didn't sleep well. The noise level, intermittent census counts, and flashlights continued all night long in the dormitory that was the size of an airplane hangar. He was in one of several housing units in the east compound. Each compound was a distinct and secure area consisting of multiple buildings including dormitory-style housing with bathrooms, inmate recreation, education, and food services.

Ira learned that inmates were prohibited from entering any unit other than the one they were assigned without authorization and that inmates could move about their compound only during the ten-minute "moves." After the move had ended, they had to wait for the next "move" to relocate.

His gaze darted to the red lights in the hallway. He was poised to sprint the second the red census lights turned off, indicating the count was complete. Every minute past five a.m., the bathrooms would get more crowded.

Ira made a mad dash to the bathrooms. He rounded the corner into the showers and was thrown back from the impact of slamming into an obstacle at full force. A thrusting blow penetrated his gut with might, and he doubled over in pain. He didn't see the face of the barrel-chested mass covered in tattoos in front of him.

"We have gas showers for you Jews." The six-foot-one, three-hundred-pound hulk sneered before he turned and sauntered into the showers.

"Don't let them see your fear," a compact, middle-aged inmate muttered and handed Ira his towel and shower bag from the cement floor. "I'm Sam."

"Thanks, I'm Ira," he croaked breathily. "Who the hell was that?"

"They call him Snake. He's been in prison since he was nineteen. They moved him here because he's almost ready for release. He's angry all the time, and he hates everyone. Don't take it personally."

"Of course not, I'm sure it's just his way of getting acquainted." Ira sneered. "Has anyone suggested he go after the smaller warm-blooded prey such as the mice and rats?" He tracked a rat that disappeared into the drain. "Or I could just stay out of his way." He palpated his abdomen and ribs, checking for injury.

"Exactly. Even if the only open shower is next to Snake, don't use it. He likes his space. It's a rule, and if you break it, there'll be hell to pay. That was just a warning."

"Thanks for explaining." Ira looked up at the wall clock. It was now five thirty.

"You new here?" Sam inquired.

"Relatively—I was transferred from Sandstone last

week, but I was only there a short time," Ira muttered miserably.

"If you'd like to meet up at breakfast, I can give you the lay of the land. You know, point out some of the unwritten rules." Sam winked.

"Sure, I'm all for getting up to speed quickly." Ira saw something in Sam he had not seen in any other inmate. When he smiled, warmth shone from his mink-brown eyes with crow's feet etched deep into his skin. Ira imagined he'd had a life of laughter and joy before his incarceration. He wondered what his story was and followed Sam into the line for the showers. This was the first normal conversation he'd had with an inmate.

Waiting for the seven a.m. ten-minute "move," Ira checked the hospital corners on his bed one last time. They were faultless. *Not bad for someone who never made a bed up until two months ago.* He wore the standard-issue khakis with an elastic waistband, white T-shirt, and blue canvas slip-on shoes. He woke up every day and wondered who he was and how he was going to get through this terrible situation.

Ira found Sam in the cafeteria and sat across from him with his all-white, all-carb breakfast tray. The lousy menu, which never included fruit, was more bearable when there was someone to talk to.

"How long are you serving?" Sam ate the watery oatmeal.

"Twenty months," Ira replied hollowly. He didn't know whether it was polite to ask about sentences and was relieved that Sam evidently did. He wondered what Sam had done that landed him in federal prison.

"Any time is rough." Sam shook his head. "Why are you here?"

"I was a doctor convicted of writing illegal prescriptions. Plea bargain got me a reduced sentence. What about you?"

"Two years for insider trading with eight months left. I've got a wife and a family waiting for me on the outside. That keeps me going. And you?"

"I don't know how I'm going to get through this." Ira slumped over his tray.

"You will get through this. Every single day you need to think about what your new life will look like and how you will make it happen. Do you have a family?"

"A wife and a beautiful daughter." Ira hung his head.

"Are they behind you?" Sam raised an eyebrow.

"They are what keeps me alive." Ira twisted the wedding ring on his finger, glad it was permitted given that it had no jewels or engraving and had limited use as brass knuckles in a fight. "I've lost my medical license, my career, my reputation, and everything else." He recognized the gold Star of David necklace Sam wore. He used to have one similar.

"I get it. I'm barred from Wall Street, lost my license, fined by the SEC, and can't expect to work in finance again. It won't end when the sentence is over."

"It's a life sentence, and I still don't understand how this happened." Ira shuddered.

"You've got time to figure that out. But right now, let's talk about what you need to know to best survive Loretto." Sam thrust an impatient hand through his black-and-silver hair. "Don't touch the televisions." He paused to shovel in the rest of the watery oatmeal.

Ira arched a quizzical eyebrow.

"White guys don't change the channel. The Blacks and the Hispanics control the television. You've

111

probably noticed prison is a very racist place." A sardonic smile crossed Sam's face.

"So Snake isn't just having a bad day?" Ira's throat muscles tightened.

"Snake has a bad day every day, which is why he took care of our very own godfather up until he was transferred to the camp."

"A bona fide mafioso inside Loretto?" He gave a shaken laugh.

"Yeah, we have our own mobsters here. I'm talking the whole cheek-kissing, back-slapping, mafia social club, leading and controlling the family from inside. If you meet Don Vece, you need to show proper respect. Nicky Vece's always got his number one and two guys with him, and they're loyal as dogs. You'll see him come from the commissary with his boys carrying cases of stuff. He shops big, his boys cook for him, and they never eat here in the chow hall. I hear he has mini banquets and parties every night with his boys and those who cater to him."

The siren blared, signaling work call.

"We'll talk more at supper." Sam nodded and was gone.

"Sure, I'm off to earn forty cents an hour," Ira muttered to himself and calculated that, at the end of the day, he'd have earned enough to buy a foil pouch of tuna from the commissary.

Chapter Nineteen—Out of Practice

Southwood, Michigan

The rabbi rang the doorbell at precisely 6:58 p.m., just as Ben imagined he'd done every Thursday for the past fifteen years. He cleared his plate and thanked Grandma for the delicious spaghetti and meatball dinner, his favorite, before answering the door. He looked forward to his standing Thursday dinner date with Grandma Ann followed by his class with Rabbi Silverstein.

Ben was getting used to the rabbi's long square beard, black hat, and warm smile. While he couldn't explain it, he couldn't deny that he liked this rabbi. They settled into leather barrel chairs at a beautiful mahogany table in Grandpa's private study. After a month of weekly study sessions, he still felt like a trespasser, as though he didn't belong in this esteemed place. The rabbi motioned for Ben to sit to his right. Grandma brought in a tray with a pitcher of water, two glasses, and a package of mandel bread, bearing the proper kosher certification. A grandfather clock in a case taller than Ben stood in the long hallway, the pendulum swung hypnotically. The clock struck seven, and bell tones counted the hour.

"Hello, Chana, so good to see you." Rabbi Silverstein smiled broadly, and the corners of his eyes crinkled. "You always have a sweet treat. I spoke with the chaplain in Loretto today and learned that Ira is doing fine. He's adjusting to the new facility."

"I'm so relieved to hear that." Grandma set down the tray. They exchanged good wishes, and she left them to their learning.

"How are you doing, Ben? Any complications from that allergic reaction?"

"I'm okay, feeling pretty much back to normal and haven't had any reactions since that Saturday night when I ate shrimp."

Ben uncomfortably spun the medical alert bracelet around his wrist and hoped they weren't going to talk about his meltdown the day of the funeral. He told himself to quit fidgeting and rested his hand on the mahogany table. "My mother won't let me eat out in restaurants anymore. She says the risk of cross-contamination is too great."

Ben scanned the built-in bookcases lining the walls. He'd never been inside his grandpa's study before his meetings with the rabbi. Now he felt he had entered his inner sanctuary.

"Given the severity of your reaction, that seems like a reasonable precaution. Maybe I can convince her to put us on the 'safe' list, and you and your grandma Ann can join us for a Friday night meal? My son Levy is back home from yeshiva for a couple of weeks, and I know he'd enjoy meeting you."

"I'd like that." Ben relaxed, and his mouth curved into a smile.

"Great. I'll have Levy reach out to you. So, shall we continue where we left off last week?" Rabbi Silverstein raised an eyebrow and opened volume one of the *Laws of Shabbos* to the bookmarked page.

"Actually, before we start, I wondered if you might help me figure out something my grandpa said when he visited me the night he passed away." Ben's eyes lifted and met the rabbi's.

"I'll try." The rabbi leaned back now and gazed intently at Ben.

"He said, '*I've done all I can. Now this mission is yours.*' "

"Can you provide some context? What were you talking about just before he said that?"

"Grandpa reminded me of the day I helped him dock the *Sunchaser*, his cabin cruiser, fighting high winds in a terrible storm."

"And before that?"

"That's the thing, I just came out of a coma, and it's all a little fuzzy. I remember asking him about Siedlce and whether coming to America was what he hoped it would be."

"What did he say?"

"There was something he regretted. Something he wanted to give me." Ben surveyed the room lined from floor to ceiling with books. He crouched in front of the bookcases, studying the volumes on the bottom shelf. "When you met with Grandpa, what books did you learn from?"

"We started with the Hebrew Bible. There are several versions two shelves up on the middle shelf."

Ben looked closer at the intimidating sets of books lining the walls of the room. He recognized a leather-bound set of the five books of Moses. "You mean these?"

"Yes, but most recently your grandpa was interested in chassidus."

"What is chassidus?"

"It's the mystical aspect of Judaism."

"When we first met, you asked me if I was bar mitzvah and if I wanted to put on my grandpa's tefillin."

"Yes, I remember."

"My bar mitzvah is going to be on Saturday, March 22nd. I was wondering if you could tell me what it would be like to have a bar mitzvah at your shul."

"We can talk about that. Let's first look at the calendar to determine your Hebrew birthday. When were you born?" The rabbi took a thick leather-bound calendar from his breast pocket and swiftly flipped the pages.

"April 14th, 1962." Ben fidgeted, awaiting the rabbi's answer.

"Your Jewish birthday is Nissan 10, 5735, and this year that falls on Saturday, March 22nd—no change there. In my shul, on your bar mitzvah, you wouldn't put on tefillin during the prayer service because it's Shabbat, but you would read from the Torah, depending on your ability. And from that day forward you will be an adult and part of the Jewish community responsible for keeping the commandments. You will be counted for a prayer service needing a minyan, a group of ten men. And you'll put on tefillin every day going forward."

"Can you teach me about the prayer service and to read from the Torah?"

"That depends on you. Three months is much less time than it takes most young men to prepare for bar mitzvah. Can you read Hebrew?"

"Yes, and I learn very fast." Ben knew it was a stretch to say he could read Hebrew, but he did know the letters, the vowels, and the sounds they made.

"Your bar mitzvah parsha is Tzav. Have you learned any portion of your parsha?"

"No, but I've learned the Hebrew blessings recited before the Torah and haftarah readings. I'm supposed to be working on a project to make the world better—*tikkun olam* they call it. And I'm in the Bar Mitzvah Club where we've got to do a good deed together. Is that what bar mitzvah is about?"

"Transforming the world is a prime directive, but that can't be accomplished without transforming ourselves. Bar mitzvah is a celebration of a commitment to keep to that path according to the laws of the Torah."

"At your shul, is there a party?"

"Each family chooses their own way to celebrate. A festive meal with friends, family, and community is traditional, but lavish parties aren't the custom. Bar mitzvah is the entry into Jewish life. I like to say it's an opening celebration, not a 'going out of business sale.'" Rabbi Silverstein smiled, looked Ben in the eye, and was quiet for what felt like a long time. "It's customary for the bar mitzvah boy to share some thoughts about what he's learned from his Torah portion and preparation for his bar mitzvah. You'd have to do a lot of work on your own."

"I can do that. I've been studying sections of my grandpa's books on the laws of Shabbos. I'm good at learning independently."

"During World War II in Belgium, there was a General Creighton Abrams who led a tank battalion. He is accredited with the wise statement, 'when eating an elephant, take one bite at a time.' Have you heard that expression?"

Ben nodded, and his cheeks got hot. "But I have a million questions."

"You're an outstanding student, Ben. I wish I had a

dozen more students like you. What do you think about talking to your parents about wanting to do something different for your bar mitzvah?"

"I've tried. I told my mother that I don't want the mega-birthday event they're planning. I keep thinking that we're missing the point. If that's what this is about, it feels like a serious letdown. Then there's my father. He's set on me having my bar mitzvah in the new sanctuary he's been working on getting built for the last ten years."

Rabbi Silverstein stroked his beard. "Ben, when you turn thirteen, you'll become bar mitzvah, with or without a party. Wherever and however you celebrate, learning Torah and Jewish law is a good thing. We can start tonight learning your parsha. I'll give you an overview and read the first portion with the proper tune, which is called trope. Then I'll make you an audio recording you can use to practice. When we meet on Thursdays, I'll monitor your progress, make corrections, and answer all of your questions. Deal?"

The rabbi extended a hand.

"Deal." Ben shook enthusiastically. "Before we start, I have one more question. When I put on my grandpa's tefillin, why did I start crying?"

"It's for you to answer that question. I could only guess that maybe you connected with your grandpa. Maybe because tefillin have the power to awaken your soul and remind you who you are. Those feelings can be overwhelming."

Ben nodded, making sense of the words as the rabbi removed a large book from the bookshelf and opened it to the portion. He motioned for Ben to come closer.

"Before the day I put on my grandpa's tefillin, there

was nothing about this bar mitzvah that I felt connected to. None of it seemed relevant. People at the temple say all these rules and rituals don't apply anymore." He immediately regretted his words, afraid he'd offended Rabbi Silverstein.

Rabbi Silverstein removed his glasses, and Ben thought he had never seen such doleful eyes.

"On his birthday in 1957, my rebbe spoke of this mistaken notion. He explained that to overcome the challenges of immigrating to the United States, some Jews had the misconception that the solution was to quickly assimilate into the new environment by giving up their Jewish way of life. They contrived some justification, that the Jewish way of life, with the observance of the Torah and Mitzvot, observing the laws, didn't fit. They looked for flaws with the Jewish way of life and convinced themselves that everything in the secular society was pleasing and precious."

Ben listened intently.

"With this approach, parents hoped to protect their children and ensure their survival in the new environment. And my rebbe asked, 'But what kind of existence is it, if everything spiritual and holy is traded for the material? What kind of survival is it if it means the sacrifice of the soul for the amenities of the body?' "

Ben was intrigued by the rabbi's words. He raked his fingers through his hair. "The thing is, I don't even know the rules. That morning here at my grandma's when I first put on tefillin, you told me to recite the Shema. I feel like that's the only thing I know because from the time I was little, Mom would say the Shema with me before bed. The Shema includes some of the commandments, right?"

"Yes, the Shema mentions the commandments of tefillin, mezuzah, and tzitzit, all signs of our love and commitment. The Shema is our quintessential faith. It reflects our fundamental belief in one God. It's a commandment to recite the Shema in the morning and at night. And the Shema are the last words we speak before we die. Through the Shema, we declare that we love God with all our heart and will dedicate our lives to carrying out his will. For millenniums Jewish mothers have put their children to bed while singing Shema to them."

"I know Shema by heart," he stated as though making the realization for the first time. "It's like an imprint."

"The Shema is what is written on the rolled piece of parchment inside the mezuzah." Rabbi Silverstein pointed to the mezuzah mounted on the doorway into the study.

"My grandparents have a lot of mezuzahs in their house. It seems they have them on every doorway."

"It states in the Shema we must place them on the doorposts of our house. We interpret that as every doorway with a lintel, not a bathroom or a closet."

"In my house we only have one on the front door." Ben got up and examined the mezuzah.

"That's good, and we should check the scroll to make sure it's been written properly and is still intact. There are many stories told about the protection afforded by the mezuzah." Rabbi Silverstein smiled warmly at Ben.

"We can use all the protection we can get." Ben rolled his eyes and laughed. He flipped up the top of the decorative case, removed the scroll, and studied it. "Can I put one on my bedroom door?"

"Yes, you should place it on the right side of the door, in the upper third of the doorpost, around shoulder height, with the top slanting in toward your bedroom, and there's a blessing…" The rabbi trailed off. "Or I can send over a mezuzah with my son Levy tomorrow. I know he'd be happy to help you put it up."

"That would be great!" Ben was relieved. "So, what do you think my grandpa meant when he said the mission is mine?"

"I'm certain that you'll discover the meaning of his message for yourself." Rabbi Silverstein smiled and placed a hand on Ben's shoulder. "We're just about out of time for this week, and we need to read the first section of your parsha." The rabbi looked at the clock.

"Just one more thing." Ben paused, awaiting the nod and acknowledgment from the rabbi to continue. "Do you remember we talked about how I'm on a swim team?"

"Yes, you told me you practice at six a.m. every weekday." Rabbi Silverstein gave Ben his full attention.

"That's right. What we didn't talk about is that some of my swim meets are on Saturday."

"I see." The rabbi nodded.

"We read in my grandpa's book on the laws of Shabbos that there is a prohibition against swimming on the Sabbath. I can't stop thinking about that. If the Sabbath is a day of rest, why aren't we permitted to swim?"

"Ben, the laws of Sabbath all have one purpose—to make it holy."

"I can already tell that I'm doing a lot of things wrong," he stammered. "Every time we talk, I learn about something else that I'm messing up."

"That's why we call it 'practicing Judaism.' " Rabbi Silverstein smiled and put an arm around Ben's shoulders.

"I've got to tell you"—Ben gave a lopsided grin—"my family is really out of practice."

Chapter Twenty—The Wager

Siedlce, Poland

Esther's wailing faded into the distance as Dovid snaked down Warszawski Street. He hugged the shadows and followed the boisterous catcalls and howling band of Cossacks. From the tracks in the dirt, he could see where they dragged his daughter Sora. Before the war, the three hotels—the Litewski Hotel of Chaim Wyszkowics and the Węgierski and Warszawski Hotels of Moszek Zubrowics—had made an urbane and bustling thoroughfare. The street was empty given the curfew from eight p.m. to six a.m. Dovid disappeared into every archway and portal in the event the Cossacks looked back—but they never did. He kept the band within his range of vision. Suddenly, the group halted in front of a tall wooden supply shed that looked like a stockade between the Węgierski and Warszawski Hotels. The windows were boarded over.

Dovid lurked close enough to hear their voices and see Commandant Aleksandrov give the brass candlesticks and silver cup to two of the soldiers. "Comrades Vladimir and Mikola, go to the railroad station to sell these valuables. There is very high demand for copper and silver. Take not less than 500 rubles!"

Without ado, the soldiers turned on their heels and marched in the direction of the railroad station where stolen items were bought and sold.

As the soldiers moved out toward the train station, Dovid moved in closer and surveyed the darkness, frantically searching until he laid eyes on his daughter.

Commandant Aleksandrov pushed on the stuck shed door with his shoulder. "Open it!" he ordered.

The soldier not restraining Sora stepped forward swiftly and attempted to pry the door open with the butt of his rifle. When this didn't work, he kicked it with the heel of his boot, and it flew open. Sora screamed as they dragged her inside. The scream pierced Dovid's heart, and it took all his strength to restrain his impulse to rush Aleksandrov and his men prematurely.

Aleksandrov entered the stockade and shoved his men into the street. "You watch and wait for Comrades Vladimir and Mikola." The commandant secured the door from inside.

Nausea and dread rolled through the pit of Dovid's stomach. He knew what would happen. Aleksandrov would press himself against his daughter, grope her beneath her dress, and force his mouth on hers.

Sora screamed, and then the sound grew muffled. An image of Aleksandrov's filthy hand pressed over his daughter's mouth burned in Dovid's mind. Fury rose within him, and he prepared to storm the shed. Suddenly, comrades Vladimir and Mikola returned from the train station. Several czar officers passed, and the comrades snapped to attention when Colonel Stayanov approached them.

"Who is your commandant?" Colonel Stayanov demanded.

"Major Aleksandrov, sir!" they shot back.

"Where is your commandant? He knows there's a

meeting at midnight." When the comrades stood mute, Stayanov stepped toward the supply shed, kicked the door open, and backed away.

Aleksandrov stumbled through the doorway, straightening his tunic, and saluted the colonel in the moonlight.

"All commandants were ordered to report to the Victoria Hotel," Colonel Stayanov barked at Aleksandrov. "Immediately!" he hissed and marched down Warszawski Street. Aleksandrov quickly followed the colonel, pausing momentarily to secure a padlock on the door, and fell into line behind Colonel Stayanov.

Dovid emerged from the shadows of the portal and bolted for the stockade door. The lock held it tight. Adrenaline surged through him, and he thought only of his daughter Sora and prayed that he was not too late. He gripped the lock in his muscular hands and twisted it until it bent, released, and dropped to the dirt. He slammed his shoulder into the door, and it flung open. Sora was curled in a fetal position on the crate, sobbing and shaking. He wrapped her in the brown wool coat and scooped her into his arms as though she were still five years old. Concealed in the shadows, he stole through the streets, carrying his daughter home.

Chana and Esther were picking up broken dishes when Dovid returned with Sora. "Thank God you're back!" His wife kissed Sora's tear-streaked face and swept back her disheveled hair. "Are you hurt?"

"Not hurt, Mama." Sora suddenly let go and vehemently sobbed. Tears streamed down her face. "I feel filthy from him touching me." Her lips trembled, and she wiped her mouth with the sleeve of her coat. "If not for that officer…he wouldn't have stopped." She shivered uncontrollably. "Tatty, why do they hate us so?"

"Sorale, that is a long story for another time. Esther, take the children to your sister's at once." Dovid pushed their coats toward them. "Stay out of sight and move quickly."

"Not without you!" Esther wiggled the sleeping children into sweaters and coats.

"Don't argue!" Dovid's jaw was set firm. He kissed each sleepy child's head and forced them into the street.

He knew Aleksandrov would be back for Sora when she was not where he left her. His appetite was whet and not satisfied. Dovid pushed down his fury, drew a deep breath, and paced as he planned a scheme to confound the commandant. While the plan was thin, it was all he had. He dropped into his seat at the head of the table, waiting for the Cossacks to return.

****

The cock crowing alerted Dovid to the first light. The dragoon hurled open the door and lined up on either side of the entry at attention as Aleksandrov stomped forward like a feral beast.

"Where's my daughter?" Dovid jumped to his feet and confronted Aleksandrov, filling the silence before Aleksandrov could speak. "What have you done to her?" Dovid willed his heart not to pound and his palms not to sweat while concealing that he knew his daughter was safe. The broken glass on the warped plank floor cracked beneath his boots.

Aleksandrov looked confused. His icy eyes darted around the apartment. "Where is your family?" he shouted in Russian. He flung open the bedroom doors and scanned every crevice. The Cossacks flew in all directions, overturning furniture and emptying closets and cupboards.

"I want my daughter back," Dovid repeated, pretending he was not the one who rescued her.

"Are you a gambling man?" Aleksandrov smiled.

"I'll make you a wager." Dovid sized up Aleksandrov. "We arm wrestle, and if I win, you back off, and I get my daughter back." He stood resolute as though unaware that he was outnumbered and outgunned.

"And if I win, what do I get?" Aleksandrov's nostrils flared, and he smiled with amusement.

"My other daughter." Dovid stood eyeball to eyeball with Aleksandrov. Neither backed down.

The dragoon gathered around the table, and broken glass screeched beneath their boots. Aleksandrov removed his saber and his tunic. Hairy as a bear, he stepped close to the table with his right foot forward and placed his elbow on the table.

Dovid removed his wool coat and rolled up the sleeves of his white shirt. While physical strength mattered, he knew this was as much about positioning as strength. He placed his elbow on the table, tightened his core muscles, and opposed Aleksandrov. The two men gripped each other's hand. The goal was to pin the other's arm onto the surface of the table, the winner's arm over the loser's.

Mikola slammed his palm on the table, and the wrestling began. In an instant, merriment filled the room, and the Cossacks began their howls of encouragement and support for their commandant. Aleksandrov tried to rotate his hand over his opponent, and Dovid rotated his shoulder and body in the direction he wanted

Aleksandrov's arm to go. Aleksandrov twisted his wrist toward his chest and applied pressure. Dovid recognized the classic top roll and countered with a pulling motion and moved Aleksandrov's hand toward him, applying force with his back and shoulders. Both men grimaced, and Aleksandrov grunted.

Dovid visualized Sora and Chana frozen in time as children playing in the park and laughing with gaiety and innocence. A surge of strength rose up in him. As Aleksandrov pushed in one direction, Dovid pulled in the other. Slowly, Aleksandrov's arm inched closer to the table's surface. Dovid curled his thumb underneath to secure a tighter grip and continued to pull, drawing strength from his back and shoulders, until Aleksandrov was pinned to the table.

Aleksandrov's nostrils flared, and then his expression quickly changed to joviality, and he slapped his opponent on the back.

"Where's my daughter?" Dovid demanded, concealing that he had knowledge of her whereabouts.

"I let her go when I was finished with her," Aleksandrov sneered, acting like he was in control. "If she comes home, she's yours." He wiped the sweat from his chest and buttoned his tunic. Then he secured his belt with the saber. With a single motion of his hand, his soldiers sprang to attention and marched behind him into the street.

Dovid slammed the door, threw his head back, and raised his arms above his shoulders in a punching motion. But within a moment, wariness and disbelief consumed him. Why did he think Aleksandrov would honor any deal? He grabbed his coat and rushed out the back, taking a circuitous route to reunite with his family.

Chapter Twenty-One—Protection

Southwood, Michigan

Levy stepped into the elegant foyer of Ben's home on Friday, carrying a hammer and a mezuzah. He was tall and lanky like his father in his white shirt, black pants, and tzitzit strings hanging at his sides. Ben thought he gave the impression of all wrists and ankles.

"I'm Ben—you must be Levy." Ben extended his hand and gazed upon Levy.

"Good to meet you. My father has told me a lot about you." Levy smiled broadly and gripped Ben's large hand with his own. His narrow electric-blue eyes met Ben's. He gazed up at the high ceiling and sparkling chandelier.

Ben's parents were in the kitchen arguing. Their voices carried into the foyer like an echo chamber.

Ben glanced at Levy awkwardly. "Sorry, they're fighting about me. It's been a little intense. Let's go up to my bedroom." He led the way up the staircase.

"I can imagine. I heard about your grandfather's passing and the funeral. Please accept my condolences. Sorry I wasn't around to come over and meet you sooner."

"You're away at yeshiva most of the time?"

"Yeah, but I'm on break next week and home for Shabbos this week and next. I heard you're preparing for your bar mitzvah. When is it?" Levy checked out the oak trim on the doorframe of Ben's bedroom and positioned the mezuzah on an angle.

"March 22nd." Ben held the mezuzah in place as Levy fit the tiny nail into the hole at the top of the clear plastic case.

"Just ten weeks away." Levy lined up the hammer.

"Your dad's a great teacher."

"He says you're an excellent student, and he doesn't say that often. So, there's a blessing we say when putting up a mezuzah. You can just answer, amen." Levy recited the Hebrew words and tapped in the nail on the top and on the bottom.

"Amen," Ben answered. "What does it mean?" The mezuzah was just the right height for him to reach it.

"The words mean 'Blessed are you, Lord our God, King of the Universe, Who has made us holy with His commandments and commanded us to affix a mezuzah.' "

"Made us holy? What does that mean 'made us holy'? Sorry. You don't need to answer that. I just keep hearing about things being holy, and I don't understand what that means. But do you know how to check the mezuzah we have on the front door to make sure it's still good?"

"My dad will have to do that. But you've now got the best security system available on your bedroom door." Levy put an arm on Ben's shoulder. "Hey, would you like to come spend Shabbos at our house?"

"You mean dinner?" Ben raised an eyebrow.

"You're invited for all of Shabbos. Stay over, and we can walk to shul, have lunch, the whole deal. I'll bring you home Saturday night." Levy scanned the books on Ben's bookcase, which were mostly science fiction.

"Yeah, I think I'd like that." He laughed to himself. "What time should I come over?" He looked at his watch—two thirty. He started thinking about what he needed to do to put his life on pause. For weeks his discomfort with swimming on Saturday had mounted. It had begun when he started learning the laws of keeping the Sabbath. He wanted to experience a real Shabbat.

"My dad invited both your grandmas for dinner too. If you're up for it, they said they'll pick you up at a quarter to five."

****

Ben showered and dressed in clothes he would wear to an event. He parted and combed his thick wet hair and brushed away the dry flaky skin on his broad forehead. Swimming took its toll on his complexion. He was packing a small bag with pajamas and toiletries when his mom and dad poked their heads into his room.

"You clean up nice!" Dad gave him a once-over. "Going out?"

"The Silversteins invited me for Shabbat."

"Nice." Mom adjusted the knot on his tie.

"You need a ride?" Dad reached into his pocket for car keys.

"Nope, Grandma Ann and Grandma Libby are picking me up in twenty minutes." Ben packed his comb and deodorant.

"Really? So you don't need a ride home after dinner?" Dad pressed.

"Actually, I'm staying for all of Shabbat and won't be home until Saturday night."

"What about your swim meet?" Dad's forehead

creased.

"I told Coach Walker that I won't be at the meet."

"You did what?" Dad's eyes bored into him.

Ben braced himself. "I called Coach and told him that I'm not swimming on Saturday." He'd hoped to dodge this conversation for the next twenty minutes until he got out of the house. He was careful not to mention he'd left Coach a message, and he specifically didn't say he wouldn't be swimming on any future Saturdays. He just wanted one Shabbat.

"Don't you think we should have discussed that?" Dad glowered.

"I think you should bring a hostess gift, you know, wine, chocolate, or flowers. How nice that the Silversteins invited all three of you," Mom interjected with bubbly enthusiasm. "Come to think of it, we have some nice cases of kosher wine for the bar mitzvah. Dad and I will check on that while you finish getting ready."

Mom took Dad's arm and pulled him down the hall. Their conversation carried like they were in an echo chamber due to the tall ceilings and marble walls and floors.

"What are you doing?" Dad scowled, his face beet red.

"Keeping you from saying something you'll regret, Counselor. Let it rest," Mom whispered. "Did you hear there was an earthquake in Los Angeles yesterday measuring 6.7 on the Richter scale?" She casually changed the subject and resumed her normal voice.

"So this must be the aftershocks," Dad fired back and followed her downstairs.

Chapter Twenty-Two—After Sunset

Southwood, Michigan

The machatunim picked up Ben precisely at a quarter to five as planned. Despite himself, Steven was delighted to see his mother and mother-in-law dressed up and excited to take their grandson to Shabbat dinner at the Silverstein's. Estie and Joel set the table for their own family dinner, and Aliza finished last minute preparations in the kitchen. He knew Aliza was right, and he needed to be careful not to push Ben further away. Winding down after a couple of hectic and crazy weeks, he relaxed with the newspaper. Ben's anaphylactic reaction, the funeral, the shooting, and Ira home on furlough was more commotion than he had an appetite for. Finally, he thought, the family would get back to their normal routines, but he wasn't a fool. He knew it was wishful thinking. Given the turbulent events let loose, it was unlikely they would ever return to normal.

The phone rang, and Steven answered on the third ring.

"May I speak to Ben?" a commanding voice boomed through the receiver.

"Ben isn't home. This is his father. May I take a message?" Steven clicked a pen, and the spring-loaded ink cartridge extended and retracted as he waited to write.

"This is Coach Walker. Don't tell me I missed him! I called as soon as I retrieved Ben's message off that recording machine."

"Well, yes, Ben's already left. What's this about?"

"It's about that nonsensical message he left. He says he's not swimming on Saturday."

Steven quickly surmised that Coach Walker didn't feel it was beyond the scope of his responsibility to provide personal influence when one of his athletes, especially one as talented as Ben, required that extra push to become a champion. "It's just a conflict this week, Coach. There's been a lot going on here." He doodled on the scratch pad.

"This is the week that matters! Tomorrow swimmers qualify for state. Swimmers who qualify will compete in the prelims. The medley team is depending on him."

"That must have slipped Ben's mind. He wouldn't let his team down."

"He's not just any swimmer. He's our strongest in every stroke. I've got to talk to him. I'm sure once he realizes what's at stake, he'll change his mind."

Steven drew three-dimensional cubes on the scratch pad and sought a solution he could live with. "Coach, I don't see any harm in you talking with Ben. He's with his grandmothers, having dinner with a friend of the family. They won't answer the phone, but you could stop over if you think you really need to see him. Looks like snow is coming, but I'll give you the address if you want to go there."

Chapter Twenty-Three—Skipping

Southwood, Michigan

"Thank you for inviting us." Ben handed Mrs. Silverstein a bottle of 1972 Bordeaux.

The rebbetzin wore a floor-length crushed-velvet hostess gown of the same burgundy color and smiled warmly, greeting them like royalty. "Good Shabbos. Thank you all for coming. It's so special to have the soon-to-be bar mitzvah boy with both his grandmothers! Anna and Libby, we're thrilled you could join us. You must know how much we admired and enjoyed Mordy. We'll miss him so much."

Grandma blanched at the mention of Grandpa. Clearly, Grandma was still not herself. Ben knew it was hard each time she had to do the things they used to do together without him. He loved how Grandma Libby sensed this too and squeezed Grandma Ann's hand.

"It smells amazing in here," Ben murmured as he inhaled the aroma of freshly baked challah bread. He recognized the smell of chicken soup permeating the house. It was heavenly and reminded him of holiday meals at Grandma Ann's.

In the dining room the table was set with fine china. Candles glowed from a silver candelabra, and other guests mingled.

"Glad to see you, Ben. Levy will show you where

you can put your things." Rabbi Silverstein shook Ben's hand and nodded toward Levy who was greeting other guests at the door.

The rebbetzin handed the bottle of wine to the rabbi.

He rotated the bottle and studied the fine print on the label. "This is a rare gift. It's not easy to find a kosher Bordeaux. We shall enjoy it for kiddush."

"Great! My mom gets credit for the wine." Ben laughed and headed across the room to greet Levy. Just being there breathed new life into him. He was excited to see what Shabbat looked like.

****

The glow of Sabbath candles shone forth from the candelabrum, and the crowded table was covered with a white tablecloth and elaborate floral centerpieces. The aroma of sweet and savory mouthwatering dishes enveloped him. Suddenly, the brass door knocker banged on the solid wood door.

The rabbi, dressed in his finest black silk coat, opened the door. Ben had a view into the foyer from his seat at the dining room table. Coach Walker stood at the entryway amidst the lightly falling snow, and the rabbi welcomed the coach into his home.

"How can I help you?" Rabbi Silverstein sounded like he was trying to rouse any recollection of a previous encounter with the unfamiliar man.

"Good evening, I'm Ryan Walker, Ben's swim coach. Mr. Friedman, Ben's father, told me I could find Ben here? I need to speak to Ben about the swim meet in the morning."

Really? Ben clearly heard Coach's booming voice. *Will my father stop at nothing?*

"I'm sorry, but we're celebrating the Sabbath,"

Rabbi Silverstein patiently explained. "But please join us."

Oh, no. Ben squirmed in his chair and couldn't believe this was happening.

Coach Walker removed his galoshes and overcoat, underdressed in corduroy pants and a sweatshirt. He followed the rabbi into the dining room and took in the scene. "This reminds me of Christmas dinner at my grandparents' house when I was a boy," he murmured.

Everyone scooted over a bit, and the kitchen help added a chair and a formal table setting for Coach Walker between Ben and Grandma Libby.

"Good evening, I'm Libby Friedman, and you are…"

"Ryan Walker, Coach Ryan Walker, Ben's swim coach."

"What are you doing here?" Ben leaned in and muttered at the coach, incredulous. He knew Coach Walker believed in him, and he hated to let him down.

"Now, Ben…" Libby reprimanded Ben's tone of voice, but the coach cut her off.

"I called your house when I got your message and spoke to your father."

"Did my father send you?" Ben snapped.

"No, I came on my own. I just wanted a chance to talk with you. This isn't like you. There's a lot at stake, and I'm not sure you've thought this through."

"I don't expect you to understand," he sputtered. He felt like his worlds were colliding.

"Try me. I'm a pretty good listener."

"The thing is, Coach, there's a lot at stake, more than you know. I can't swim tomorrow for religious reasons."

"Why now, Ben? You've swum on Saturday before.

There will be other Saturdays. Now's the time for you to qualify! You're part of a team—you can't let down your team." Coach Walker banged his fist on the table. "You'll be letting your school down too."

"Then I quit the team, as of right now." Ben jumped up, trembling, and backed away from the table.

"We don't want you to quit the team—quite the opposite. Let's make this work. There'll be other meets that don't fall on Saturday."

"Did my son send you here to bully Ben?" Grandma Libby intervened, louder than she probably intended.

"Please understand. Ben has a gift, a talent, and he's ready to qualify for the state meet. He could break records tomorrow and really establish himself as a coming champion."

Then Grandma Ann spoke up. "Ben has more gifts and talents than you know. He'll choose *what* he'll do and *when* he'll do it!"

It was so quiet Ben could hear his own heartbeat. No one in the room spoke or even moved as the conflict became public.

The rabbi seized the silence that hung in the room. He stood at the head of the table, cleared his throat, and held his wine goblet high. "I want to make a special toast to Ben Friedman on the occasion of spending his first Sabbath with us. I am certain his grandpa Mordy is here in spirit and is filled with naches. May Ben be blessed and may the master of the universe give him strength and protection. *L'chaim*, to life!

"Next I want to make a toast to Ben's grandmothers, Libby Friedman and Anna Rosen. Welcome back to Anna and a first-time welcome to Libby. May we spend many wonderful Shabbosim together! *L'chaim*, to life!"

the rabbi exclaimed.

"To life!" the guests answered back with equal enthusiasm, and they all drank wine from their crystal glasses.

Coach Walker seemed unable to summon forth or articulate any further argument to convince Ben to reverse his decision. He thanked the Silversteins for their gracious hospitality and left.

The front door was open, and guests were leaving when Dad arrived. He stormed in without hesitation. Ben looked up from his conversation with Levy and wasn't totally surprised to see his father coming at him with the force of a cannonball.

"You have a responsibility to the team. You can't let your team down!" Dad seemed bigger and more menacing with his fury.

Grandma Libby cut Dad off and stepped between her son and her grandson. Firmly positioned with her hands on her hips, she looked more substantial than she was. "Steven, it was so thoughtful of you to come. I was nervous about driving home in this blizzard." Grandma gripped Dad's forearm forcefully and brought him to a halt.

"Son, you'll face serious consequences if you don't keep your commitments," Dad still thundered.

"Won't you please get our coats from the front closet, Steven?" Grandma Libby stepped closer and glared at her son, only inches from his face. Neither Dad nor Grandma looked away.

"Dad, I've learned I have other responsibilities. This is really important to me," Ben began, trying to explain, but Libby put a finger to her mouth and shushed him.

"You'll lose everything we've worked toward!"

Dad's face was beet red, and his hands tightened to fists.

Ben ducked behind his grandma Ann. It was nearly midnight now. The snow had been accumulating, and driving had become hazardous. Succumbing only to reminders of his own familial obligations, Dad reluctantly fetched the fur coats from the closet and departed in the guise of ensuring that both his mother and mother-in-law arrived home safely.

The morning after the Sabbath dinner, Ben tiptoed to the bathroom. His internal clock was set, and he was the only one moving in the Silverstein home at five thirty Shabbat morning. He reflected that ordinarily he would already be on the bus with the team for the prelims. His times were good enough to qualify today. He hoped that his team, when given the chance, would step up and fill his shoes. The rich aroma of cholent—beef and bean stew cooking overnight in the crockpot—planted him firmly in this new sphere. The bathroom light was left on, covered by a plastic switch cover, he assumed to ensure it would not be habitually turned off. The toilet paper was ripped into short segments of four sheets and stacked neatly in a rattan basket. He wondered if they were rationing the toilet paper. His heart was beating so fast that he was breathless—as though he'd just completed 200 yards freestyle—and the endorphin rush flooded him. He wasn't sure he'd slept at all—he recalled a sense of hovering in a twilight sleep while the songs from the Shabbos table echoed in his mind and his father's fury ran over him like a wave. He was grateful he could always count on his grandmothers to take his side—and no one could stand up to his father like Grandma Libby. Had she not been there, he would have been a hot mess. He tried not to think about what would have happened next.

He dressed silently and went downstairs to the kitchen. A fruit bowl and a selection of coffee cakes and cookies were laid out on the counter near the hot-water urn. Ben prepared a cup of tea and helped himself to sticky cinnamon babka. The dining room table and white tablecloth showed no sign of last night's crowd. Across from the ornate silver seven-branch candelabrum was a vase of pink roses and Asiatic lilies. Last night the lilies had been in bud form, and this morning they were beginning to bloom. The candles that were lit before Shabbat had gone out, but he still felt their festive peace.

Ben tried to remember the names of the people he'd met at the sumptuous feast before Coach Walker arrived. He was not good with names, but he remembered faces. The family with the two teenagers had sat across from him, making jokes and passing him salads, Moroccan fish, roasted chicken, and potato kugel. He had never tasted such delicious food and wondered if it was wrong to have enjoyed the food so much—he felt like a glutton. As he recollected the evening, he still felt high. The joy went beyond the food. The stories, the songs, the Torah, and thoughts Rabbi Silverstein shared at the meal uplifted him. Even his father could not spoil it. He wished his grandpa had really been there too.

It was seven thirty a.m., and the house was still. Ben browsed the bookshelf and helped himself to a book of Chassidic tales. He settled into a recliner and lost himself in extraordinary stories that he yearned to be a part of.

"Good Shabbos." Levy sat down on the sofa with a cup of orange juice and a chunk of babka.

"Good morning." Ben startled as he hadn't heard Levy come in.

"Did you find something interesting?" Levy leaned over and inspected the book cover. "That's a good one."

"Do you believe these stories about people skipping across water and visiting the heavenly court?" Ben tried his best to remain respectful.

"Do you?" Levy peeled a layer of the sweet, fluffy dough with raisins and cinnamon.

"I don't know." A sudden chill swept through his body. He remembered his plate of babka and took a bite. "Cake for breakfast just might be my favorite part of Shabbos."

"Mine too." Levy ate leisurely. "You're up early."

"I always get up at the same time—I swim at six a.m.," he said bleakly.

"Swim where?"

"At school. I'm on the swim team—I should say *was* on the swim team. I've been swimming since I was a kid."

"Yeah, I picked that up last night. Was that your coach who joined the meal and sat next to you?"

"First my coach, then my dad. Together they're a force to be reckoned with. There's a swim meet this morning they wanted me to attend." Ben rolled his eyes.

"That's a tough one. From as far back as I can remember, my father always told me, 'More than you keep the Shabbos, the Shabbos will keep you.' "

"Well, it's not like that in my family. My father thinks I have other responsibilities and need to give it my all to get a college swimming scholarship."

"Do you need the scholarship to go to college?" Levy asked, looking confused.

Ben considered Levy's question. A smile creased his cheeks, and a bubble of laughter rose in his throat and escaped.

"No, I'm sure I don't *need* a scholarship." Suddenly, he was laughing from the depths of his gut. It was that contagious kind of laugh that he couldn't stop.

"Then I don't see the problem." Levy roared with laughter too.

In between gasping for air, Ben exclaimed, "Levy, I like the way you think!" Fresh energy filled him.

When Rabbi Silverstein joined them at eight a.m., a broad smile spread across his face, and Levy jumped to his feet.

"Let's get ready—we'll go to shul early for my father's nine a.m. chassidus class." Without delay he took the dishes to the kitchen and returned with their coats.

It was snowing, but Ben didn't mind. The snowflakes landed peacefully on their hats and coats, and they made fresh tracks along the sidewalks.

"Just as a heads up, I don't know how to pray, at least not in your shul," Ben confessed.

"Here's the thing. I'll announce the page numbers, and you can follow in English—you do read English?"

"Yes, I do read English." Ben punched Levy in the shoulder and knocked him into a snowbank.

Levy brushed off the snow and got serious. "I love something Rabbi Aharon of Karlin used to say. 'If you don't know the Zohar, study Talmud. You don't know the Talmud? Open the Bible. You don't know the Bible? Say psalms. You don't know psalms? Do you know the Shema Israel? No? Then just think of your people and love one another. That will be sufficient.' "

****

Upon the appearance of three stars, Rabbi

Silverstein ended the Sabbath with the closing multisensory ritual including fire, wine, and spices. They wished one another a good week, and Ben gathered his few belongings and prepared to leave. He felt dread at the prospect of leaving the cocoon of calm protection.

"Rabbi, thank you for a beautiful Shabbat. I'm sorry about all the commotion with my coach and my father," Ben apologized. "My father gets like this. He won't let me make my own decisions. He thinks he knows what's best for me."

"We enjoyed having you with us, Ben, and we hope you'll come again. The Torah directs us to honor our parents and observe the Sabbath in the same sentence. Both parents, as partners with God in creating us, and Sabbath observance testify that God is the Creator and Master of the universe. I can talk to your father and try to help."

"That would be great! But what if he doesn't change his mind? What do I do then?"

"Our sages are clear that a parent's command to violate the Sabbath or any other part of Torah must not be obeyed. You are to honor your parents, but God's commandments take precedence over the wishes of your parents."

They brushed what seemed like a foot of snow off the 1970 Monte Carlo and shoveled, which allowed Levy to cautiously back down the driveway and inch through the side streets, most of which were not yet plowed. After stopping at the intersection of Greenview and Lincoln, the tires only spun in the deep snow when Levy gently pushed on the gas pedal. The classic white Chevy would not move. Levy tried to rock the car out of the drift, moving from reverse to drive, repeatedly, but to no avail.

He turned the radio to the local news channel.

The announcer reported, "Southwood received a record fourteen inches of snow over the last twenty-four hours. Residents are encouraged to stay off the roads until the snowplows have cleared the main thoroughfares. Roads continue to be hazardous. We just received an exclusive WDTR update on the tragic bus accident that occurred early this morning. The swim team en route to a meet in Pontiac slid off the road and rolled into a ravine off North Telegraph Road. The coach and four team members have been hospitalized. Stay tuned for updates on the hour."

"Did you hear that?" Ben buried his face in his hands, overcome by the horrific news, rocking back and forth like a metronome.

Chapter Twenty-Four—Linden Trees

Siedlce, Poland

Dovid lifted and stepped in sync with five others and carried the plain pine casket from the wagon toward the mound of earth, pausing three times along the short journey as though reluctant to remove their dead. He exhaled into the cold air and watched the vapor disappear. With no substance the breath of life vanished into thin air. Micah's mother followed the casket and wept into her chapped red hands. Micah's father, recognizable by his red hair and beard, supported his wife. The community followed behind. The pallbearers rested the casket on ropes suspended above the grave. Slowly, the ropes were released, and the casket was lowered into the grave.

Noach was the first to shovel earth into the grave. The thud of dirt on the casket marked the finality of death. No one spoke. Dovid took the shovel next, dropped a shovelful of earth onto the casket, and said his personal good-bye. One by one the community stepped forward to pay their respects and express their final sentiments. Silently, each one replaced the shovel in the diminished mound of earth, never passing the shovel from hand to hand, a gesture expressing that the tragedy of death should not be contagious. Micah was returned to Mother Earth.

"The Lord has given, and the Lord has taken. Blessed be the name of the Lord," the rabbi concluded.

Micah's father recited the burial prayer in ancient Aramaic, "*Yitgadal ve-yitkadash shemeh rabba…*"

The community responded, "Amen."

Before turning to leave, Dovid placed a small stone on the covered grave. He paused and closed his eyes. In a whisper he asked for Micah's forgiveness. Then he joined Esther in the parallel rows of men and women lined up facing one another. Micah's mother and father passed through the walls of friends as they left the grave of their only son. Together the community recited the traditional words of consolation in Hebrew, "May the Lord comfort you among the other mourners of Zion and Jerusalem."

Dovid and Esther left the cemetery and walked down Zydowska Street toward home, following the tall brick wall that contained the gravestones. They passed the beit midrash, but neither spoke of the upshernish and the drama that had begun that night. He relived the events of the last week over again. It was a familiar pattern of escalation.

"Sora was grieved that you did not allow her to be at the funeral." Esther broke the silence.

"She needs to stay out of sight. This is not over." Dovid surveyed the area, on guard, awaiting what would happen next.

"We cannot hide them away forever." She looked up into the canopy of linden trees. "Where will we be when they bloom again? In June and July they will dangle creamy-yellow, star-shaped flowers beneath their pale-green branches and exhale the sweetest, most powerful perfume of honey and lemon peel." She inhaled deeply.

"You know that linden trees can live for a thousand years?" He gazed into the canopy of trees eighty feet tall and forty feet wide.

"I ran beneath these trees as a child, and my mother also ran beneath these trees, and my grandmother before her ran and smelled their scent. These trees with their hairy stems watch us come and go. They were here when things were different. They welcomed us."

Dovid abruptly turned one hundred eighty degrees, and his gaze nervously swept the wide street behind them toward the horse market. Wagons and community members on foot still flowed from the cemetery.

"Men under the age of fifty-five are now forbidden to leave the country. They will draft you a third time." She brushed her tears away.

He dried her face with a handkerchief and whispered, "You must stop weeping. My petition for a permit has been rejected. We need to focus on Sorale. I cannot keep her safe here."

Esther bit her lip, and silence was consent.

"Sorale wants to marry Aaron and go to America. I want to give her our blessing." He spoke gently.

Esther took a step back, and tears pooled in her eyes. "Sorale get married? She is just a child."

"She is a young woman the same age you were when we were married." He smiled in memory.

She nodded and smiled tenderly. "I can see that her heart is drawn to him. How will Chana survive without her? One has never been without the other."

"Chana will go to America as well—in her own time. She is strong. You will see." He held her elbow firmly, guided her away from the cemetery, and suppressed the dread that rose from deep within him when he pictured life without Sorale and Chana.

"The two of them have dreamed of emigrating to America since they were little girls, studying and perfecting their English. They write to your cousin Isadore in New York."

"Isadore will help." Dovid stroked his beard. "I will write to him."

"Surely, there is no hurry." Esther gripped Dovid's solid forearm as if to slow him down.

"But there is. When it comes to a wedding, our sages tell us that we should not delay. Particularly with *chassan* and *kallah* in the same city. A delay will cause more harm than good."

"How will we find the funds to make a proper wedding? There is no meat to sell, and if there were, those thieving Cossacks would take it for their own! And how will Aaron provide a livelihood in America?" She twisted the thin gold ring on her finger.

"Lack of funds is no reason to delay a wedding. Our sages, of blessed memory, tell us that God provides man with sustenance in the merit of his wife. The month of Adar is coming in six weeks. It will be an entire month of joy and gladness. All days in the month of Adar are of equal goodness." He squeezed her hand, and it was decided.

****

The copper wood-fired samovar was heating when Dovid and Esther returned home from the cemetery. Chana poured a measure of extra strong tea sense from a small pot into the faceted glass teacups in silver cup holders and turned the ornate key of the samovar to fill the cups with boiling water for her parents. Sora set out sugar cubes and fresh chocolate rugelach on the dining table, covered with a lace cloth. The younger children fixed their gazes on the rugelach but held back until their parents were served first.

Dovid was pleased no sign of the turmoil that had occurred over the last forty-eight hours remained. His daughters had spent the morning toiling to return the house to a neat and tidy appearance. He interlaced stiffened fingers as he recalled previous pogroms and patterns of escalating violence. After learning of Aleksandrov's run-in with Stayanov, he was reasonably certain that Aleksandrov would keep a low profile, at least for a while.

At the nod and wink of their tatty, the young children rushed to climb onto his lap and helped themselves to chocolate rugelach. When they'd had their fill, they climbed down to play. Dovid's white shirt was stamped with small chocolate handprints. He laughed and poured himself another glass of tea, and the younger children rushed outdoors.

Sora passed her father the glass bowl of sugar cubes. "Tatty, will you tell me now?"

Dovid responded with a questioning look. The events of the prior week flashed before him—the home invasion, Sora's abduction, the marriage proposal, the emigration to America, Micah's murder... He could not guess what his daughter wished to talk about.

"Could you please tell me, why do they hate us so?" Sora sat down, her posture straight and tall, resembling royalty, and poured herself tea in the thick-walled glass cup.

This was not the question he'd expected as he sipped tea through a sugar cube in his teeth. He'd assumed Sorale was occupied with other matters—love and marriage and steamships to America.

"You said it was a long story." Sora broke the silence and sipped her tea from a spoon with a sugar cube.

"I did say that. Actually, there are many stories from different times and places, but they all repeat the same pattern of events. So really, Sorale, it is the same story over and over again." Dovid blinked his daughter into focus.

Chana moved from the sofa to an empty chair at the table. Esther reclined on the sofa and closed her eyes.

"Our rebbe tells us, 'One must live with the times.' This does not mean what you think. He explained we should live with and experience in one's own life the Torah portion of the week. This is Shemot, the week that 'A new king arose over Egypt, who didn't know of Joseph.' "

Dovid kneaded his swollen knuckles, rubbing his hands back and forth. He compressed his lips and continued. "Gratitude for Joseph's monumental contributions was forgotten. The Jews had become too strong and therefore dangerous but too useful to let go. The search for a solution to this 'Jewish problem' goes back to Pharaoh, and it repeats again and again.

"It was King Casimir the Great himself who invited the Jews to Poland. My zaidy said it was an offer you couldn't decline. You see, in the fourteenth century the Jews were persecuted in Western Europe, and there was nowhere else to go. In 1481, the Inquisition started in Spain and ultimately surpassed the Medieval Inquisition. The Polish noblemen were averse to work, and they saw a shrewd and competent workforce in the Jews. In a short time, the nobility depended on the Jews to serve as their leaseholders, agents, and financial managers."

"What did that have to do with the Cossacks?" Sora coaxed her tatty to continue.

"The Polish nobility owned everything, including the land and the churches. The Jews were there at every christening and funeral, collecting taxes. And when the Polish nobles settled in what is now Ukraine and built palaces and castles, Jews were again their trusted agents and managers, leasing their estates, mills, inns, rivers, lakes, and all other sources of income."

"So the Jews lorded over the Cossacks in Ukraine?" Sora leaned in toward her father.

"They were the hand of the Polish noblemen. Both the Polish peasants and the Ukrainian vassals, which included Cossacks, were incensed to be oppressed by the lowly Jew."

Sora served her father another glass of strong tea.

"Still, it was a time of growth and prosperity for our people. We built great synagogues, communities, and yeshivas. There were many Torah scholars and kabbalists. It was only a matter of time until the Poles' hatred escalated into violence, and the Cossacks rose up and took revenge on both the Jews and the Poles. And the violence was contagious, leading to brutal massacres and pogroms." Dovid leaned back in his chair as he unveiled the tragic events.

"Now they hate and terrorize us..." Sora slowly rocked back and forth, deep inside her own world.

"No matter how great the threats, we've existed by refusing to abandon our practices and Torah study. When the Eternal appeared to Moses in the burning bush, He showed us He is with us in our suffering. We're the burning bush that isn't consumed by fire."

"Tatty, I don't want my children to be born in Siedlce." Sora began to tremble. "And I don't want to leave you," she said in a choked voice.

Dovid took her hands in his own and kissed her forehead. "I know, Sorale, but you must leave, and I'll give you my blessing."

Chapter Twenty-Five—Late

Southwood, Michigan

Huddled with a small group of parents whose names she'd come to know, Nanci observed Rubie in the pool with the swim instructor through the wall of glass. She was giggling and wearing pink goggles. Her face bobbed in and out of the water. She was blowing bubbles and elated with herself. Nanci mentally patted herself on the back for sticking it out and patiently allowing Rubie to overcome her fear of the water. She was grateful to be on the other side of water hysteria and encouraged to see that Rubie would soon be floating. The plainclothes officer assigned to them for protection stood vigilant by the door.

Her cycle was late. Nanci told herself there could be many reasons. And the exhaustion could be from the stress of the new job. What was she thinking going back to work? She felt crampy. Like her period was just around the corner, but it never came. The pill was reliable contraception had she continued to take it. How could she have let this happen? She reminded herself that it was her OB-GYN who'd told her to take a break from oral contraception. No one expected Ira would be home on furlough. The breast tenderness was the clincher. She'd finally brought herself to make an appointment for a pregnancy test that afternoon.

Rubie sang in the floor-to-ceiling tiled shower room painted with goldfish and turtles. She used excessive amounts of shampoo, conditioner, and body wash to lather her small form and twisted her sudsy hair into exotic fairy-tale princess hairstyles. Nanci hardly noticed. She pressed the button to make the swimsuit spin. The centrifugal force extracted all the water. She felt schizophrenic—anxious one moment and excited the next, carrying a secret. Glancing at her watch, she saw they needed to meet Aliza for lunch in twenty minutes, and she hurried Rubie along.

The Friedmans' house was quiet when Nanci and Rubie arrived.

"Good morning! It's turning into a blizzard out there. Where is everyone?" Nanci gave Aliza a quick hug, and Rubie threw her arms around Aliza's legs.

"Steven's at the office. Joel is over at a friend's house, Estie is at Northland Roller Rink with friends, and Ben is spending Shabbat with the Silversteins."

"Really?" Nanci was genuinely surprised.

"You haven't heard about last night's drama?" Aliza sighed and bit a nail.

"Not yet. What have I missed?" Nanci leaned in, smiling playfully.

"Steven orchestrated something of an intervention with Coach Walker at the rabbi's Shabbat dinner last night. He intended to pressure Ben into attending the swim meet today."

"What happened?" Nanci pressed.

"Let's just say the intervention failed. Rather than persuade Ben to alter his course, I think Ben's probably dug in more deeply. It seems Steven was pitted against both his mother and mother-in-law, who interceded on

Ben's behalf. I'm guessing Steven completely lost it. Early this morning, he retreated to his office, which is what he always does under pressure."

"So, it's just us girls today." Nanci squeezed Aliza's hand.

"Indeed, Estie may never come home again—Cheryl's mom is taking the girls to Northland Center to shop for event dresses after skating. Did you know Northland is the world's largest shopping center? Hudson's has four levels."

"Let's put a video on for Rubie. She's crazy for that movie with the jungle animals, but be forewarned you'll have to replay the catchy theme song about a half dozen times, and fast-forward past that terrifying Bengal tiger, or she'll become hysterical with fear. Do you have peanut butter?"

Aliza slid the video tape Nanci handed her into the deck, and Rubie snuggled into the overstuffed cushions of the large leather couch with a crocheted afghan, already spellbound.

"Peanut butter's in the pantry." Aliza set a platter of spinach dip in a pumpernickel bread bowl on the table. "What time is dinner at Mom's tonight?"

"Six thirty. I'm picking up a few things at the market for her right after lunch. Is it okay if I leave Rubie here? She'll take an afternoon nap."

Nanci spread peanut butter on white bread, then cut off the crust for Rubie.

"Sure, leave Rubie with me while you run out, and we'll all meet you at the house later."

"This bread bowl is delicious, and I'm famished!" Nanci tore off a chunk of pumpernickel and scooped it into the dip.

"I'm glad you brought an appetite. The Cajun fish will be done in a minute. Can I get you a drink?" Aliza sat across from Nanci and watched her eat.

Nanci tore away at the pumpernickel bread bowl and looked her sister-in-law in the eyes. "What's happening? You really look down in the dumps."

"It's these bar mitzvah invitations. They were supposed to be mailed last week."

"Let me help with that," Nanci offered good-naturedly.

"No—it's more than that." Aliza sounded fatigued.

"What's bothering you?" Nanci gave Aliza her full attention.

"This isn't what Ben wants." Her face paled, and her trembling mouth turned down in a frown.

Nanci furrowed her brow. "So, it's not too late to make changes, is it?"

"But this is exactly what Steven wants." Aliza pretended to shoot herself in the head.

"I see." Nanci rubbed her temples, feeling a headache coming on, then rested her hands on her rounded tummy.

"The whole affair has been planned for months, scratch that, years." Aliza kneaded her shoulders. "I feel like I'm sitting in a house of cards." She shivered and then jumped to her feet to remove the pan of fish from the fire.

"Why do you say that?" Nanci devoured the fish, rice, and green salad.

"Well—Dad passed, and Ben had an anaphylactic reaction that nearly killed him. Then the shooting at the funeral, and did I mention that Dad appeared to Ben in a dream before he died?"

"No!" Nanci exclaimed.

"We can go into that another time. So, in the middle of all this, Dad leaves Ben his tefillin." She gave a mirthless laugh and wilted into the chair across from Nanci.

"Okay, is that significant?" Nanci stretched and reclined back in the chair.

"To Ben, it is. He had some kind of experience putting them on with Rabbi Silverstein that's now linked to his bar mitzvah." Aliza pushed her untouched plate away. "Ben is looking for more than a bar mitzvah party. He's on a spiritual quest."

"Maybe he's got the right idea." Nanci cleaned her plate.

"Maybe. And I keep dreaming about having babies. Everything from giving birth to holding a beautiful baby boy that we named Mo, after Dad." She looked away.

"I miss him too." Nanci held her breath and was just about to say something when Rubie came dancing into the breakfast room singing that catchy theme song. She pulled Nanci and Aliza to their feet, and with hands on one another's hips, the three of them danced through the house, singing the lines over and over as Rubie insisted they play it again.

****

Anna tuned the radio to the weather channel and looked out the kitchen window into the thick windless blizzard, watching for Nanci. She chopped an onion into the ground beef for meatballs and felt uplifted by the thought that Sara and Aaron were coming for the bar mitzvah. They were her connection to where she came from. No one else was left from Siedlce. She switched on the small fan she kept on the kitchen counter to minimize the onions burning her eyes. Nevertheless, tears ran down her face. It was getting dark, and Anna worried about Nanci. She should have arrived hours ago.

Suddenly, a blue-white light flashed outside the kitchen window, accompanied by a loud purple boom. The lights and the fan went off. The high voltage lines down the street formed an electric arc to a tree limb. A buzzing enveloped Anna.

A moment later Estie, Joel, and Rubie stampeded through the foyer into the kitchen, howling. Aliza wasn't far behind.

"We need to call DTE to report a downed power line." Aliza raced to the kitchen window. "We saw it go down from the driveway. Those high voltage lines can be lethal." She opened the kitchen window to get a better look through the falling snow while the buzzing got louder.

"What's that electrifying humming?" Anna covered her ears, alarmed.

"That's the wet limbs touching the power line, shorting out electricity to ground. We're going to need flashlights. Mom, light some candles from the gas burner on the stove. It will be pitch black in here shortly. Looks like we'll be having a candlelit dinner." Aliza gave her mother a quick kiss on the cheek.

"Where's Nanci?" Anna stopped rolling meatballs, her hands shaking.

"Her car is stuck in the snow down the street. Road service is backed up for hours, so Steven is on his way to help get her out. I'm walking back to wait with her. Yummm, the meatballs already smell wonderful. We'll be home soon. Estie, take the kids to play in the living room."

Rubie cried and called for her mother. Estie stepped in and handed her a frying pan and a spatula, which she put on the pretend stove and began flipping pretend pancakes and serving up plates of breakfast. Joel dumped the tub of Legos and built a multicolored tower. Anna set a bowl of chips on the coffee table to hold them over until dinner, pleased to find the three of them playing together nicely. The sound of the full chime and strike filled the house. It was five o'clock, and the gloom of dusk settled over the room as they immersed in imaginative play. Snow fell at the rate of an inch an hour. She watched out the window for their moms and dad, aunt, and uncle to come in from the storm, while the aroma of meatballs and mashed potatoes wafted from the kitchen.

****

Aliza trudged down the street toward the intersection where Nanci's white Volvo was stuck in the snow and was relieved to see Steven's green Lincoln town car already there. As she got closer, Steven blared on the horn and shouted through the open door, "Stay away!"

Aliza shined the flashlight on Nanci's vehicle, and her heart stopped when she saw the power line draped across the roof of the Volvo. The plainclothes policeman was on his radio. The policeman in uniform yelled from the street, "Nanci, help is coming. Stay inside your vehicle!"

"Steven, I've got to get out of here," she bellowed through the open window from the edge of her seat.

"Don't get out! And don't touch anything metal!" Steven blanched as he spoke.

The color drained from Nanci's face, and she went white as a sheet. A vortex of wild auburn curls framed her sober expression as she scooted back into the driver's seat. She looked suddenly overcome. "This can't happen without Ira. Who'll take care of Rubie?"

Aliza flinched at the sight of the downed power line as it sparked and squirmed, demonstrating that it was energized and live, carrying a lethal dose of electricity. Nanci sobbed, and Aliza yearned to hold her. She could see that Nanci was near her breaking point, feeling that she couldn't do this alone.

"I can't touch you, or we'll both be shocked. The ground around the car is energized by the power line," Aliza shouted.

The policeman advanced closer but maintained a good distance of twenty-five feet.

"You don't understand." Nanci's lower lip trembled. "Rubie needs me. She needs at least one parent. This can't be happening..." Her impeccably made-up face twisted as she fought back tears.

"Listen carefully to what I'm saying. If you make any sudden moves, you may electrocute yourself." Steven used his hands like a megaphone, and his words echoed off the snow-covered landscape.

Aliza gave Steven a dirty look, reproaching him for frightening Nanci. "Rescue vehicles are coming. You're going to be okay. You just need to keep still. Don't panic. Breathe with me," she said and chewed on her bottom lip.

"I can't be electrocuted." Nanci took in a deep breath. "Aliza—I'm pregnant." She hugged herself, and tears ran down her cheeks.

Aliza tried to absorb the news and realized the pregnancy dreams she'd been having were about Nanci. She struggled to stay in the moment, but she couldn't keep herself from thinking ahead. How would they deliver this baby without Ira? How could they possibly have a child while Ira was in prison? A tremor shook her body.

Nanci's words echoed off the soft white landscape and reverberated through Aliza. She reached out her arms to Nanci from afar and fell onto her knees in the whiteout. Elation arose from within her, and she wanted to scream out in joy at the start of a new soul. The force of life surged through her.

"We're getting you out of there now," Steven bellowed to Nanci, and Aliza begged him to hurry. "Nanci, you need to stay calm and listen carefully. Be cautious moving around within the car and make sure you don't touch anything metal. I want you to take extreme care to unlatch the door and push it wide open."

With Aliza at his side, Steven shuffled as close to Nanci's white Volvo sedan as he dared to give her instructions. "Nanci, grip the black leather steering wheel, avoid the silver spokes, and pull yourself forward and toward the door. Now, inspect the interior. Is the handle metal or vinyl?"

"It looks like black vinyl."

"Good. Now pull the handle toward you while you thrust your feet against the door panel and push it open."

She screwed her eyes closed, and suddenly, the door flung open. She hugged herself against the blast of cold air.

"Good, very good," Steven whooped.

The policeman stepped forward. "Nanci, you'll need to jump out of the car. It's crucial that both your feet land on the ground at the same time. If one foot hits the ground while the other is still touching the car, your body will become a conductor for the electricity, and you could be electrocuted. Keep your knees bent and make sure you jump cleanly from the vehicle, rather than sliding yourself from your seat. Again, if your legs connect to the ground while your body is still touching the car, you run the risk of being electrocuted. Do you understand?"

Nanci nodded silently, counting to three, and without warning, she jumped and landed with two feet planted firmly in the snow.

"Don't move!" the officer shouted. "You're not entirely safe yet. The ground around you is still electrified. You need to shuffle or hop. If you shuffle, you need to make sure both your feet are touching the ground at all times. Keep your feet close together and shuffle until you're clear from the electrified zone. Or you can hop away, but both feet must land at the same time as you hop."

Nanci began to shuffle. "I feel tingling in my feet and legs!"

Aliza's heart raced as Nanci hopped wildly away from the car. Aliza bolted and embraced her, and she sobbed with relief.

"I need to go to Rubie." Nanci brushed away tears and began trudging toward Anna's home with all her power.

Arm in arm, basked in thankfulness, Aliza slogged through the whiteout, infused with the almost religious feeling of a miracle, the divinity of life, when suddenly they were thrown by the force of an explosion. The Volvo burst into flames.

****

Anna sat in the candlelit kitchen, drinking tea, and

was startled by the second flash and boom in the last two hours. She checked again on Rubie, Estie, and Joel who were all in the living room, happily building towers in the candlelight from the glass memorial candles. She realized it was now dark in the Midwest, and Shabbat was over. Grateful for the reliability of the telephone, powered by just a nine-volt battery, she called the Silversteins to check on Ben.

Chapter Twenty-Six—Friends

Southwood, Michigan

Alan strutted across the stage, slid onto the polished floor in splits, and crossed the raised platform doing the knee drops he'd performed the night of his bar mitzvah. Ricky and Howard hooted and jumped onto the stage with Alan and tried, clumsily, to mimic Alan's moves. Ben watched the entertainment from the podium where he arranged the agenda and notes for the meeting.

Alan was the official president of the Mitzvah Day Committee at the temple, and he'd talked Ben into being secretary. They'd been best friends since kindergarten, and Ben always had trouble saying no to him. Ben lifted his heel and tapped to the beat that played in his head. He marveled at Alan's ability to attract and hold everyone's attention. He was a born showman.

The lanky, pimpled, adolescent boys, captivated by Alan's performance, assembled from the hall, the stage, and various places around the large multipurpose room that functioned as a sanctuary, a social hall, and a meeting place, at least for another month until the building expansion was complete.

After one more strut across the stage, Alan planted a hand on his hip while he pointed and scanned the crowd. The group of nearly two dozen boys lost their minds, clapping and foot stomping. Alan took a deep theatrical bow, assumed his place at the podium, and banged the American walnut gavel on the sound block.

"I officially call to order the first meeting of the 1975 Mitzvah Day Committee." Alan motioned for applause from the group. He then signaled for the clapping and foot stamping to stop by making a swift cut across his throat, and it was instantly silent.

"Most of you know that Mitzvah Day is the project of the bar mitzvah class. Let us commit today that we, the Bar Mitzvah Class of 1975, will pull off the most outstanding Mitzvah Day event ever!"

Alan fist-pumped and jumped into the air. The applause and foot stamping was deafening. He made the swift cut across his throat again to silence the room. He looked to Ben who gestured to the agenda he'd prepared on the podium. Alan glanced at the notes and read the script Ben had written as though it were projected on a teleprompter.

"Gentlemen, we'll devote ourselves to social action through volunteering where we'll dedicate our time, not our money, to a cause for those in need in our community for a single day. *Tikkun olam*, or repairing the world, is our responsibility as we become bar mitzvah. It's up to us to set the world right! And the first order of business today is a brainstorming session to decide on our Mitzvah Madness Event! I'd like to call upon our dynamite secretary, Ben Friedman, to give some background on past Mitzvah Day events and lead us in this brainstorming. Drumroll, please…" Alan presented like a news anchor.

Ben came to the podium and spoke extemporaneously. "The goal is to have fun and feel great about the good deed we'll perform. We want to

166

choose something that one, we're good at. And two, we like to do. And last, fixes something that bothers us. Also, think about who you know that can help us. To ignite all of your imaginations, I'll share the types of Mitzvah Day projects that have been done in the past.

"They include distributing food and clothing to the poor and homeless, volunteering to tutor homeless and underprivileged children, volunteering to help the environment, and assisting the elderly and sick. We also helped those with special needs and their families and single parents with their kids."

Ben uncapped the red permanent marker and inhaled the smell of hydrocarbons, alcohols, and aromatic compounds that reminded him of the whiteboard markers he'd drawn with as a child at his father's law office. He'd used the blue, red, green, and black markers to draw stick figures of his family, all with wide red smiles. On the flip chart he wrote with the red squeaky marker *MD Projects* across the top of the page. He capped the red permanent marker and pulled out the blue one, awaiting anyone to say something.

"Ideas, gentlemen? There are no bad ideas. Ricky, I see your hand. I knew we could count on you to get us started."

"I was thinking we could give blood," Ricky called out as he kicked at the leg of the table.

Ben made a blue bullet and wrote it down. He questioned himself as he transcribed. Hadn't he explained this was supposed to be a *team* activity? This was a project they would work on together, not a trip to a local blood bank.

"How about reading to the blind?" David shouted.

"Good." Ben nodded, made another bullet, and

captured the suggestion, slightly encouraged.

"Our band could put on a concert for special needs kids," Michael proposed after a drumroll on the desk.

"No one would sit through that misery," Alan jibed.

"Snide remarks will cost you a dollar, Mr. President," Ben chided.

"It was worth it," Alan shot back and threw a dollar onto the podium. He was the master of happy talk.

"We could paint a public mural on an ugly building or on a concrete barrier."

Ben wrote faster to capture the stream of ideas the group was now generating.

"Maybe we could clean up the environment somehow or spruce up a rundown space."

"I think it's nice to visit old people who are lonely."

"We could mow their lawns and rake their leaves while we're there. You know, spruce the place up a bit."

"Yeah, that's like two kindly acts in one. I like that," Alan chimed in.

The group eventually unanimously supported the initiative to find isolated elderly people in the community, visit them, and do their yard work.

"Good progress. For our next meeting, everybody brings two ideas about what we'll need to make this happen. In the meantime, I'll talk to the rabbi and get his approval. Meeting is adjourned!"

Alan banged the walnut gavel.

Ben tore the pages from the flip chart and rolled them into a tube. Howard hung out with Ben as he gathered the papers and notes.

"Just a couple weeks until your big day. Are you ready?" Ben asked lightheartedly. With all that had been going on, he hadn't seen Howard as often as usual.

"Not exactly…" Howard replied. His hand tightened on Ben's arm. "I wanted to talk to you about that."

Ben froze and considered what Howard might need. "Something I can do to help?"

"I was hoping you could." His mouth turned into a grin. "I haven't been able to put my speech together." Howard was talking really fast.

"Well, what part are you stuck on?"

"I haven't been able to come up with a funny story or a joke—you know, to warm up the crowd."

"What about that joke where the dog wants to have a bar mitzvah?"

"Yeah, that's a good one. I forgot about that." Howard drummed his fingers on the podium.

"Is there something else?" Ben bit his lower lip, uneasy. Howard's fidgeting was making him anxious.

"And I can't think of a story or idea from my Torah portion that I could talk about." Howard laughed nervously.

"Gotcha." Ben tapped the paper tube on the podium. "It's usually easier if you choose an idea that's connected to something in your life—like a lesson you can relate to so you can make it personal. What's your portion?"

"Mishpatim." Howard cracked his knuckles.

"Isn't that about social legislation, the kind man would have invented if God hadn't?"

"That sounds right," Howard said, narrowing his eyes.

"What about talking about the difference between laws we understand and laws we can't understand?" His grandpa had spoken about this portion at a Friday night dinner last year, and he remembered it well. They had all gathered around Grandma and Grandpa's dining room table and had just finished bowls of Grandma Ann's rich chicken soup loaded with thick egg noodles, chicken, and round matzah balls. While the main course of brisket was coming out, Grandpa usually talked about the Torah portion, but that week he was very serious.

It seemed to Ben that Grandpa was speaking directly to Ira as he discussed the commandments pertaining to business and community dealings in specific detail. Grandpa culminated, as the brisket arrived, with the statement that the Torah was an instruction booklet for peace. At the time, Ben couldn't understand his grandpa's unusual tone. No one had known about Ira's trouble with the FBI yet.

"Yes! I can always depend on you when I'm in a jam, Ben. If you'd write something simple for me by next week, I could still turn it in to the rabbi." Howard slapped Ben on the back.

"You want me to write your speech?" Ben whispered incredulously.

"Well, not all of it," Howard stammered. "Just that middle part with the social legislation stuff that comes easy to you."

"The thing is, that's the part about your Torah portion. Don't you want to look at how it might apply to your life?"

"Maybe if I had more time. But it's already overdue, and the rabbi has called my parents. Everybody is all over me now, and it's going to ruin the whole party."

Ben felt trapped. His loyalty to Howard was strong, but he felt so uncomfortable like he wanted to run out of the building. He couldn't explain why he should care. For years Ben had given Howard the answers to math homework, and that had never bothered him. Howard would see this as no different.

Ben and Howard headed out to the parking lot where the others waited for their parents to pick them up. As they approached, they were bombarded with snowballs. Alan and Ricky had built up quite a pile of nice round and dense snowballs that they hurled at Ben and Howard. The snow was wet and packing good. Ben and Howard scooped up snow and retaliated with half-formed snowballs. They stormed the stockpile, launching a free-for-all brawl.

Alan stuffed a snowball inside the back of Ben's coat and down his shirt. "And that's for the drama you pulled at my bar mitzvah."

"Yeah, I hope it didn't cut down on the gifts." Ben smashed a snowball in Alan's face.

"It was a night to remember, even if they don't remember me." Alan jumped on Ben and rubbed snowballs into Ben's hair.

"No one could forget you, Alan!"

"Right. So why did you eat that shrimp?" Alan pinned Ben down with his knees on his shoulders and smashed snowballs in his face.

"You gave it to me." Ben spat snow out of his mouth. "You told me to try it. What, you think I knew I was allergic?" He was uncertain whether this was a joke.

"How could you not? Who never ate shrimp?" Alan stuffed snow down the front of Ben's shirt and laughed.

"What's wrong with you guys? Cut it out." Howard pulled Alan off Ben, jumped on Alan, and then Ricky leaped on Howard as though in a choreographed dance.

"Get off of me!" Alan pushed Howard with two hands in the chest and tried to roll away.

D.G. Schulman

"You need to cool off." Howard shoved snow down Alan's shirt.

When Aliza arrived for pickup, they were in a pile on top of each other, punching and grappling with snow flying in all directions. Ben saw a worried expression cross his mother's face. Dad often had to explain that boys this age roughhoused and did horseplay for sport. She rolled down the window and called out, "Everyone having fun?"

No, Ben thought. *I'm really not having fun.* For as long as he could remember, Alan always looked after Alan and used Ben to get what he wanted. It dawned on Ben that he had nearly died, and Alan was mad that it took the spotlight off of him.

Chapter Twenty-Seven—Mail

Siedlce, Poland

Chana's skin prickled with anticipation as she looked over her father's shoulder. Dovid sat at the head of the table and sliced open an envelope with a United States postmark. The news had spread like wildfire, and the house was bustling with excitement. Even the dreadful cold didn't curb the steady stream of neighbors and relatives from coming. With wild arm waving and fist pounding, the gathered men exchanged views on the war and the growing list of recruits, some already injured or missing. Cousin Yosel shared the news that in May they would be drafting nineteen-year-olds.

When tatty unfolded the letter, a stillness fell over the room. He read the letter from the cousins in New York aloud.

November 3, 1914

Dearest Dovid, Esther, and family,

It has been over three months since the start of the war, and we hear that Siedlce has been under attack and occupied. We have received no mail from you since August 1, 1914, (the 9th of Av) when Germany declared war against Russia. Faygie and I fear that you are all dead and worry for your safety day and night. More than anything we wish to hear that you have survived and are all well. Please tell us how we can help.

With high unemployment in New York, upholstery work is scarce, but Faygie is still busy working as a seamstress and a milliner, designing, making, and selling upscale hats for women. Despite unemployment being very bad, there are still many rich women buying fancy expensive hats. We do not mean to complain as we have enough to buy coal to keep the small apartment warm, a wide selection of delicious food is available, and we always manage to cook a hot meal. Please, God, may everything go well, we are expecting a baby in December. With God's grace may you come to America, and together we will celebrate. We are sending prayers and wishes that our beloved friends and family in Siedlce were sheltered from danger and are out of harm's way.

Looking forward to hearing good news,

Isadore and Faygie

Tatty handed the letter to Mama. She collected the envelope from the table and held it to her breast while rereading the letter as if to glean something more between the words. A cluster of dollars fell from the upside-down envelope and settled on the mottled wooden tabletop. Mama's eyes opened wide, and she covered her mouth with the envelope. The room gasped at the sight of American dollars.

The letter circulated and finally came back around to Chana. She retreated to a corner, reread the letter, and imagined herself in New York with Faygie, working as a milliner and sending American dollars home to Tatty and Mama. She was supposed to be happy preparing for Sora's wedding, but she felt like crying. Sora would be married soon and would go to America with Aaron. When would she see her again?

"Mama, I just need to see him for five minutes. I

can't bear it!" Sora crumbled onto the chair she'd stood on for the alterations. With the wedding only a week away, Sora and Aaron were now not to see one another again until the chuppah.

"Closeness at a time when one should be distant may well lead to distance at a time when one should be close." Mama held the pins, waiting for Sora to stand.

"Mama, you always say that!" Sora centered herself on the chair again.

Mama smiled. "I was once a young kallah myself."

"I know you're right. You don't need to worry. We've resolved to conduct ourselves properly."

"There's so much to do. The week will go quickly. You'll see." Mama knelt and continued to pin the hem.

The table was piled high with mandel bread, babka, rugelach, and candied nuts for the festive celebration. Mama and Chana were baking continuously. The iron was perched on the stove for pressing the mountain of trousers, shirts, jackets, blouses, skirts, and dresses that were all borrowed from the community recycling agency.

Chana surveyed Sora in the gorgeous floor-length ivory gown. It was nearly flawless with only a small yellow stain on one sleeve. She imagined the satin undergarment cool against her skin. It was exactly what she imagined she would wear one day on her wedding night.

She pictured the moment Sora would see Aaron the day of the wedding at the veiling ceremony. Sora would be sitting like a queen on a white satin chair flanked by her mother, herself, and Aaron's mother. The younger siblings would be off playing in their fancy festive attire. Sora would be reciting psalms, and the men would be singing a soulful wordless melody as they approached in their black hats and jackets. Aaron would be escorted, like a king, by his father, soon-to-be father-in-law, relatives, and friends as he proceeded to meet his bride. He would look pale and nervous. They would both be fasting until after the wedding ceremony. Sora's eyes would be focused on the psalms, but she'd feel his approach. When she looked up, he'd be smiling at her, and she would be resplendent. Everyone would be looking at her, and she'd welcome the privacy that would come when Aaron placed the opaque veil over her face.

That night Chana dreamed that she arrived at the dock in Rotterdam just as the *Noordham* ship was leaving the harbor for America. She awoke on a pillow wet with tears and cried silently in the night. Her body trembled with the power of her emotions, which she could barely disentangle. Of course, she was happy for Sora. She was thrilled to see her in love, excited, and embarking on a new life. Yet the pain of losing her and being left behind was too much for her to bear. She repeated over and over in her mind, *I wish my sweet and loving sister my heartfelt mazal tov on her wedding. May God give her all the blessings for her future life and give her all that she needs to build a peaceful and happy home.* The last thing she wanted was for her selfish thoughts to cast an evil eye upon her sister. She would never forget the Friday night that Sora stepped forward and let herself be taken by the Cossacks. Chana wept and felt she could never love anyone as she loved Sora, her best friend and her sister. But Sora now had Aaron, and Chana would be alone.

****

Ten days after the wedding, Cousin Yosel arrived at

dawn with his horse and wagon to take Aaron and Sora to the train station. Tatty helped Aaron load the wagon with a single trunk that contained their wedding gifts and worldly possessions. Both Sora and Aaron also carried a suitcase packed with the clothing, toiletries, and food they would need for the journey across the Atlantic.

"Esther, please stop this weeping. We agreed to take action, and you must stop weeping and making it hard for everyone." Tatty gently wiped the tears from her face with a handkerchief. Mama nodded and put away her tears.

For as long as she could remember, Chana dreamed of nothing other than emigrating to the United States, and now she stood locked in place as her sister and new brother-in-law departed for the Holland America ship dock.

"Sora, I wish you every happiness and every blessing." Chana embraced and kissed her sister. She attempted to swallow the knot in her throat, but it wouldn't move.

"Promise you'll write to me." Sora pressed the paper with the address of their destination into Chana's hand, a tiny flat in Boston that Aaron's uncle had secured for them in the neighborhood of his shul.

"I will, I promise I will," Chana breathlessly repeated as Sora squeezed her hand one last time, hugged the little children, and was swept out the door with Aaron to the wagon.

Chana parted the curtain and watched the wagon leave. Was she strong enough to endure what was ahead? A bigger world not full of only hardship, suffering, and bitter disappointment was out there. She envisioned herself at the dock in Rotterdam boarding the *Noordham* and set to sail for America. She vowed that she *would* find a way out of Siedlce.

Chapter Twenty-Eight—Accidents

Loretto, Pennsylvania
Monday, February 24, 1975

Ira searched the mess hall for Sam and spotted him at their usual spot at the end of the long metal table in the back of the mess hall. Sam waved for Ira to join him. It was four thirty.

"Hey, buddy." Ira set down his compartmentalized tray, which was double wrapped in foil, and slapped Sam on the back.

"What have you got there?" Sam leaned in to inspect the novel presentation.

"Well, this seems to be a fish filet meal with tomato sauce, white rice, and lima beans." Ira read the meal description aloud and ripped open the foil to let the steam escape.

"Where did that come from?"

"Thanks to our resourceful chaplain/rabbi, I am now enrolled in the kosher meal program." Ira tasted the cod and nodded approvingly.

"Who knew? What do you think?"

"So far, this runs circles around anything else I've had here. This is actually a solid filet, not reconstituted."

"Any chance I can get on that plan?" Sam scrutinized his taco. "What is that isolated protein?"

"Claim your Judaism and swap out routine prison

food for tastier cuisine. I get the feeling the rabbi would be happy to sign you up. Ya know, I had no idea I liked lima beans." Ira shoveled the food into his mouth. He was ravenous.

"I've wondered whether these meals even meet the USDA standards or worse whether they're contaminated. I'm all in for an alternative meal plan, not to mention, my bubby and zaidy will be thrilled that I became kosher while incarcerated." Sam laughed and pushed the taco away.

"Tell them we also eat dinner at four thirty and meet up with our friends for the early bird special. But seriously, do you ever call them?" Ira wondered whether Sam burned through phone minutes like he did.

"I haven't been able to work up the nerve. So what, I just say things are great in prison?" Sam poked at the taco.

"What did you used to talk about with them, you know, before?"

"Work, family, their health…"

"That's good, ask about their health. They'll be glad to hear from you."

"Or maybe they'll just hang up. I'll think about it. How's your family?"

"Nothing new really. Since coming back from furlough for my dad's funeral, it's been really tough. All I think about is my wife and the feel of her beside me." He resisted the urge to check his watch. It felt like an hour had passed, but he knew it was only ten minutes. Time collapsed in on itself and seemed not to move at all.

"No one in your family is giving you the cold shoulder?" Sam's eyes sank.

"Funny you should ask. My nephew started ignoring me, then let me have it after the incident at the cemetery. Sometimes he answers the phone when I call my sister's house, but he's very abrupt and hands the phone off to my sister or brother-in-law right away. We used to have a good relationship."

"What happened at the cemetery?"

"Well, as we were dropping dirt on my father's coffin, someone in a black Cadillac parked in the circular drive and took a couple shots at me. The body of the shooter was identified and allegedly connected to organized crime." Ira cleaned his plate and pushed it aside.

"The body of the shooter?"

"Yeah, I don't think I mentioned that my seventy-four-year-old mother pulled out her 1911, shot, and killed him." Ira smiled, unable to hide his admiration.

"Holy crap! Interesting family you've got. Seems you've pissed off someone who is set on exacting revenge." His eyes flashed ominously.

"The FBI has protection on my wife and daughter now. They're also watching my mother's house. So my nephew blames me for all the family troubles and the death of my father to boot. Honestly, I don't blame him."

"What a mess. I thought isolation from your family was the worst part. If I were you, I'd be a wreck worrying that my family is safe." Sam thrust a hand through his salt-and-pepper hair.

"So tell me about the mobster boss in the minimum-security satellite. What's he in for?" Ira threw his napkin over the empty tray.

"Story goes, our Sicilian guy is responsible for flooding the US with heroin. He's credited with creating the Sicilian-American heroin pipeline." Sam kept his head down and spoke in a hushed tone.

"Very impressive. I heard the federal prison is filled with a lot of wannabe mafiosos."

"Used to be, but recently the FBI has taken on the mob in a big way. On a tapped line they heard about 'tangerine trees bearing lemons,' which they decoded as a pending heroin deal. Busted our Nicky in a 1973 heroin shipment to a Buffalo tile warehouse." Sam glanced around. "This compound has its share of gangsters who make millions in the drug trade—although they deny it. They've become savvy businessmen."

"I'd think they'd brag about it." Ira shifted his eyes nervously and looked around the mess hall, which was starting to empty out.

"The old-school mafiosos wouldn't touch drugs— gambling, prostitution, all that was okay. Then things changed—too much money to be made. Mobsters were holding back drug money from the bosses. It all started falling apart when they began snitching on each other, breaking the code of silence. Word is they've moved to more legitimate entrepreneurship. Even the wannabes show Nicky respect. Make no mistake, he takes his business very seriously. He's sharp, makes difficult decisions, and stands by them, still stackin' loot, enough for the family on the outside and to keep himself living relatively comfortably on the inside."

"I saw him leaving the commissary with some muscle guys carrying boxes of stuff."

"Word is they make feasts every night with their summer sausage, pepperoni, anchovies, crackers, cheese, and olives. They live large with their mini banquets."

"I thought there was a monthly spending limit at the commissary." Ira straddled the bench.

"Three hundred a month, but Nicky bought all the dorms around him and moved his people close. Are you starting to get the picture? The camp is supposed to be dedicated to the nonviolent white-collar inmates, and capacity is less than fifty—it's not easy to get in. There's maybe one guard, and they don't even lock the doors. No one walks out. They would just land back inside, not in a camp next time, with another seven years added to their sentence."

"How did I get here?" Ira shook his head, distressed, talking more to himself than to Sam. "How do I work this?" He felt so out of his element.

"You'll get the lay of the land. The important thing is you learn who you can trust and who to stay away from. Same with the guards. Learn when to keep your head down and toe the line. They enjoy the power—especially over the white-collar inmates. Now the tables are turned, and they can make you get on your knees and scrub the tile with a toothbrush."

"I noticed some attitude." Ira succumbed to the urge to look at his watch. It was 4:50 p.m. He felt like he'd fallen into a time warp.

"Have no doubt, they notice your attitude too. Two kinds of people wind up here: those who had nothing and those who had everything. If you're one of those who had everything, good chance you think you're better than everyone else. They smell that in an instant. Lose it fast, or they'll beat it out of you."

Ira nodded slowly, absorbing his meaning. "How do you pass the time without going crazy?"

"I spend most of my time here in the law library

preparing for life when I get out," Sam said without missing a beat. "Don't waste time feeling sorry for yourself and jerking off. How about we hit the rec room—you play basketball?"

"Yeah, but I didn't bring my varsity sweater." Ira grinned, making a joke, albeit a lame one, for the first time in weeks. "Let me call home first, and I'll meet you in a half hour."

"That's optimistic. The bank of phones is always busy after dinner. I'll catch ya later." Sam stood and tossed his tray into the trash like it was a basketball. "Score!" he yelled and raised his fist in the air.

Ira was on his third cigarette when one of the four wall phones freed up. He dialed home and perched on the metal circular seat. His heart pounded at the thought of Nanci, and he smelled her herb-and-wildflower-scented auburn hair. He took a deep drag on his cigarette and exhaled the smoke. It was almost the end of the month, and he didn't know how many minutes he had left.

"Nan, it's me." He faced the white cinder-block wall and swiveled the seat. "Is Rubie still up?"

"I was hoping you'd call. She just went to sleep. She's loving the swim classes, putting her face in the water, and blowing bubbles now."

"That's great. It's important that she learns to swim." Ira kicked off the wall and recalled his summers at Edgewood Swim Club. He yearned to hold Rubie in the pool and make her feel safe in the water. "What are you up to?"

"Unpacking. There are still boxes all over the house. And I sent you some magazine subscriptions."

"So, I got my first kosher meal today."

"And?"

"A little bland but a vast improvement over the standard prison fare." Ira could sense she was distracted and envisioned her unpacking puzzles and baby dolls.

"I need to tell you something. I know it's not the best timing." She hemmed and hawed, which was not like her. "But I'm pregnant."

He could no longer hear her respiration. Was she holding her breath while she waited for his response?

"You're sure?" Ira felt a total shutdown of his mental processes. This was the last thing he expected.

"Yes, I saw the doctor."

"I'm the dad?" Before the words left his mouth, he knew this was a hopelessly stupid question. He needed time to think and couldn't blame her for being angry.

"We're going to get through this," she said.

Was that excitement he heard in her voice? "Nan, you can't have a baby while I'm in prison." He knew this was another serious blunder.

"Really?" She cut short her words, and it came out snarky. "The fact that ninety-two percent of inmates in federal and state prisons are fathers would indicate otherwise."

The warnings and fears ran through his brain like ticker tape. *Children with fathers in prison are destined to go to prison. Children of convicts will never amount to anything.*

"You have a short sentence. You'll be home soon, and we'll be a family again."

"How will I support you? This baby won't have a chance. Don't you see that I can't be there to take care of you!" He couldn't think of a single positive statement.

"You're shocked. I was shocked and scared too. You need some time to think this through," she said, her voice husky with tears.

Ira realized too late that they should have discussed this with Sydney Blackwell. He was the expert on keeping families together. Now Nanci would need to explain this whole mess to him.

****

"Rosen, get up!" A guard shook Ira roughly by the shoulder.

"What's going on?" Ira squinted. It was still dark, and flashlight beams blinded him.

"There's a medical emergency." The guard pulled on Ira's arm, and he rolled off the top bunk, staggering onto his feet.

"What the hell is this?" Ira backed away across the cold tile floor.

"There's been an accident in the UNICOR factory. We need a doctor."

"Get one of those Loretto fed doctors. I'm not supposed to be a doctor anymore." Groggy, Ira turned to climb up to his bunk, but a guard pulled him back.

"There's nobody else. The ambulance is twenty minutes out. There isn't time to put on your shoes. We're going to the satellite."

Two guards spun Ira around and drove him through the barracks, down the corridors, and out into the raw night air. Large snowflakes blew against his face, and he fully awoke, shivering. He was alone in the yard with the guards, and adrenaline rushed into his system.

The satellite door was unlocked, like Sam said it would be, and they shoved him through. They led Ira down a long green corridor to a sterile room that looked like an infirmary, and a patient lay wheezing in a bed with rails. Ira became alert at the scent of fresh blood. A red stain spread across the white sheet over the patient's chest. He lifted the sheet and layers of gauze and saw the chest puncture. It was a normal sight in the downtown Detroit ER where he'd done his training. Detroit Medical Center was one of the best places to learn trauma.

"This man is in critical condition and needs emergency care immediately, or he won't make it through the night." Ira knew that, without a chest tube thoracostomy, the patient would die from a collapsed lung due to traumatic hemothorax.

"No one is dying on my shift—especially not Don Vece. Do something, Rosen!"

"I'm not looking for any trouble here. I've lost my license. You know I can't do anything."

"What are they going to do? Take your license away, throw you in jail? Don't overthink it, Rosen. Just save his life. You'll be taken care of."

"I've heard that line before."

The inmate moaned, and against his better judgment, Ira's instincts kicked in. He pulled on a pair of latex gloves from a box on the metal cart next to the bed and leaned over the patient. He palpated the patient's chest, and the sufferer winced in pain and had greater difficulty breathing. A penetrating injury to the man's thoracic structures damaged his lungs and caused blood to fill the outer cavity. Blood had already filled the pleural cavity, and if the pressure wasn't released, the don would die.

"Nicky isn't dying on my shift!" the guard shouted. "See, he's quieter now."

Ira leaned over the body and listened. The wheezing had stopped, which meant the lungs were no longer expanding. They were now minutes away from the organs shutting down.

"I need an advanced first aid trauma kit and that Coke bottle. Stat!"

The guards extended an empty two-liter Coke bottle from the counter and a box of medical supplies. Ira sorted through and selected gauze, tape, a sterile pad, a scalpel, and a chest tube.

"Prep, insert, secure." He talked himself through as he opened the sterile bags and laid out the supplies on the cart. He palpated and felt for the sixth or seventh intercostal space at the posterior axillary line. This would be the best placement.

When he was only a resident, physicians had turned to him to perform exacting procedures where variance of one or two millimeters was the difference between success and death. His understanding of physiology was innate, something they couldn't take from him. The healer within him was steadfast and intact.

Using the scalpel, he cut into the chest, making an opening wide and deep enough to insert the hollow, flexible tube. He inserted the other end of the tube into the bottle and secured the chest tube with tape and gauze. Immediately, blood began to drain from the pleural cavity into the two-liter bottle. He breathed a sigh of relief that despite the lack of a sterile chest-tube drainage system with the proper one-way valve to prevent return of the air or fluid back into the patient, this jerry-rigged system seemed to be working for the moment. He just needed to buy enough time for the paramedics to bring in a proper drainage system. Later, he would instruct the paramedics that the tube wasn't to be removed until the lung was fully reinflated and there was less than 200-300 ML of fluid—at least twenty-four hours. He then went to work repairing the puncture wound.

While Ira sutured the don, he lost track of space and time. He was in the zone where only he and his patient existed. He was covered in Don Vece's blood. When he finished, he peeled off the latex gloves and breathed in the sweet scent from his blood-soaked scrubs. He sat in a straight metal chair beside the bed and watched the don breathe.

The guards escorted Ira across the courtyard under the star-studded sky. He pulled himself onto the top bunk and curled into a fetal position. The instants of life and death triggered arousal of his fundamental drive to heal and protect. He remembered the bright-red postpartum bleeding after Rubie was born. The blood of life he cherished. Would he be there to catch this new baby when he was born? In the green, fluorescent lighting, he had sudden clarity. He had lost sight of his calling and ruined it all. His career, his marriage, and his family. His life. He had been given every privilege. He felt broken, and despair submersed him. He started to cry for what he had lost. He cried for the hurt, the shame, the stigma, and the dishonor to Nanci, Rubie, his mother, his father, and himself. He was in a dark hole, and there was no light at all.

Chapter Twenty-Nine—Honking

Southwood, Michigan

"Hey, Andy, awesome to see you working out." Ben braced himself as Luna jumped on him and nuzzled her white face and triangular ears affectionately into his chest, shedding her double thick husky coat on his navy peacoat and pants. He scratched behind her ears, and she looked up at him lovingly with her pale-blue eyes.

"You've got yourself a friend for life." Andy stood panting behind a chair, practicing shifting his weight onto one leg, swinging the other to the side, and balancing on the first. "This is the most exciting part of her day."

Ben had been walking Luna for five weeks since Andy's blow to the head when the swim team's bus slid off the road and rolled into a ravine. At first, Ben came by just to keep Andy company, but then he saw that his family was exhausted and stressed with Andy's medical appointments, therapy, and daily care. Walking Andy's dog, Luna, was a welcome service he could offer while Andy recovered from a mild traumatic brain injury. The swelling and bruising finally healed to the point that Andy was able to stand and practice walking. The fatigue, dizziness, and blurry vision were gradually going away, but it would be a while until he swam the 200 meter backstroke.

Ben hooked the leash onto Luna's collar, and she lunged for the front door. "We'll be back." He waved, and Luna pulled him forward.

Once on the sidewalk, Ben lured her into a sitting position and rewarded her with a treat from his pocket when she was calm. "Let's go," he commanded and walked purposefully. Luna was hanging out at his side with a loose leash as they headed to the park. "Good girl," he rewarded, proud of the progress they'd made.

Ben continued to ruminate about the accident. No one seemed to know the exact cause. Someone said the driver got distracted and took his focus off the road, but most agreed it was caused by hazardous road conditions. He'd learned injuries were often worse in bus crashes due to no seat belts to provide restraint.

True to his relentless nature, Coach Walker reinstated swim practice a week later, wearing a soft foam neck brace for whiplash and a sling immobilizing his right shoulder to support a broken clavicle. At the sparsely attended morning swim practice, Ben learned that Chris Boyce had been slammed against the dashboard in the crash and was still recovering from broken ribs, internal bleeding, abdominal pain, light-headedness, chills, and fatigue. Along with Ben, Andy and Chris were the team's strongest swimmers. Half of their medley relay was out of commission. No telling when Andy and Chris would be back in the water and ready to compete. Before his injury, Andy's backstroke had been extraordinary. Tom Peters had escaped injury in the bus accident and could cover the breaststroke, but Chris was a long way from the butterfly with broken ribs. It didn't look good for winning the state championship.

Given the Sabbath restriction, my record-setting

freestyle is of little help. At least Coach had agreed that they would find a way to make it work for him to remain on the team. But the team was in poor condition and pretty much out of action until they could mend and rebuild. He kept thinking what might have happened to him had he not chosen that Saturday to keep the Sabbath.

Luna stopped and sniffed a tree, and Ben checked his watch. Today was Howard's bar mitzvah, and Ben needed to meet his family at home to leave for the temple in forty-five minutes. He walked quickly.

His last conversation with Howard replayed again and again in his mind. "I know this might sound silly, but I'm really just not comfortable doing that."

"After everything I've done for you? I'm always there for you," Howard pleaded.

"I'm here to help. I'm just not writing it for you."

"When did you become holier than thou? You've given me answers on a math test."

"It's one thing to cheat on a math test and another thing entirely to cheat on the Torah. Howard, we're talking about your soul. You're asking me to help you cheat your way through a spiritually significant rite of passage." Ben could see that he had totally lost Howard. "I don't expect you to understand why I don't feel right about this, but if we talk it through, I think there's a way I can still help you."

Ben felt miserable. He liked Howard, and their friendship was important to him.

"That's just stupid. No one will know that you wrote it."

"Howard, if we have to keep it a secret, we shouldn't be doing it. Don't put me in this position. I said this isn't something I'm comfortable doing. Why do you keep asking me to do this?"

Ben was sure that a part of Howard knew what he was doing was not right. The more Howard insisted, the more frustrated he became.

"You're ruining my bar mitzvah!" Howard looked desperate. His eyes glistened with tears, and he bulldozed Ben across the family room to the door. "You're a rotten excuse for a friend! Get out of my house!"

"Shove it, Howard. I'm trying to help you. This is your issue, not mine." Ben had slammed the door behind him on the way out.

This morning he reflected that Howard hadn't rescinded the invitation to his bar mitzvah, and he intended to attend. He was curious what Howard had come up with on his own.

Ben pulled off the navy pants scattered with Luna's white fur and pulled on his suit slacks with the crisp crease for Howard's coming-of-age event at the temple. He looked in the mirror and straightened his tie. He flicked some dry skin from his forehead and licked his fingers to smooth his bushy eyebrows that very nearly formed a unibrow, which he'd read was a sign of intelligence and great beauty in ancient Greece.

The gala mega birthday event was going to be tonight at the Raleigh House. His throat tightened at the thought of another Raleigh House event. He hadn't been there since the shrimp incident the night of Alan's bar mitzvah.

"We're waiting for you…" Estie said through her teeth as she passed by Ben's room.

"Coming now…" Ben's eyebrows shot up, and he ran down the flight of stairs.

The family was dressed to the nines for Howard Greenberg's bar mitzvah service. Ben followed a trail of Old Spice behind Dad into the car in the garage. He could barely breathe when Mom closed the passenger door and he was engulfed in a cloud of the Oriental fragrances of sandalwood, cedarwood, and tangerine that dominated the perfume Mom wore like a new dress. Ben took shallow breaths and felt crushed by the big aromas, big shoulder pads, and big hair surrounding him.

It was a short drive to the temple, and the emerald Lincoln town car moved slowly through the snow-covered streets. The snow crunched beneath the tires, and the car stopped at the red light at the corner of Pierce and Southwood. At exactly that moment, in his black coat and hat, Rabbi Silverstein crossed the street directly in front of the car.

"Why, isn't that Rabbi Silverstein?" Mom exclaimed. She stretched across the front seat and honked the horn with one hand and waved with the other.

The rabbi slowed his stride and looked through the windshield. With a glimmer of recognition, he smiled warmly. Everyone waved. Ben wanted to disappear and slid down in his seat.

"Ben, why are you sinking into the footwell?" Estie prodded.

The entire family was now looking at Ben, awaiting a response.

"Because it's Shabbos, and we're driving in the car and waving at the rabbi! Doesn't that seem wrong to any of you?" He felt the heat in his cheeks.

"Ben, don't you think the rabbi knows you drive on Saturday? You're not accountable to the rabbi. You're only accountable to the almighty God, and believe me,

194

he knows. If you aren't comfortable with that, don't drive." Dad spoke to Ben through the rearview mirror.

"You're right. You are so right, Dad." Ben had a flash of clarity. "I need to get out." He opened the back door and stepped onto the street. The light changed to green, and the string of cars behind the town car started honking.

Mom opened her door. "I'm going with him, Steven."

"I'm going too!" Joel stopped the door from closing behind Ben and jumped out after him.

Then Ben, Mom, and Joel were on the sidewalk, walking alongside Rabbi Silverstein. While they weren't going to the same place, they were walking in the same direction. Dad and Estie were left alone in the car.

Ben glanced back and saw his dad pound his palms on the steering wheel. His face was grim with anger, and his lips seemed to mouth the words, "Damn it!" The light turned red again. The cars behind continued to blare their horns.

Ben slipped on the sidewalk slush in his dress shoes and caught himself. He looked ahead at the unshoveled sidewalks. *I should have worn boots.*

"Ben, Good Shabbos—where are you going?" the rabbi greeted Ben, warmhearted.

"Good Shabbos, Rabbi. We're going to the temple for a friend's bar mitzvah." They walked in two pairs, he and the rabbi in front and his mom and Joel behind.

"Nice. Which friend?"

"Howard Greenberg."

"Mazal tov! Please wish the family mazal tov from me."

"For sure." Ben avoided stepping in the deeper piles

D.G. Schulman

of slush. "Rabbi, I kind of have a problem with a friend and wonder if you can help me?"

"I'll try."

"We had an argument because my friend asked me to do something that I wasn't comfortable doing, and he wouldn't let up. I didn't do it, and he said I was a rotten friend."

The rabbi didn't pause or show any uncertainty. "*Ethics of our Fathers* says, '…acquire for yourself a friend; and judge every person meritoriously.' "

"What if the friend disappoints you?"

"Every person needs a friend to whom he can reveal his inner feelings. When friends expose themselves to one another and share their innermost feelings, they're likely to see parts of one another that they don't like. That's why we're told to look favorably upon every person, even one who seems spiritually inferior. Together they can work on self-betterment."

Ben suddenly remembered his collar tightening around his throat, struggling to breathe at Alan's bar mitzvah, and Howard yelling, "Ben's in trouble! He's going to die. Do something!" He had no doubt how much Howard cared for him and felt ashamed that he had been looking down on him.

"A person generally judges himself too favorably and judges others too harshly." Rabbi Silverstein slowed down and placed a hand on Ben's shoulder. "This is my stop. I'll see you Thursday night. Good Shabbos."

Ben looked up, surprised they were already in front of the familiar red-brick house that had been converted to a shul. His feet were getting cold. He thought of his Uncle Ira and considered for a split second that maybe he was judging him too harshly too. He regrouped with

Mom and Joel, and they rambled down the street. Joel was telling Mom jokes. The temple was just a half mile away.

Chapter Thirty—Sanctuary

Southwood, Michigan

They arrived late. The Torah reading was over, and one of the board members carried the Torah through the aisles of the sanctuary for congregants to kiss the Torah before it was returned to the ark. Ben, his mom, and Joel blended into the standing crowd. They slid into an open row in the back near the entry and sat together with the congregation when the ark was closed.

Howard stepped up to the microphone and tapped to make sure it was on. He took a deep breath. "A man walks into a synagogue with his dog. He goes up to the rabbi. 'Rabbi, I want my dog to have a bar mitzvah, and I want to do it here.'

" 'What are you crazy?' the rabbi says. 'We can't do that!'

" 'Please, I'll do anything.'

" 'It can't be done,' the rabbi insists.

" 'Rabbi, I don't think you understand. I'm willing to donate twenty thousand dollars to this synagogue.'

"The rabbi says, 'Why didn't you tell me your dog was Jewish?' "

A few uncomfortable laughs came from pockets of the sanctuary. The dog joke was stale.

"Okay. I have one more. What does Arnold Schwarzenegger say at a bar mitzvah?" He paused for

198

comedic timing. "Muscle. Tough."

Laughter exploded.

A smile flickered across Howard's anxious face. "Thank you all for coming. Especially my friends and family who traveled from far away and took the time to be here. My Torah portion is Mishpatim. It's the Hebrew word for laws, and the portion contains fifty-three commandments—twenty-three you must do and thirty you must *not* do. Don't worry, I'm not going to talk about them all."

There was a little more laughter.

"Actually, I know very little about them. Truth is, I tried to get a friend of mine to write this part of my speech for me. He refused. He said it would be cheating, and we had an argument about it."

The sanctuary became totally still and quiet. Ben scanned the crowd. *They can't tell if he's joking.*

Howard licked his lips and jiggled his foot. "I said some things I wish I hadn't, but I couldn't stop thinking about what he said. That we were talking about my soul and the Torah isn't something you want to be deceptive about. Exodus 23:7 commands us: 'From a false matter you shall keep far.' In short, the Torah is very anti-deception. So, this is what I learned from my portion." Howard felt a tinge of heat in his cheeks.

"I want to thank my parents for everything they do for me because I wouldn't be here without them. They didn't give up on me even when I gave up on myself. Thanks to Aunt Millie and Uncle Syd, Aunt Ruthie and Uncle Irving, Aunt Thelma and Uncle Sol, and all the cousins for coming from out of town. Special thanks to my grandparents, Freda and Jacob Greenberg and Lily and Nathan Schill, who never give up on trying to make me a mensch. Thanks to the rabbi who wouldn't let me off the hook. Last but not least, a big shout-out to all of you who came to share this special celebration with me."

The applause erupted, and Ben clapped too. He locked on to Howard who was searching the faces in the crowd. Finally, their eyes met, and Howard gave Ben a broad radiant smile.

Chapter Thirty-One—Time

Siedlce, Poland

When Chana slipped into the millinery shop ten minutes after nine o'clock, Mrs. Eckstein made a show of tapping her wristwatch and recording the time in her log. Chana was breathless and had run the whole way from the Siedlce Jewish Community Center where she dropped Yitzchak with his classmates in the courtyard. She was usually prompt, but this morning Yitzchak had dillydallied over every little thing—getting dressed, making breakfast, even walking—which put Chana late. She didn't sleep well and felt lonely and overworked since Sora left—all of which made her irritable. She regretted that she wasn't more patient with Yitzchak.

Chana could see her breath in the frigid air of the cluttered shop and groaned as she realized that no one had started the stove or brought any wood. She remembered that Sora had cautioned her when she agreed to fill the job about the miserly milliner who refused even to provide heat in the winter.

"Mrs. Pincus will be picking up her hat at noon. Be sure it's ready, and Madame Frank will be in at two o'clock to select a hat for her daughter's wedding. And remember, dear, that time is money. A kopek will be deducted from your wages." Mrs. Eckstein tapped her pencil on the ledger while taking inventory of bolts of velvet, satin, silk flowers, feathers, ribbons, even thread, all items that were no longer available since the war.

Chana hung her coat and scarf on a wooden peg, despondent that she was in the hole before she even started. She reclaimed the hat she'd begun the day before for Mrs. Pincus and settled into a hard wooden chair next to her co-worker, Neche.

Wire hat frames were stacked on every surface with notes and swatches of fabric pinned to them. Her fingers were numb from the freezing and bleak morning, and she didn't even feel it when she stuck herself with a needle. A bright-red bead of blood came to the surface, and she instinctively put her finger to her mouth to keep from staining the white satin bow.

"Excuse me, Mrs. Eckstein, if you would arrange for wood in the stove, we could move our cold and stiff fingers ever more skillfully and swiftly." Chana gazed into her eyes, cold as ice, and set the hat in progress in her lap. She cupped her hands, blew on them to generate heat, and looked down, as though praying, awaiting a response and bracing for the wrath of the milliner.

Mrs. Eckstein made a clucking sound and sighed deeply but called to her son, Jakub, to bring a few logs of wood to start a fire. Chana slowly released her breath and resumed sewing the large satin bow on Mrs. Pincus' hat as the warmth from the crackling logs reached her. She thought for a split second that today might not be as miserable as she anticipated.

Sora had told Chana that staying late never changed Mrs. Eckstein's mind about docking her pay, and so she thought, *keep your pitiful kopek.*

She left the hat shop at five o'clock sharp with a spring in her step as she sensed the birth of spring in the air. The temperature had risen throughout the day, and the sound of melting ice dripping and water running was all around her. She resisted the yearning to take a short detour through the park and linger in the last hour of daylight because she had promised to help with the children while Mama prepared supper.

When Chana arrived at their white two-story apartment house on Piekna Strasse, the form of a fine gentleman in a tailored gray flannel overcoat stood on the wide busy street, gazing at the black, scorched, and gaping hole in the wall of the second story.

"Looking for something?" Chana slid him a wary look.

"I believe I've found it." His expression softened. "Such a pity, though, before the war this was one of the loveliest homes. If I remember correctly, there were shutters on the windows and balconies with ornate iron railings on the second story. Tell me, when did it happen?"

"In September of the occupation, during the night of explosions, a cannonball was shot through the wall. The family who owned the building lived in that apartment on the second story, and the very next morning they left with whatever possessions they could load in a wagon." She looked him straight in the eyes.

"They were fortunate to escape with their lives. It's unlikely they'll return." His forehead creased.

"If given an alternative, would anyone choose between invasion by the lesser of two evils, Russians or Germans?" Chana cringed.

"It would be better for Russia to win the war rather than Germany. I can think of no worse fate than being ruled by Germanic militaristic barbarians. Do you know the family who lives here?"

"Who's asking?" She took a step back but couldn't take her eyes from his face.

"Pardon me, I'm Mordechai Rosen, and I'm looking for a young woman to pen a letter to my uncle in America. The dressmaker, Masha, told me to look for the apartment house with the hole in the wall." He gave a half smile.

Chana was arrested by his moss-green eyes, glossy black beard, and windblown hair. "My sister has married and gone to America," she said as she tucked a lock of loose hair behind her ear.

"Is there no one else who can write an English letter?" He looked askance at her.

Chana was wearing her shabbiest skirt and sweater beneath the wool coat and felt like a child with her long raven hair in a braid. "Come back tomorrow at seven thirty p.m., and I'll compose your letter," she said, feeling her heart skip a beat. She whirled around and let herself into the apartment, fell back against the closed door, and clutched a hand to her heart, which was beating strangely fast.

The following evening, when Yitzchak, Reva, and Raizel were bathed and tucked into their beds, Chana bathed and clipped her nails. She toweled her freshly washed hair as she looked through her bureau for a suitable dress. Again, she found herself thinking about the Prusses' vacant residence upstairs and what they'd left behind. She imagined the four Pruss daughters' finest European high-fashion apparel deserted in their hasty departure at the break of dawn.

Searching the bureau, she was delighted to find Sora had left some dresses behind. Chana held a bold printed

Russian peasant dress against her in front of the mirror. The hemline fell above mid-calf, and Chana was sure Mama would complain of immodesty. She swapped it for an Edwardian silhouette lacy shirtwaist and long, narrow skirt that fell to the top of the foot. She surmised that Sora had deemed these dresses as either skimpy, out of fashion, or not sophisticated enough for a married woman in America. The last was a soft hunter-green crinoline, without a hoop but with a wide, full mid-length skirt and a white collar and cuffs. Chana had always loved this dress. She spun and chose it for its freedom of movement and striking color. She pulled her hair loosely into a soft roll at the nape of her neck and then decided she would look older if she piled her hair loosely on top of her head. She was now fifteen. The smooth sides with gentle waves resembled a bob haircut.

Reasonably satisfied with her appearance, she hummed a waltz and filled the samovar. Then she straightened the living room, swept the scarred wooden floor, and cleared the dining room table. Finally, she sat down with a pen, a box of writing paper, and a copy of Sigmund Freud's *Totem and Taboo,* which she found very readable.

"Are you expecting a caller?" Mama asked and took the seat next to Chana at the table with her sewing.

"Just a gentleman who needs a letter composed in English. He should be here shortly." Chana hid the book cover.

"You continue to read that outrageous book by Freud?"

"It's interesting, Mama...his idea about the origin of religion."

"Speculation taken to the point of absurdity."

"He says we have powerful desires that we must repress." She felt color rush into her cheeks.

"The Torah tells us as much. If someone wasn't doing it, God wouldn't have told us it was prohibited." Mama laughed. "And who is this gentleman?"

"Mordechai Rosen."

"Yes, the eldest son of the clockmaker—a fine man." She turned to a knocking at the door. "That must be him now." Mama set down her darning and received Mordechai Rosen graciously.

"Good evening." Chana set her book aside, and her mouth went dry.

"Good evening. I regret that we weren't properly introduced yesterday. I'm Mordechai Rosen, and you are?" He removed his hat.

"Chana Weisman." She met his eyes. "Please sit down." She motioned to a chair.

"How shall we get started?"

"Tell me to whom the letter will be addressed. Then you can proceed to speak naturally, as though the person were seated across the table, and I'll take notes. When you're finished, I may need to ask some questions. Then I'll write the letter, capturing your meaning and feeling to the best of my ability."

Chana arranged the stack of writing paper in front of her and held a pen at the ready.

"The letter is to my father's brother, my uncle Julius, in Detroit, Michigan, United States," he said in a deep voice.

Chana scribbled quickly to keep pace with his speech. She focused entirely on his voice and the nuances of his expression, and she felt the kindness and sensitivity of his soul and the passion and hope that burned within him.

"Am I going too fast?" He paused to ask.

"Not at all." Her breath caught in her throat. "Keep going." As she wrote, she detected his gaze studying her face.

When he finished speaking, she stood up, and her cheeks heated. "You must be thirsty. Would you like some tea while I arrange my notes into a letter?"

He nodded, his eyes held her captive, and she turned away to prepare a cup of tea. Before the clock struck nine, Chana presented the letter to Mordechai. He inspected her small, meticulous, cursive letters and placed a gold ruble on the table. "Would you kindly read back a translation?"

"Of course." Her eyes flashed to meet his. She swallowed the nervous dryness in her throat and began...

Dear Uncle Julius,

How lucky you are to have made it to America before the war. The suffering is unbearable, and dread for what is yet to come is great. As much as we dislike the Russians, we absolutely despise the Germans. You can imagine how dire the times are when we see a Russian victory as the best option for survival. In the end, the war will ruin all. For now, we remain in our homes but hear of evacuations in many neighboring towns. We keep debating whether to leave Siedlce but fear that it will be worse wherever we go. Expulsions are accompanied by pogroms, started by Cossacks hostile to Jews and seeking to seize Jewish property and possessions.

All males aged eighteen to forty-five are now required to register for the draft. We fear that our father will be taken for a third service, and in six months I will turn eighteen and be eligible for the draft myself. Daily, we get reports of those who are wounded and those who have died. Father is seeking papers and steamship tickets to leave at the soonest opportunity.

This brings me to the purpose of my letter. Father would like to bring our family to Detroit to be near you and yours. I have been learning watchmaking and have a passion for it. We expect you are still a watchmaker in a jewelry store and hope you would consider becoming a proprietor yourself. Despite the war, at present Father is still well-off and wishes to establish a business partnership together. We pray for your reply. May God bless us all.

Your beloved nephew,
Mordechai Rosen

Mordechai caught her gaze and held it for an extended period. "Your writing is beautiful and quite perceptive. I believe you make me sound more knowledgeable and quick-witted than I am. May I call on you again, for another letter?"

The eye contact was like a touch. Chana felt him close to her. His attraction was palpable, and when he looked in her eyes, she knew he wanted to know her.

Chapter Thirty-Two—Visiting Day

Loretto, Pennsylvania

Nanci slipped quietly into her sister-in-law's house with Rubie, woozy, in tow in her fleece onesie Pooh Bear PJ's.

"Are you sure you want to go alone?" Aliza slid Rubie's backpack off her shoulders, and they plopped down on the couch together. Aliza was still in her ankle-length, blue scotch plaid flannel nightgown. It wasn't yet sunrise.

"Here's Rubie's blankie and her favorite Pooh Bear she always sleeps with. Peanut butter on white bread with no crust is her go-to food. That's practically all she eats right now, except for bananas, granola bars, and sometimes noodles. She might eat three bananas in a day. It's fine. You know about that jungle animal movie and fast-forwarding through the Bengal tiger part. Bed at seven o'clock after bath and story time. Her favorite books are in here, and I always let her pick three, which are usually *Goodnight Moon, Are You My Mother,* and *Corduroy.*"

She didn't want to forget anything. She had never left Rubie overnight, and she needed to stay focused for fear of losing her resolve.

"Ben or Mom could go with you." Aliza snuggled with Rubie.

"Pajamas, toothbrush, and fresh clothes are in her backpack. And she only likes the bubble-gum flavored toothpaste. You can drop her off at preschool in the morning anytime between seven thirty and eight thirty, and you don't need to pack lunch. Pickup is at four o'clock." She took hold of Aliza's right hand.

"You'll tell him about the Volvo?" Aliza asked, shuddering, and Nanci knew she was referring to the explosion.

"Yes," Nanci whispered. "We have a lot to talk about."

Aliza surrendered and hugged Nanci who kissed Rubie on the head. Nanci had worried about a difficult good-bye, but Rubie was sleeping softly.

"Tonight I'll be at the Holiday Inn in Altoona. Here's the phone number." Nanci pressed the scrap of paper into Aliza's hand. "And don't worry, I've got this." Her tone became brighter.

"Right, but let's not forget how useless the protection officer was at the funeral. Be safe." Aliza offered a forced smile and embraced Nanci in a tight extended hug. "Give my love to my brother."

Nanci agreed with her sister-in-law about the competency, or lack thereof, of the security protection. Nevertheless, this was something she had to do on her own.

The car rental included unlimited mileage, and the tank was full. Given she was now in the market for a new car, she considered the Cutlass as she adjusted the mirrors. While both white, the luxury coupe and her Volvo were like night and day, and it would take some time to get used to the soft ride and light touch required by the power steering and brakes. She reviewed the map and directions to Loretto and calculated she would be there by noon, even with pit stops. She'd submitted the proper visitor paperwork, BP-Forms 224 and 629, and had a valid picture ID, adhered to the dress code, and carried nothing forbidden. Clear weather was forecasted. She pushed her sunglasses onto her head, like a headband in her whorl of auburn curls, and backed out of the driveway. The headlamps projected a beam of light in the darkness. She accelerated confidently onto the illuminated road ahead.

Inhaling deeply, she sped onto I-75 S., which she would take to exit 1A where she would merge onto I-80 E. toward Cleveland and continue for one-hundred forty-eight miles where the Ohio Turnpike/I-76 E. would take her into Pennsylvania. It had seemed closer when she first learned Ira was transferred from Sandstone, Minnesota, to Loretto, Pennsylvania. Three hundred seventy-two miles each way was hardly a day trip.

She was glad to be alone. She needed the time to think about what to share with Ira. She felt like she was keeping a beach ball underwater and worried that she would let herself go and the ball would unexpectedly pop up. Their last conversation had gone badly. She was in uncharted territory and felt her instincts couldn't be trusted. She no longer knew what Ira was thinking, and that's what frightened her most.

She had moved past feeling betrayed and rejected. She knew that Ira never meant to hurt her. He sometimes said stupid things when he was shocked, insecure, and emotional. Her goal was to rebuild their connection and make a unified plan. She hoped he was able and available but expected to be disappointed. Fear splintered her heart. After talking with Sydney Blackwell, she understood that she couldn't lean on Ira and the bonding she hoped for wouldn't be possible. She expected there would be an opportunity to be together in private for some extended period. Surely, the facility had a designated room, trailer, or small cabin for that purpose, but Sydney explained that very few states had conjugal visit programs and that federal prisons didn't.

****

Sam dribbled out to half court and called the shot, "Straight in." Just as he predicted, the basketball went into the basket without touching the backboard or rim.

Ira stepped into position to match the shot. He aimed and threw. "Damn, bank swish."

The ball bounced off the backboard and into the basket without touching the rim. "That's E and two out of three. Should we go for three out of five?" H-O-R-S-E was their favored game, and they went back and forth on who won the shoot-out.

"It's not exactly satisfying when you're hardly there. Distracted, buddy?" Sam dribbled and practiced his hook shot.

"Yeah, my monkey mind is producing a drama worthy of an Oscar." Ira caught a hard pass from Sam and dribbled down court.

"Rosen!" A guard shouted from the door of the rec room.

Ira signaled to Sam he was heading out and wrapped a towel around the back of his neck to absorb the sweat. The large institutional clock on the wall showed ten o'clock. His stomach flipped with nervous excitement, and he counted the hours until he would see Nanci.

"Hey, what's up?" Ira approached Rodney, the same guard who had dragged him out of bed in the middle of

212

the night last week. They were now on familiar terms.

"You're moving, Rosen." Rodney led Ira out of the rec center and down the long linoleum corridors to his cell unit.

Rodney's words sent panic signals racing through Ira's body. "I can't move now—my wife is visiting in two hours."

"You're going to the camp, old buddy." He laid a hand on Ira's tense shoulder.

"You mean the satellite across the courtyard?" Ira's brain froze. That would mean he was moving from low security to minimum security. Certainly, Sydney Blackwell, their pricey prison consultant hired to accomplish this exact development, would have notified him. Did Nanci know? While he instantly rejoiced at the realization that he was free from Snake's harassment and attacks, he was filled with unanswered questions. And he already missed Sam. Could they still meet up for basketball? His elation was tempered, and he wondered who was behind this move.

The camp's dormitory-like setting differed from the low-security facility with its individual cells and airplane-hangar-size dormitories. The relaxed wooden furnishings in the camp reminded Ira of a college dorm. He threw his bag of minimal belongings into a bright-blue metal locker and sprawled across his bottom bunk. Just two bunk beds—four to a room and a round wooden table. A TV with a built-in VCR was mounted on the wall. But the biggest change was that "counts" weren't taken. He was free to move around most of the facility, inside and out, and inmates could wear their own clothes. He wished he'd known before Nanci left this morning. She could have brought him some casual clothing, and he could get out of the prison uniform. In his own clothes, he speculated, he might feel himself again.

The striking of hard knuckles on the wooden doorjamb jolted Ira to the strangeness of the situation.

"You're the doctor?" the lone guard inquired.

Ira nodded, and confusion engulfed him. No one here addressed him by that title.

"You have guests." The guard signaled to a tall olive-skinned inmate with blue-black hair and a broad barrel chest who came forward carrying a box.

"The don welcomes you and wishes to acknowledge his indebtedness to you for saving his life." The broad olive-skinned inmate set down an unopened box of foil-pouch Albacore tuna packs and stepped to the side only to be replaced by another olive-skinned inmate.

"The don welcomes you and wishes to express his gratitude to you for saving his life." The second inmate set down an unopened box of pink salmon packs and stepped aside. He was quickly replaced by a third.

Ira raised his hand to stop them, but it was of no use. The third came forward and placed an unopened box of mixed-nut packs, and a fourth followed and offered a variety pack of instant oatmeal, which he stacked on the top of the tower of boxes. He was completely out of his element and racked his brain to process what it meant to receive a procession of gifts from a mafioso boss. Intuitively, he knew it was a bribe, a threat, a form of extortion, or all three. Accepting the gift meant the don could call in a favor in the future. He saw clearly that refusing the gift was not an option but would be insulting, showing a lack of respect. He had to accept. Either way, he was screwed.

"Please tell the don that I thank him for the gifts."

Ira surveyed the boxes, attempting to show appreciation and pleasure. He tore open the box of foil-pouch Albacore tuna packs, held up a fistful, and smiled broadly.

"You can tell him yourself. The don requests your presence. I'm Matteo, and Don Vece asked me to bring you these gifts and invite you to visit him." Matteo and his cohorts didn't move and stood at attention on either side of the doorway, waiting as though they had all the time in the world.

Ira understood this wasn't an invitation he could refuse and allowed himself to be escorted to the dormitory at the end of the corridor where Matteo stopped and announced, "The doctor is here," before turning and leaving.

The first thing Ira noticed was a microwave and what appeared to be a private commissary stock of salami, beef stew, spaghetti sauce, pasta, summer sausage, chicken, and foil pouches of mackerel. He registered the foil packets of mackerel, called macs, that were the prison currency. The macs represented both wealth and power to obtain all manner of services. Then he saw his patient sitting in an upholstered recliner with his feet elevated.

"Welcome, Doctor, I'm Nicky. Please take a seat."

The don motioned for Ira to sit on an institutional metal chair at his right side. Nicky's chest rose and fell with rapid breaths, and a faint flush tinged his cheeks. He was no longer the ashen man Ira had met, wheezing and gasping for his life. "Thank you for coming. You received my gifts?" His voice was both jubilant and intense.

"Yes, thank you and really not necessary." Ira

quickly added, "You picked out the items I prefer. I'm sure I'll enjoy everything." He remembered what his mother had taught him about receiving gifts he didn't want and did his best to sound genuine.

"I give you my word that you are now a protected man." The don held up a finger and spoke with a gravelly voice.

"The way I see it, we're square. All those gifts were more than enough. Really." Ira's skin prickled with alarm.

"I do not remain in debt," he said, folding his arms defiantly. "The gifts meet your kosher meal plan, yes?" His piercing eyes focused intently on Ira's face.

Ira nodded and didn't dare look away. How did Nicky know about his meal plan? What else did he know? Every instinct he had told him that he was anything but safe.

"Don, your selection from the commissary was just right, and I'll enjoy it. You appear to be healing well and getting back to normal."

"I'm feeling better than I've felt for years. I haven't had decent medical care since I entered this joint. The on-staff physician couldn't recognize me in a lineup, and he's never around when I need him. I'm certain this new arrangement will provide the personalized, comprehensive care that I need." Nicki beamed at Ira.

"New arrangement?" Ira wasn't following.

"This is the perfect patient-physician relationship."

A sense of impending doom filled Ira. His rapid, pounding heart rate was loud in his ears, drowning out everything else. All he could think was what he would say to a patient on the verge of a panic attack. *Follow the three-three-three rule. Name three things you see. Then name three sounds you hear. Finally, move three parts of your body.* He couldn't move his feet. He realized he was suffering from temporary paralysis triggered by the don's alarming power in the minimum-security camp.

****

Nanci understood Ira needed to know that the forensic team determined that the explosion was no accident. She remembered very little about the explosion. Instead, what she vividly recalled was trudging through the snow, arm in arm with Aliza, infused with the almost religious feeling of a miracle, the divinity of life, when she was propelled forward into the drifts by the force of the blast. She was overjoyed and overwhelmed, and she wasn't going to give it up. She was alive, and she had life within her.

She put on her sunglasses and merged onto I-76 E. toward Pittsburgh as the morning sunlight filled the sky with a blaze of pinks and reds. High rock walls rose up on both the east and westbound shoulders—the road appeared to cut through a mountain. A snowplow filled her rearview mirror, tailgating. A glance in her side mirrors reflected open road behind the plow. Nanci slowed gradually, hoping to force the plow to pass. Terror gripped her stomach when the plow didn't move to the left lane, appeared to be right on her, then rammed her rear end and jolted the Cutlass forward.

She clenched the steering wheel with white knuckles, and the plow came at her from an angle and attempted to ram her into the rock wall. Fear clutched her heart, and she reactively spun the wheel to move to the left lane but oversteered and found herself skidding into a one hundred eighty degree turn in the westbound lane. Her heart beat like a hammer in her chest, and she hit the accelerator pedal to the floor, peeling forward and pushing the Cutlass to performance specs of 0 to 60 mph in 8.9 seconds.

Nanci parked in the center of a busy truck stop off the next exit. Her heart was still racing, and her body trembled uncontrollably. She breathed in deeply, steadied her hands, and opened the driver's door to check the condition of the car. The left rear and side fender were crushed. A brawny trucker jumped down from his cab and crossed the pavement toward her.

"This just happen?" He inspected the wheel well and the tire for alignment.

"Yeah, a snowplow rammed me on eastbound I-76."

"She looks drivable. Hit your brakes and let me check your taillights."

Nanci slid onto the smooth brown leather seat and tapped the brake pedal.

He gave her the thumbs-up and went around to the passenger window, motioning for her to roll down the window. "How far ya going?"

"To Monroeville, Exit 57."

"I'm heading that way east on I-76 myself, ma'am. I'll follow you to make sure you don't have any problems."

"That's very kind. Thank you." She made a note never again to complain about truckers on the road. Her best calculations indicated she was just over an hour from FCI Loretto.

She tried to relax into the upholstered seat and merged onto the interstate with the trucker in her rearview mirror. She smiled at the thought that no one would believe the maneuver she'd pulled back there. She loosened her grip on the steering wheel and resumed her course eastbound. As much as she struggled against admitting what was self-evident and unmistakable, she recognized the indisputable fact that someone was trying to kill her.

****

After a simple sign-in and a flash of her driver's license, a guard led Nanci outside and across the court into the minimum-security satellite referred to as an FPC, Federal Prison Camp, known for having no fences, no walls, and a low staff-inmate ratio. The guard directed her to wait in the visiting room. Sydney Blackwell had prepared her for more intense questioning and screening. She was exhausted and grateful that for once something was less complicated than she anticipated. The incident on the interstate had delayed her arrival, and it was already one o'clock. She knew visiting hours ran only until three p.m. and no one would be processed in after two.

At the sight of Ira, hot tears filled her eyes.

"We're going to get through this together," he said, drawing her into his arms.

Her tired body yielded to his. He pressed his torso against hers, and her heart was so full of love that she thought it would explode.

"Nan, I need you, and I'll make this up to you."

She knew they had to separate but could not let him go. She felt his body react to her. Sydney had warned that visiting protocol allowed limited displays of affection—an embrace upon greeting and another upon departure.

She drew away, and he cupped her face in his hands, studying her for a long moment. "Come with me," he said, taking her firmly by the hand to a pair of chairs in the corner. She gave the place a once-over, and they appeared to be alone.

"Forgive me, Nan. I was an idiot on our last phone call." He touched her hair.

She couldn't argue and rested her head against his shoulder.

"Plenty has happened in a short time," he whispered in her ear. "I was dragged out of bed in the middle of the night to save a man's life. Then this morning, out of the blue, they moved me to this minimum-security camp. Did Sydney make this happen?"

Nanci shook her head. "I don't think so. Maybe the rabbi? The same one who arranged your furlough for the funeral?"

"I hadn't thought of that." His brows drew together. "But you must be tired from the long drive. Did you have any trouble getting here?"

"Funny you should ask." A frown creased her forehead. "In fact, a snowplow tried to ram me into the rocks."

His spine stiffened at the words.

"It was only by the grace of God that I oversteered myself into a hundred and eighty degree turn onto westbound I-76." She combed her fingers through her curly hair and gathered it into a scrunchy. "And the forensic team said the Volvo explosion was no accident."

She felt him shiver. "Ira, I'm getting a distinct impression that someone is trying to kill me. Do you know why anyone would want to do that?"

He buried his face in his hands, and she sensed the pieces of a complex puzzle starting to come together.

Chapter Thirty-Three—Dance Lessons

Southwood, Michigan

"Grandma, I don't feel much like dancing today." Ben had woken up in a foul mood and had been grumpy all day.

"I know, honey, there are days like that. If I only danced when I felt like it, there'd be no dance school at all. Just wait till you see this Cuban action." She pressed the start on the boombox and took the lead with his hands in a low hold. Latin music drowned out his objections, and she demonstrated. "Rock step, one-two-three, rock step, cha-cha-cha. Take that triple step quickly—on the balls of your feet, Ben, switching your weight." Grandma was light on her feet, lively and playful. She swayed to a rhythmic pulse, and her arm movements became vibrant and flamboyant.

Ben couldn't resist the light and bubbly feel. He smiled, certain that no one had a grandma like his. Years of dance training kicked in, and his body poised, his spine pulled him up, and the arm action came instinctively from his core, sending his energy out through his arms as he walked forward and back, digging down with Cuban action.

"Rock step, cha-cha-cha. Small movement under your body with hip action, rock step, cha-cha-cha. No rise and fall, keep it compact, rock step, cha-cha-cha.

Dance it forward—masculine. There ya go!"

Grandma mirrored his movements, adding quick spins, strong hip movement, and sharp action.

The purple neon *Got To Dance* sign glowed on the paneled wall above the mirrors. Ben's eyes traced the bright cut-to-shape letters, and he wondered whether Grandma really had days when she didn't feel like dancing. His earliest memories were here in the basement studio playing on the expansive classic parquet dance floor. The mirrors and the wooden bar stretching the length of the longest wall made it irresistible. Grandma insisted everyone in her family learn to dance. Her contagious enthusiasm converted even the most reluctant students, both those related and those unrelated.

Got To Dance was the neighborhood studio for every coming-of-age boy and girl in the community. Everyone had fun, and parents found it more convenient than the dance studio in the strip mall because the kids could walk there and back on their own. Initially, Grandma taught ballroom dance for bar and bat mitzvah kids and their parents. Driven by demand, she later offered couples classes and private wedding dance lessons. When the demand for jazz, tap, and Latin dance kicked in, she hired a couple of instructors who matched her enthusiasm.

Grandma tossed a white towel to Ben and took one for herself. They wiped the sweat from their faces, draped the towels around their necks, and perched on stools with bottles of cola. Some days he was lucky enough to get a private lesson. He cleared his throat and spun on the stool. "I hope you won't be disappointed if I don't have the kind of bar mitzvah where we're going to do this kind of dancing."

"Is there another dance you'd like to do?" Grandma raised an eyebrow and looked at her grandson in a way she hadn't looked at her son.

Ben sensed she saw the fire smoldering within him. He didn't know how long he could contain this suppressed combustion.

"I think so, but it's not a dance we know."

"Try me. I bet I can learn some new steps." Grandma had danced long enough now to appreciate how her students found the rhythms, steps, motions, and patterns that moved them. How they moved in their own way and made the dance their own.

Ben noticed the time on the large atomic wall clock and was startled to see how late it was. He jumped down from the stool, kissed his grandma on the cheek, and said, "I need to get going. There's a Mitzvah Day Committee meeting at the temple."

****

Ben reviewed his notes and set up the flip chart and permanent markers on the easel. Their last meeting had been the week before Howard's bar mitzvah. He never expected that to go down the way it had. He had underestimated Howard. He had overestimated himself. Lately, he felt emotion in every fiber of his body. He felt more alive than he could remember ever feeling before. Heat spread from his chest. He was glad to still have a friend.

"Meeting is called to order!" Alan banged the walnut gavel and read from the notes Ben prepared. "At our last meeting, we unanimously voted to go out into the community and do spring cleanup for seniors—you know, mowing and raking leaves. And we'll visit with isolated elders. Five minutes are allotted for review and discussion. Does anyone have any questions?"

"How are we going to find the old people?" Ricky raised his hand more in protest than to be called upon.

"Good question, Ricky! I think our secretary, Ben, has some thoughts on that?"

"Yeah, the Jewish Family Service Agency has lists of seniors who have requested services. They're happy to have our help."

"What about equipment and transportation? We're not exactly in the lawn care business," Howard reminded them.

"Right," Alan said. "So that leads us into today's agenda. Everybody was supposed to bring two ideas about what we'll need to make this happen. Ben will capture these pearls on the flip chart. No need to raise your hand—just call out, gentlemen."

Ben stood poised with his blue aromatic marker. When no one said anything, he made a round bullet and wrote: *recruit drivers, i.e. ask your parents.*

"Borrow lawn mowers and rakes," Ricky yelled out.

And then the ideas began to flow: ask a gas station to donate gas; get a trailer to haul the mowers; maybe a rental company will donate; and get matched up with seniors through the JFS.

Ben couldn't write fast enough as more ideas floated through the air: get drinks, snacks, and lunch; everybody sign up for a shift; create work teams; schedule teams to assigned seniors; and get rabbinic approval.

"Good progress. A couple more things before we adjourn today: one, everybody look at the list and pick something to work on before our next meeting. Write your initials next to the job you pick. Two, I already talked to the rabbi, and we have rabbinic approval.

Mitzvah Day of the 1975 Bar Mitzvah Class will be on Saturday, May 24th!"

Alan banged the walnut gavel.

Ben went rigid hearing the words. "Wait a minute, we need to talk about this. Mitzvah Day can't be on a Saturday." A wedge of anger mixed with outrage consumed him.

"The rabbi said it's always on Saturday." Alan stacked the papers together.

"That doesn't make any sense!"

"Why not?"

"Because Saturday is our Sabbath—the seventh day when God rested and commanded us to rest, *not* to mow lawns."

"This isn't work, Ben. The rabbi explained we're doing a good deed. It's a mitzvah."

"Keeping the Sabbath is a mitzvah. The Torah we read from, carry, and kiss says to keep the Sabbath and lists the forbidden activities."

"Well, I guess sometimes it's a mitzvah *not* to do a mitzvah." A glimmer of laughter came into Alan's eyes. He gave an exasperated humph. The room broke into spontaneous boisterous hoopla.

"Then I'm out." Ben's cheeks burned as his gaze swept over the room.

"Come on, Ben, we can talk about this later." Alan flashed a smile at his anxious face.

"I can't do this. I don't belong here." Ben choked, his eyes filling with tears of insult, shock, and hurt.

Howard held back while their classmates jostled with rowdy horseplay and left the room like a stampede of buffalo. Ben tore off the oversized paper from the flip chart, his hand shaking, and rolled it into a tube. He said, handing it to Howard, "You'll bring this to the next meeting." A rush of strong emotion stormed through his body.

"Hang on." Howard held up a hand like a stop sign and backed away. "Let's think this through when you're not so upset." He thrust his hands in his pockets, refusing to take the tube.

"It won't change anything!" Ben smacked the hollow cylinder on the podium. "This is wrong. Something here is so wrong. Don't you feel it?"

"The thing is, you don't have to do this. Your bar mitzvah is three weeks away. When it's over, none of this will matter. Two months later, on Mitzvah Day, you can just be sick."

"Don't you see how off and dangerous this masquerade is? The lip service to adorn and honor the Torah? It's false, Howard. Whatever truth was here is covered by a thick cloak." A tremor shook his body as he spoke.

"Ben, I know what they'll do. Your participation in Mitzvah Day is required. If you do this, the rabbi will cancel your bar mitzvah. Your father is going to have a conniption fit," he charged, gripping Ben's wrist with his clammy hand.

"The rabbi can't 'cancel' my bar mitzvah. This sham of a ritual with its fabricated requirements has nothing to do with my becoming bar mitzvah." Now every nerve in his body seemed to scream out.

"I don't really get your fire, Ben, but you're my friend, and I'm begging you to just slow down. I do see how dangerous this is. They'll stop you with their esteemed board and the divine authority invested in their rabbi. Especially with this building dedication coming up, the ongoing fundraising, and the big to-do honoring all the major donors. I saw the hammer when I hadn't written my speech. I'm telling you they'll take you down."

Ben paused. His face grew hot, and his eyes narrowed at the words. He could imagine his father having a conniption. He remembered the Friday night at the rabbi's when he refused to attend the swim meet in the morning, and he was strengthened with the knowledge that with that single act he'd eluded a life-threatening tragedy. Rabbi Silverstein's words were distinct in his mind. He reasoned that if God's commandment to honor the Sabbath took precedence over the wishes of his own parents, it certainly took precedence over the wishes of this institution. A light smile spread across his face, and he had clarity. He put an arm around Howard's shoulders and said, "I couldn't ask for a better friend." He passed Howard the hollow roll of paper recording the notes from the meeting, and this time his friend took the baton.

Chapter Thirty-Four—Foraging

Siedlce, Poland

Chana crowbarred the door to get into the Prusses' dwelling place on the second floor of their two-story apartment house. She felt like a burglar and thought to herself that she well should. Here she was breaking and entering a dwelling with the intent of theft. Mama wouldn't approve, and she'd said as much, but that was when they thought the Prusses might return. Chana reasoned it was different now that they'd learned the Prusses had gone to America. Far across the ocean, and what was left was now abandoned.

She jumped with fright at the sight of sheets hung like ghosts over furniture in the sprawling drawing room. Teardrop crystals in the overhead chandeliers clinked together in the wind. She saw clearly that the laughter and footwork of dancers they'd heard aloft had come from this room in more gracious times. This had been the Prusses' residence until the night of the occupation when the cannonballs blew through the exterior brick, exploding and breaking down interior walls. They were surely traumatized. Her empty stomach growled loudly as she pulled back the brocade draperies from the large windows, letting in light, and looked into the wide and muddy street that was well-traveled by horse-drawn carriages. At one time this view of Siedlce had been glorious, extending to the fountains and concerts in Aleksandria Park.

She was ashamed to admit that from the dawn the Pruss family had fled, with whatever they could load on their hastily packed wagon, she'd wondered what they had left behind. What was forsaken in deference to the yearning for survival? That was six months ago, and just last week they'd heard the Prusses had settled in America. No one was coming back, she reassured herself. She moved across the plush tapestry rugs and pushed through stately french doors into the dining room where she faced the wind and the gaping black hole open to the forces of nature. The beams creaked. She wrapped her arms around her body, shivering, remembering the terrifying night of explosions. She'd thought the world had come to an end.

She clutched the crowbar in her left hand, a flour sack in her right, and explored the kitchen, seeking the pantry. There above the door she found another black gaping hole in the wall, wide open to the elements. But the storeroom door was stuck shut, expanded from moisture. She pulled with all her strength until suddenly the glass doorknob detached in her hand, and she flew across the kitchen, landing on her bottom on the floor in a most undignified way. She pushed her Russian peasant dress down from over her face, pulled herself up, and brushed herself off. For the past three weeks, meat was nowhere to be found, and the pantry was nearly bare. She was tired of being hungry, and this door would not be her undoing.

She retrieved the crowbar from where it had slid across the kitchen floor and hit the storeroom door in earnest until it split and sprang open, displaying a surplus of flour, sugar, salt, spices, oil, and racks of wine. The shelves on the opposite side held rows of canned peaches, pears, green beans, corn, carrots, pickles, sauerkraut, pickled beets, and bins of apples, potatoes, cabbage, and onions from the fall harvest. The pantry was as cold as a root cellar, due to the wintry outside air, keeping some of the fresh produce in a still usable state.

Chana was ecstatic. She *knew* a storehouse of provisions had been left behind. How much could one carry? It would take several trips to move the prized food supply. Mama would be amazed and relieved, she hoped. Lately, the only expression Chana saw on her mother's face was worry. When had a butcher's family ever been at risk of starving?

She loaded up the sack with flour, sugar, salt, spices, and oil and hauled the first load down to their pantry. She imagined waking up in the morning to the smell of freshly baked bread. Something else she couldn't stop thinking about was Mordechai Rosen. Which reminded her that she should search the upstairs apartment for dresses left behind by the four Pruss daughters. He was unlike any of the boys she had been around, not that she had been around many. He was intelligent and polite. He was more than polite, she corrected; he was thoughtful and kind. And she thought he was attractive, more attractive than she was. He certainly had nicer clothes.

Mama wasn't yet home from the Balabusta Homemakers Meeting at the synagogue. The women were meeting to pool resources to feed their families. She calculated she had time for one more haul of provisions before Mama returned home with the children. She couldn't wait to see Mama's face when she showed her the pantry full of produce and fine flour. With that thought, she raced up the back flight of stairs, carrying the empty flour sack and a wooden crate to bring down the fruits and vegetables. But before she headed to the kitchen, she couldn't resist a quick peek in the bureaus and tall mahogany armoire in the Pruss daughters' bedroom.

She had never seen so many dresses in one place—crinolines, ball gowns, Edwardian shirtwaists, long skirts in deep jewel tones—burgundy, purple, blue, and forest green—velvet, satin, and silk. She oohed and aahed at a stack of white, ivory, and pinstriped cotton blouses and held one up to her breast with a stand collar edged in lace, a ruffle with a lace-trimmed front yoke, and a row of tiny buttons at the front bib. She adored how the elongated cuffs below the bell sleeves were trimmed with ribbon and imagined herself in the crisp cream blouse and narrow purple velvet skirt. Promising herself she'd come back once she finished with the storeroom, she swiftly returned the garments to the armoire for safekeeping. Right now, she refocused. Transferring the produce and canned fruits and vegetables to their pantry was paramount.

Chana sat on the floor in the storeroom, her legs extended into the doorway, and loaded the firm apples, onions, cabbage, and potatoes into the flour sack. When it was full, she slid it outside the storeroom door and positioned the wooden crate on the floor in front of her. The wind howled, and the beams groaned and creaked. Mama would be incredulous when she saw the colorful jars of corn, carrots, tomatoes, and beets loaded into the crate. A sudden loud cracking startled Chana, and she looked up just in time to see the ceiling and doorframe collapsing on her. Huge four-foot chunks of plaster and the chandelier came crashing down on her at the same time the doorframe caved in, trapping her legs. She threw her arms over her head to protect herself from the sheets of stucco plaster that continued to rain down, but the agony in her legs was excruciating. A cloud of dust and debris enveloped her, and she choked and coughed while she wailed for help.

****

Mordechai Rosen stood in front of the two-story apartment house on Piekna Strasse, working up the nerve to rap upon the door of the home he'd visited just two nights ago. He'd tried to shift his thoughts, but they kept drifting back to her. She was beautiful, inside and out, sensitive and intelligent. She'd interpreted the words of his soul in a way even he couldn't articulate. His mind told him that he hardly knew her, but he felt like he'd known her for a lifetime. Pacing the street in front of the apartment house, he determined it was too soon to claim he needed to send another letter when he heard cries for help coming from the second floor. Was it his imagination? The wind? Wasn't it a woman's desperate scream?

Mordechai stood below the scorched holes from the cannonball shots, and the calls grew louder. It was a woman's urgent and hopeless shout.

He ran around to the back of the building, seeking a way in, but located only the doors to the ground-level apartments. Continuing around to the side, he found a black wrought-iron fire escape that led directly to the second story. He took the stairs of the emergency exit two at a time to the platform outside the escape door, busted the glass with his elbow, and reached in, closing his fingers around the knob to open the door. The desperate calls for help were close. His heart drummed against his ribs as he darted from room to room, calling, "Hello, hello? Where are you?"

"The kitchen—in the storeroom! Please help me. I'm trapped!"

Mordechai recognized Chana's pained and strained voice and stopped when he came face-to-face with a pile of wooden beams, plaster, and rubble. He looked up and realized that what he saw before him was the collapsed doorframe and ceiling. The screws in the saturated wooden beams had detached from the crumbling plaster and lay in a heap. At the bottom, beneath the debris, he saw a pair of small, black ankle-high button shoes sticking out.

"Chana!" Panic gripped his stomach muscles, and he wildly pulled chunks of plaster and wood off of her.

"It's me," she whispered faintly, with a sob caught in her throat.

"I'm going to get you out of there." He was sweating and removed his gray flannel overcoat, threw it aside, and tossed timber and plaster across the room until he'd removed the mountain of debris. He rushed to her.

"Chana! Are you okay?" Her eyes were closed, and blood seeped from a gash on her forehead.

She opened her eyes. "Mordechai?" she whispered. "My leg, I think it's broken. It hurts so much." She blinked back tears.

Thank God she was conscious and knew who he was. He took a handkerchief from his shirt pocket, wiped the blood from her face, and applied pressure to the cut across her forehead. A nasty bruise the size of a goose egg was forming. He was so close he could feel her breath. "Can you hold this?"

She lifted a dusty arm and pressed the handkerchief in place. She winced in pain and closed her eyes.

"Talk to me. Tell me what happened." Her stockings were torn, and her right leg was badly bruised and swelling.

"Mama will be angry that I came up here. I only pried open the storeroom door since we learned the Prusses have gone to America and the children are so hungry. There are wonderful foods and delicacies. See for yourself the jars of corn, carrots, green beans…" Her voice trailed off. "We must take them for the children." Chana held a jar of corn up to the sunlight filtering through the scorched hole in the wall.

"Your mama isn't a woman to get so angry." He took the golden corn from her and placed it in the wooden crate. "Though I know she'll be worried about you. Before anything else, we need to get *you* out of here." He forced his mouth into a smile. "Can you walk?" He slid his arm around her waist and lifted her to her feet.

She flinched and collapsed against him. "I don't think so," she said weakly, her arms encircling his neck.

"Let's take it slow." He inhaled deeply to steady himself and gently lowered her down. "Does it hurt when you're still?" His eyes met hers.

"Not as much." She closed her eyes and breathed, combing her fingers through her hair. "Does everyone call you Mordechai?"

"Pretty much, except my grandmother calls me Cai." Mordechai inspected the exposed ceiling rafters directly overhead and sized up the intact plaster across the kitchen and dining room. He feared the rest might collapse on them any moment. They needed to get out of there.

"I'd like to call you Mo. Do you mind?" she murmured, her head resting on his shoulder. It sounded like a soft moan the way she said it.

"We need to get you to a doctor." He was certain she didn't know what she was saying. The swelling and discoloration on Chana's forehead and shinbone were increasing before his eyes. Even her knee was swelling. The possibility that more of the ceiling would give way made him anxious to move her quickly.

"I should have known something wasn't right when the door was stuck so tight," Chana rambled.

In one swift movement, he lifted her into his arms and carried her out. She rested her head against his chest, and he was sure she could hear the pounding of his heart.

"Are you okay?" he asked as he carried her down the fire escape.

"Yah, I'm good." She closed her eyes. "Mo, I feel like I could fly." She fell unconscious, his arms tightly around her.

His eyes focused on her lips as she spoke, and he gazed at her and thought, *why do I need feet when I can fly?*

Chapter Thirty-Five—Inside Out

Loretto, Pennsylvania

Ira dribbled, spun, wrapped the ball behind his back with one arm, and released a behind-the-back shot, flicking it toward the hoop. The ball went straight in. He punched the air and then retrieved the ball. "It's up to you." He passed to Sam.

"Lucky shot, my friend, easy to execute and difficult to sink." Sam dribbled from center court and mimicked Ira's moves, making the exact same shot. He grinned. "My turn again." He dribbled all the way across the gym and sat cross-legged on the bench, aimed, and heaved. The ball sailed across the full court and banked off the backboard and into the basket without touching the rim.

"Nice one! It's a slop shot." Ira pointed out that Sam had not "called" the shot.

"Agreed. You just need to sink it from the bench. Any way in counts."

Ira took a seat and arranged himself cross-legged on the bench, feeling cut off from the strength of his lower body. The only power he could get was from his arms. Harder than it looked. He aimed and attempted to duplicate the shot, but the ball fell short of the rim and bounced out of bounds.

Ira didn't even mind that Sam was kicking his butt. He was having fun and grateful they could still meet up for sports since he'd been transferred to the camp.

"This one will get me to match—best two out of three." Sam retrieved the ball and dribbled confidently to the free-throw line.

"Really? Come on, no mercy!" Ira was incensed that Sam would go easy on him now.

"No worries." Amusement glinted in Sam's eyes as he lay down on the court, aimed, and prepared to shoot from his back. The ball arced and went straight in.

"Damn." Ira's face crinkled in despair. Sam was a real sleeper. He had mastered every shot. That on-the-floor shot was new to Ira, and he didn't expect a lucky break to carry him. He loved basketball and didn't approach it as a serious competitive sport. With a strong academic focus from the time he was young, he'd had no room for an earnest sports commitment that required thousands of hours of practice, coaching, camps, and after-school games. Basketball was one of the few things he did that he didn't feel he had to be the best, and he enjoyed that. Just having fun was freeing. He settled himself in a lying position at the free-throw line. A crowd of inmates gathered around, betting on whether Ira would make the shot. He laughed low in his throat at how little it took to entertain them or him.

He could normally swish a free throw, but he quickly realized that shooting from his back destroyed his rhythm—no dribble, no one-two step that was part of his fixed shooting form. This was worse than sitting. He felt like a fish flopping on the beach. The question suddenly came to him—one hand or two? Definitely two, and he focused on pushing the ball up and out through his fingers, reminding himself to finish with his index/middle finger pointing at the hoop. The basket was so far away.

The inmates whistled and cheered. Ira barely heard them. He visualized the ball sailing toward the basket, and then he released. Swish. He couldn't believe it. He jumped to his feet, on top of the world! Applause exploded in the gym while some inmates slumped, chopped the air, and pushed one another.

"Nice shot. Let's finish this another time." Sam slapped Ira on the back.

"Absolutely. It's getting a little wild in here." Ira was intent on making sure he wasn't part of any ruckus.

They settled at an empty table in the corner of the lounge.

"How's the camp?" Sam spoke with his head bowed, keeping his voice low.

"All right," Ira said, as a vein throbbed on his forehead. "Nicky's befriended me. Sent me all kinds of gifts from the commissary. Invited me to his banquet tonight. Said he would protect me and appointed me his concierge doctor."

"Be careful." Sam pressed his fingers to his forehead.

"I tried to refuse the gifts. Told him it wasn't necessary. He said he doesn't remain in debt." Ira felt a knot of nerves in the pit of his stomach.

"You can't refuse." Sam's eyes sank, and he sighed.

"Someone's trying to kill my wife." Ira felt as if drops of ice were running down his spine.

"What?" Sam's eyes flashed in shock.

"First there was the hit at my father's funeral. I told you about that—I seemed to be the target. Then a bomb was planted in Nanci's car, and she luckily escaped the explosion. Last week a snowplow tried to ram her into the rocks."

"Who exactly did you cross on the outside?" Sam narrowed his eyes as he searched Ira's face.

"I need to know if Nicky can protect her." He felt as if his heart had come into his throat.

****

The smell of summer sausage wafted down the hall, and Ira followed the scent. Three of the dorm rooms were set for tonight's mini banquet with long tables covered in white cotton tablecloths and platters of pasta with sausage, olives, anchovies, and marinara sauce. Ten chairs awaited around the dining table. An appetizer table was laid out with platters of crackers, cheese, pepperoni, anchovies, and olives; a drink bar sported cans of soda stacked in a pyramid and a punch bowl, and a buffet was set with foil pouches of fish—mackerel, salmon, tuna—mixed nuts, and pretzels.

The don poured red wine for all. Ira was incredulous to see that the rumors were true, and impressed with Nicky's ingenuity to find a way to live large on the inside. He immediately recognized Nicky's imposing boys, Angelo and Tony, his number one and two, who accompanied him on his shopping trips to the commissary.

"Hey, quiet down, everyone! Angelo, Tony, hold up on the serving. I want to introduce someone." Nicky motioned for Ira to come close and draped an arm around his shoulders. "I wantcha all to meet Doc. He saved my life, and he's a part of the family now. He's like a son to me." Nicky smiled broadly and clapped slowly, gesturing for the others to join the applause.

Cheers erupted from pockets of the room, and Matteo, accompanied by the boys with blue-black hair who delivered the gifts, came forward with extended hands and back-slapping. Ira noticed the quick exchange of glances between Angelo and Tony while they participated in punctuated hand-clapping, their black eyes boring through him. His eyes narrowed as he searched their formidable faces for a hint of hospitality but found none. His mouth compressed into a hard line, and he wanted to disappear. This was not a family he wanted to be a part of.

Nicky was ebullient, hooked his arm in Ira's, and led him around the room for introductions while chatting with him on the friendliest terms. "Doc, you may not have been here long enough to know that medical care in the FCI is notoriously second-rate. We seem to merit what is widely known as 'problem doctors.' I'm guessing the federal prison system isn't a physician's dream career path." Nicky chuckled. "I know I was a dead man the night they dragged you out of bed. But now that you're here, I no longer worry. You take care of me, and I'll take care of you." A glimmer of laughter came into his eyes.

Ira kept his mouth shut, and his mind whirled with questions, fears, and images he couldn't control. Now he wondered whether the don's life-threatening wound was really an accident. He had quickly ascended to a position in Nicky V's inner group. However, he didn't need to be a prophet to see that being the don's favorite and personal physician would quickly cause jealousy to swell among the family. He swiftly sensed that he was surrounded by few friends and many enemies. Outsiders were not typically welcomed into Nicky's inner circle. He'd been catapulted to the rank of Nicky's physician and was regarded with special favor. But to make matters worse, he was a Jew, and some family members didn't think he belonged. He now understood the arrangement. Here on the inside they would look after one another. But the bigger question was how far did the don's sphere of influence extend?

Chapter Thirty-Six—Vigilant

Southwood, Michigan

Nanci helped her mother-in-law, Anna, clear the table. Unexpectedly, a wave of profound sadness overwhelmed her as she stacked the dishes, thinking of the loved ones that were missing. No one sat in Pa's place at the head of the table or in Ira's place beside him. The despair and shock of losing Pa merged with the loss of Ira, making the grief unbearable. She knew it wasn't the same and reminded herself she was hormonal. *Ira will come back to me.*

Aliza loaded the dishwasher in the kitchen and yelled to Estie to get up and help. All the while Ben concentrated on solving the Rubik's Cube. Grandma Libby and Estie looked on. Steven glanced away from his newspaper to track Ben's progress. The bottom face of the puzzle was completely white. The top now displayed a yellow cross, but the squares along the top edges didn't match the side colors, which were uniform on the bottom two rows. Ben kept rotating clockwise and counter-clockwise, inevitably breaking the solved pieces while fixing new ones.

"How do you know what piece to move next?" his father asked.

"It's a pattern you repeat on all six sides. See, the center pieces always stay in the same position and determine the color of each face," Ben said.

Estie rolled her eyes and walked away, taking two empty platters into the kitchen to appease her mother. Anna sat across the table from Ben and watched him twist the moveable segments of the cube. Nanci appreciated how Anna made space and time for each of them, and she had an abundance of love for all. Despite the heartache of the last year, or maybe because of it, she was grateful for her mother-in-law. Anna was the glue that held the family together. Two years before she and Ira were engaged, her own mother had died of cancer, and Anna had become more mother than mother-in-law. During that sad first year, Anna checked on Nanci and did small acts of kindness. She picked up fun trendy gifts that Nanci adored, like strawberry lipstick, large hoop earrings, and ribbed sweaters. On desperate days, she delivered chewy chocolate chip cookies they ate with hot cups of tea. When Nanci rambled, she never interrupted. When she asked a question, she listened to the answer, not waiting for her turn to talk.

Anna was the one who hit Ira upside the head and told him to put a ring on Nanci's finger before she came to her senses. And he'd listened to her, proposing with an exquisite half-carat diamond engagement ring, part of a set Pa gifted to Ira that he'd received from his brother Julius as repayment of a personal loan. The stone looked bigger than it was due to its antique cut that brought out its fire. Nanci cherished the set and spun the ring on her finger.

As their lives became more intertwined, she'd grown closer to Anna in a way she never expected. While her friends and colleagues at the hospital complained about their in-laws, she was silent. Since she was a little girl, her mother always told her, *count your blessings, not your troubles.* Anna was a blessing, always an ally. The kids raced back to the table when she brought chocolate cake for dessert.

"Nanci, we can take you home whenever you're ready." Steven folded the newspaper and sipped black coffee.

"I think Rubie and I will stay on with Mom for a while," Nanci said. She served Rubie chocolate cake and avoided Steven's gaze. She didn't want him to see the fear in her eyes. They all knew what had happened on the way to Loretto.

"I rarely use the car, and there's no reason for anyone to be alone." Anna poured coffee.

"Ira's not the only one serving time," Steven murmured and nodded, signaling that this plan made sense to him. "When is the hearing at the state parole board for Ira's early release?"

"Sydney Blackwell is working on it—should be this month. Did you hear that Ira's on the kosher meal plan in Loretto now? The rabbi/chaplain arranged it. Seems the cuisine is better, not to mention Ira earns mitzvah points." Nanci winked. "Seriously, though, I've been thinking I would like to do the same here at home. Can you help, Mom?"

"Truth is, I'm a little rusty and could use a refresher myself. Rabbi Silverstein can help. I'll give him a call."

"That sounds interesting." Aliza handed Steven a slice of cake.

"Whoa, slow down." Steven held up his hand in protest. "Let's not go crazy."

"Estie, please start the bath for Rubie. Her Pooh Bear footie pajamas are on the bed in the guest room. She loves when you do bath time with her." Nanci was struck by how Aliza always found ways to make single parenting easier.

****

When the clock struck nine, Rubie was asleep, and Nanci and Anna sprawled on the sofa reading.

Nanci put down her book and broke the silence. "What if they come here looking for me?" The words half died in her throat, and a shiver of emotion ran through her body.

Anna went down the hall and returned carrying the Colt 1911 semiautomatic pistol she'd employed at Mo's funeral. Nanci felt the blood drain from her face.

"Of course, we have police protection, but just in case." Anna raised an eyebrow. "The Torah tells us that murder is the most serious crime one can commit, yet commands that if someone is coming to kill you, you should kill them first. We're not talking about a burglar trying to take your stuff. Someone is trying to kill you. Let me show you how to protect yourself and Rubie." Anna unloaded the weapon for demonstration.

Nanci trembled, and Anna stood beside her with one hand on her shoulder. Her touch had a calming effect. Anna looked directly into Nanci's eyes with a contagious strength. Nanci became still and focused. Her eyes were fixed upon Anna.

"Listen carefully to what I tell you now and don't get distracted thinking about what's happened or what might happen. Focus your mind." Anna instructed Nanci.

Nanci nodded, her hazel eyes unblinking. She was a quick study and in short order had mastered the grip, sight acquisition, trigger control, and safety protocols.

245

She had no uncertainty about when or if she should pull the trigger.

Anna reloaded the weapon and turned on the safety. "You have the mindset you will need if your life is in danger." A satisfied smile spread across her face.

Chapter Thirty-Seven—Fire

Southwood, Michigan

"Parsha for fifty—what is the meaning of the name of your Torah portion?" Rabbi Silverstein leaned back in his chair, folding his arms across his chest.

"Tzav and it means to command." Ben was amused playing parsha *Jeopardy*, and he desired more challenging questions. "Parsha for one hundred, please," he petitioned.

"What did God tell Moses to command Aaron and his sons?" A playful grin crossed the rabbi's face.

"To make sure the fire on the altar never goes out. Parsha for two hundred, please."

"What's the spiritual significance to the command that a fire must be constantly burning?"

"The altar is like our heart. We each have a private altar within. For the fire to be continual, it must be fed by a constant attachment to Torah and Mitzvot."

Rabbi Silverstein nodded approval, and Ben beamed. For two months they'd been learning together in Grandpa's study, and he had grown comfortable sitting with the rabbi in the leather barrel chairs at the beautiful mahogany table, poring over the books and interpreting the text. He had followed the plan they laid out and learned nearly a portion a week, except for the third portion, which was the longest and took two weeks.

D.G. Schulman

Ben practiced, and a stream of corrections flowed from Rabbi Silverstein, who focused intently on the pronunciation of every word. Ben made the necessary adjustments. He wasn't offended or discouraged as the number of mistakes were a fraction of what they had been at the start.

He was now able to chant aloud the entire parsha with the correct incantations.

"Your grandpa is basking in splendor with pride. This is the greatest gift you could give him." The rabbi rested a hand on his arm.

"I wish he was here." Hot tears welled into Ben's eyes.

"Oh, be certain, Ben. He's here, and he's *kvelling*."

"*Kvelling*?"

"Bursting with pride!" The rabbi closed the oversized leather-bound book. "You're nearly ready. Over the next two weeks, keep practicing, and we'll keep meeting to delve deeper into the questions you have. Anything else before we finish today?"

"Just one other thing…" Ben was aware his lips quivered as he tried to put his thoughts into a coherent sentence. "It doesn't look like it's going to work out for me to have my bar mitzvah at the temple after all."

"Oh, and why is that?"

"They have a rule that bar mitzvah boys need to be in the Bar Mitzvah Club, and the purpose of the club is to plan and participate in the Mitzvah Day project. And well…I quit."

"I see. Have you discussed this with your parents?"

"No, this just happened on Monday, and I'm sure the rabbi will be calling my father, if he hasn't already…" He broke off, and a frown spread over his

248

face.

"Ben, why did you quit?"

"Because Rabbi Greene refused to move Mitzvah Day from Saturday to some other day. They said it's okay to mow lawns because we're doing a good deed." Ben's voice shook with fury. "They laughed and told me sometimes it's a mitzvah *not* to do a mitzvah."

Ben didn't know if he should be telling Rabbi Silverstein all of this, but he didn't know anyone else who would understand.

"I see." Rabbi Silverstein's face grew dark and somber.

"So, I wondered if I could read from your Torah?" Ben knew this request was complicated. He was also certain that this was exactly Rabbi Silverstein's purpose, so he didn't wait for an answer. "There is something else on my mind. It's kind of personal."

"We have some time."

"I've been thinking about the advice you gave me when I had a problem with my friend."

"How did that turn out?"

"Good. You were right. A true friend is hard to find. Not to mention, it's harder to be a true friend than I thought."

"I'm glad to hear that." The rabbi paused and waited expectantly.

"So lately I've been thinking about my uncle, you know, the one in prison."

"Indeed, we actually met at your grandpa's funeral."

"Then you know all the trouble he's caused." Ben shook his head in disbelief. "I keep thinking the heartache and shame he heaped on my grandpa is what actually killed him," he clarified, his eyes glittering with anger.

"Ben, that statement has far-reaching implications. While I'm certain that the problems that befell your uncle caused your grandpa heartache, it's quite another thing to imply that your uncle is responsible for your grandpa's death."

"You don't know how it affected him. Rather than face the public humiliation, it was like he disappeared."

"Your grandpa didn't commit suicide—which is what some people do when they can't bear shame and humiliation. You're assuming that your grandpa blamed himself and judged himself so harshly that he couldn't find a way out. I don't think that's the case."

"What makes you say that?" Ben challenged.

"He learned Jewish mysticism, and those concepts were integrated into who he was. We had deep and heartfelt discussions every week. Your grandpa had complete trust in God. He knew God was running the world. He knew that God is stronger and smarter than everyone and that he can find solutions to problems that seem impossible."

"I hear what you're saying, but I still think all that pain made his heart weak and triggered the heart attack that took him from us."

"And now you want to heap that blame and shame on your uncle?" The rabbi's question hung in the air.

Ben's stomach twisted in knots. He had been so angry at his uncle, covering up his sadness, loss, and fear. He'd overwritten all the memories and good times with hostile emotions, disrespectful rants, and certainty that Ira deserved every bad thing that came to pass. As the negativity lifted, he remembered the day at Strawberry Island on Lake Erie when he was six. They were all on the sand bar, with Uncle Ira and Steven playing Frisbee. He had taken off his water wings during low tide when the sand bar was more like a vast wet beach. The tide came in fast, the armbands floated out of reach, and the cold lake water rushed in and swept him off his feet. He barely kept his head above water until the wind picked up and turned him over.

Ben was drowning in plain sight until Ira dove into the dark waves, swam underwater, and came up with him in tow, choking and gasping for air. The safety he'd felt in Ira's arms engulfed him, and the gratitude he experienced when he was rescued was eternal.

"No, I wouldn't want to do that to him. He's dealing with enough. Maybe together we can figure a way out of this mess."

****

Rabbi Silverstein was in the kitchen with his head in the oven. "If you don't have a self-cleaning oven, we can completely clean the oven and kosher it with a blow torch."

Anna looked at the antiquated control panel on the 1960s oven. "That sounds like a difficult and dangerous procedure. Maybe I should just buy a new oven?"

"Really, not a problem. We do it often. There are plenty of other things to spend money on."

"Well, at least I have a self-cleaning oven," Nanci interjected. "So, I just clean it and leave the racks in the oven while running the cycle?"

"Yes, with a self-cleaning model, koshering is fairly simple." He straightened up and scanned the kitchen. "The stainless-steel sink can also be koshered. However, sorry to say, the dishwasher will need to be replaced."

"Mine is loud and doesn't clean the dishes very well

anyhow." Nanci added a dishwasher to the list.

"I'll drop off instructions on going kosher in thirty days—no pressure, though. I suggest you start by getting used to buying only foods certified kosher by a reliable supervision agency. There'll be a list of symbols to look for on packages and canned goods. I'll have my wife, Miriam, call you about this. She's the expert on keeping a kosher kitchen."

"Can you just tell me why again?" Nanci didn't mean to be disrespectful. She was embarrassed to say she'd never learned anything about the kosher dietary laws, or pretty much any other Jewish laws, for that matter.

"The simple reason is we eat kosher because God commanded us to, and by fulfilling his divine will, we connect to him."

"Do we get points for that?" Nanci grinned.

"You definitely get mitzvah points." Rabbi Silverstein's eyes sparkled.

"Can I cash them in for something, like S&H green stamps?" Nanci laughed, but she had never been more serious. Like everyone else in the country, she had an S&H Green Stamp quick saver book in the kitchen drawer—fifty stamps on a page and twelve hundred to fill the book. She was saving nine and a half books to get a Timex men's electric watch for Ira, but now she thought they could use the new CorningWare menuette saucepan set with the spice o' life design for their new kosher kitchen. She really wondered if she could redeem mitzvah points for Ira's early release from prison.

****

When Ben got home from his class with the rabbi, his parents were in the living room. He was halfway up the staircase when they called to him.

"Son!"

A hand of fear clutched at his heart, and he froze. They knew. He was sure they knew. They only sat in the living room when the state of affairs was serious. He could hear it in his father's voice. He always called him "son" just before a stern conversation.

He moved slowly, considering his options, and saw none. His parents sat on the ivory sofa, crystal highballs in hand filled with the usual. His father drank whiskey watered down with soda water while his mother stirred a glass of mostly ginger ale with a splash of whiskey. His mother's face showed signs of exhaustion. Dad set his glass on the coffee table and traced the rim slowly with his finger, his face livid with anger. He pointed to the upholstered chair, directing Ben to sit.

"Rabbi Greene from the temple called tonight." His father's lips were tightly pursed.

Ben was deciding whether to fess up and tell them everything or exercise his right to remain silent. He chose to take the Fifth—certain that's what his father would have advised his client. He steeled himself for the onslaught.

"Is there anything you would like to tell us?"

Ben's mind was whirling. That question was a game-changer. This might be his only chance to explain. "Yeah." He sat up straighter. "Things weren't working out as I expected, and I had to quit the Bar Mitzvah Club and Mitzvah Day project on Monday." His mouth went dry.

"And why was that?"

"I don't belong there." It was the truth, and he couldn't think of anything else to say that would make

any more sense to his father.

"But you do belong there," his father roared. "Our family has belonged there for a dozen years, and I've paid the membership dues to prove it. You can't quit."

"If I'm becoming a man, as you've said, it would seem that it would be up to me to decide where I belong and where I don't belong." He intended to come off as more deferential, but he couldn't get the right mix of standing up for himself and being respectful. He should have planned this out better.

"I don't like your attitude." His father's face was blotched with redness from his anger.

"I'm sorry." Ben stopped talking. He needed to take the Fifth. The more he talked, the more he incriminated himself.

"I have a meeting with Rabbi Greene tomorrow. I'll fix this."

Mom hugged Ben and kissed his cheek, whispering, "It'll be better tomorrow."

His parents went up to bed and left Ben sitting alone in the living room. He wondered exactly what his father was going to fix.

Chapter Thirty-Eight—Symphony

Siedlce, Poland

News of the war was worse than ever. Chana was despondent about the never-ending stream of war reports from which there was no escape in her confined and immobilized state. Earlier in the month, all the men were up in arms about the German infantry occupying large forts around Przemysl after a Russian counterattack failed. And over the last weeks, everyone's hopes were dashed when Cousin Yosel reported that French and American allies repeatedly failed to break through the German line on the Western Front, suffering over one-hundred-thousand casualties.

Everyone in the house was a bundle of nerves, anticipating that any day Tatty would be required to report for a third draft. If not for Mo's daily visits, she'd have lost any glimmer of hope. His sparkling eyes, small thoughtful gifts, stories, and kind smile had the knack to overtake her thoughts and mind, making her forget all the other dismal events. Yesterday's visit had elevated her spirits beyond her wildest dreams when Mo brought the surprising announcement that the Warsaw Philharmonic Orchestra, forced from their bombed concert hall in Warsaw, was performing in Aleksandria Park today. And Mo would be escorting Chana to the Johann Strauss Gala Concert!

For months she imagined the day her bones would be mended, and she'd be able to go out again, capable of walking on her own, something she would never take for granted again. Refreshed from a bath at the women's wash house, she selected a crisp ivory blouse and a billowing crinoline purple skirt for the afternoon concert in the park. The narrow skirt would be more flattering, she assessed, given how thin she'd become, but it was impractical for sitting on the grass. She silently blessed the Pruss sisters for leaving behind such a beautiful outfit. Of course, pre-war amenities, like benched seating for the audience and abundant refreshments for sale, were unlikely. Still her heart was light. The sweet fragrance of blossoms was in the air, and despite the way the accident had left her, off-balance and with a stiff ankle, Chana felt on the verge of dancing. She adjusted her elongated cuffs, trimmed with darling ribbons below the bell sleeves, and checked her wristwatch, which Mo had given to her as a gift so she would know when to expect him. In fifteen minutes he would arrive to take her to the park. She loved that he was always right on time.

Mo took Chana's arm to keep her steady as they stepped over moss-covered rocks and passed through the dell on their way to the green. The trails through the forest were shorter than the long tree-lined, circuitous, and charming walkways leading to the bandstand. Chana was immersed in the smells of damp moss and sweet pine needles that covered the path. Time seemed to disappear. She breathed deeply, and an unexpected calm coursed through her.

How I missed the forest. This was the forest she and Sora played in during endless summers of outdoor festivals and concerts. Fallen tree trunks lay crisscrossed before them, and the forest called to her, reminding her this was a haven to rest. They sat on the trunks that beckoned like benches, facing one another at eye level because Mo's trunk was closer to the earth. Looking up into the trees, she basked in the light filtering through the leaves, its shadows, colors, and the sound of gurgling water in the distance.

Mo had sunk his hand into the soft scented earth and seized a sharp rock. With a strong grip, he carved into the trunk, first Chana's initials, then his own. Any question Chana had about his feelings for her, and hers for him, vanished. A dreamy smile was spreading over her face. He wore a flirtatious look and continued to carve a heart encircling their initials. Then he threw his head back in joyous laughter and clasped her hands in his.

"I didn't know I could feel this way," she said, a fluttery feeling in her stomach.

"Now that I've found you, I will never let you go." A whimsical smile twinkled in his eyes.

Her heart leaped with joy. "When I'm with you, the troubles of the world melt away."

He cupped her face in his hands, and his eyes held hers captive. "Without you, Chana, I'm missing part of my soul—the better part. I want to journey through life with you." His voice shook, revealing his emotion.

"I want to be there for you for the rest of my life," she said breathlessly. Hot emotion rushed through every fiber of her body.

The flutes and violins began warming up. Random scales, melodies, and assorted musical odds and ends drifted in the air. The summer breeze blew through the linden trees, and Chana closed her eyes, inhaling the fragrance of sweet, enchanting blossoms. Her pulse raced, and she felt safe and complete.

Mo kissed her hands and whispered, "I wanted to be patient and slowly show you my love, but this feeling consumes me. I can't hold back any longer. I'm deeply in love with you. I promise to protect you with all my strength."

Mo helped her up, she stood with her arms encircled around him longer than necessary, and he led her out of the dell to the lawn that stretched out before the modest bandstand overlooking the pond. It was picturesque with its backdrop of tall, wooded hills. He spread a blanket on the lawn, and they got comfortable on a soft bed of high uncut grass.

"You look wistful," Mo said as he delved into their picnic basket.

"It's just that all this reminds me of a time before the war. Mama loves music and always took us to the summer music festivals. One summer Tatty and Mama took us to the amphitheater in Lazienki Park in Warsaw for a Chopin concert. I'll never forget that large piano on the stage surrounded by the architecture of ancient Rome. Columns, arcades, and triangular tympana formed magical scenery. I can still feel the cool evening air brush across my face under a star-studded sky as I listened, enthralled, to a pianist playing for an audience of one thousand."

"You'll have to teach me more about music. My repertoire doesn't go far beyond Strauss' most famous works. 'The Blue Danube' and 'Voices of Spring Waltz' are my favorites."

"Oh, yes, mine too! If it weren't for my stiff ankle, I wouldn't be able to keep from dancing. My sister Sora and I made up stories to go with the music, running through the forest, jumping over fallen trees, chasing one another. We twirled in our best dresses, shaded by nature. Summertime open-air concerts and festivals were our happiest times. I was always dancing with Sora."

"You miss her."

"I do. Maybe if there are summertime open-air concerts in America and Sora goes, she'll think of me too." Chana's voice caught in her throat.

"Maybe one day we'll have a lovely evening of stunning music under the stars in America." Mo poured Chana a cold refreshing lemonade.

"What a dreamer you are, Mo."

The orchestra began to play, and the magical strings swept her away.

"I'm not dreaming, Chana." He sat up straighter, lifted his head, and gazed into her eyes. "I want you to come to America with me and be my wife. May I speak with your father?"

Shimmering violins and a horn spilled out the familiar waltz theme of "The Blue Danube," answered by staccato wind chords. Mo wrapped an arm around her waist, and Chana was swept away. She nodded, rested her head on his shoulder, and leaned against him.

****

In the kitchen, Mama rolled cabbage leaves filled with ground meat and rice and dropped them gently into a pot of bubbling tomato sauce on the stove. Chana sat on the sofa with her feet propped on a chair, and Mo paced the floor as he verbalized his thoughts for a letter to his uncle in America. She was still heady from their afternoon together. As much as she loved the concert, the walk to and from Aleksandria Park was a strenuous first outing, and she was tired. She held her notepad and pen, concentrating intently, and captured Mo's passion and dreams.

Dear Uncle Julius,

We have a vibrant Jewish life in Siedlce, and I wonder what it will be like in Detroit, Michigan. Our beit midrash was built about 1700, and there are many pious and scholarly Jews. It is a large square building with red brick and an iron gate. Over the years, additional rooms were added to the north and south, which house a yeshiva and a women's section. Since its establishment, they've followed Ashkenazic prayers, but in recent years our number of Hasidim has grown. It is hard for me to understand how it has transpired that the Hasidim, who pray using the Nusach Ari of Rabbi Yitzchak Luria, have now been relegated to the smaller shul upstairs and the Ashkenazic minyan will remain in the larger shul on the street level. It was never a problem for all of us to pray together as the differences were not disruptive. Sadly, the Ashkenazim are very particular about not mixing the two styles of worship, but it seems they did not expect that both the Torah reader, Rabbi Asher Meisel and his son, Aron Meisel, the cantor, would both align with the Hasidim and no longer pray in the large shul. So now, the large shul is quite empty, and the small shul upstairs is packed with our Hasidim, who are always in good humor and satisfied with their lot.

Do you have such folly in America? Our prayers are fervent, imbued with boundless faith and devotion at every service. On the Sabbath, the Ashkenazim below were worried the floor would collapse with our unrestrained joy and wild dancing to welcome the Sabbath Queen. We think perhaps now they would prefer to be in the shul upstairs. I have been upset by this division and fear that it will cause harm to us all.

Father expects to have our papers and passenger ship passage soon, and we are anxious to come to America to start our new life. We do not speak of it, but we are cognizant that any day men under the age of fifty-five may be prohibited from leaving Poland. At any moment a knock at the door could notify Father that he is required to report for the draft.

We hope you have reflected on our business proposition and are optimistic and predisposed to move forward. With God's blessing, I will arrive in America as a married man, with the most beautiful woman that God has created. I cannot wait for you to meet the love of my life. Please keep your eye out for a pleasant flat, furnished, with an abundance of natural light.

We will contact you once we arrive in New York. My bride-to-be has cousins in New York and a sister in Boston she wishes to visit before we leave the East and travel to Detroit.

Your beloved nephew,
Mordechai Rosen

****

The bed was large without Sora, and after four months Chana was still not used to sleeping alone. She tossed restlessly and for the first time thought that it would not be long before she would be a married woman sharing a bed with Mo. Excitement stirred in her, and a shiver ran through her body.

She had many questions and wished more than ever that Sora was there and they could talk all night about how things would be. She couldn't stop thinking about Mo, and her heart raced when she anticipated the upcoming marriage commitment ceremony, vort, Yiddish for "word." Tomorrow they would gather in shul, and both she and Mo would give their "word" and formally pledge to marry one another.

With Sora's vort so fresh, Chana vividly saw in her mind's eyes what it would look like. It was an engagement party. The community would be dressed in their Sabbath clothes and prepare something nice to say. They'd have a shot of the good schnapps or fine wine and raise their glasses to wish the couple "*L'chaim*" and "Mazal tov!" which were wishes for life and good luck. And the tables in the shul would be laid with platters of baked goods, smoked meats, and delicacies for the celebration.

Mo studied day and night, memorizing a Hasidic discourse for the occasion. He would take an oath that he would marry Chana, and she would take an oath that she would marry him. Up to now, Chana had never taken an oath, a serious testimony requiring witnesses and sworn declaration.

Chana blessed the Pruss sisters again, wherever they might be, as she reflected on the selection of dresses she had inherited from their abandoned wardrobes. She could choose a different dress for the vort and for each Sheva Bracha, seven days of blessings and celebration. She finally fell asleep and dreamed that she and Mo and the whole family, even Sora and Aaron, were at an open-air music festival in the park, dancing.

In the morning, the house was topsy-turvy. Chana waltzed with an imaginary partner from the living room through the dining room to the kitchen where Mama was bent over the oven removing two more apple cakes. Ingredients from the storeroom were put to good use.

Mama had been baking for a week, and poppy seed rolls, apricot rugelach, raisin nut babka, and mandel bread were at the ready on the dining table. The community had not forgotten the credit Tatty had extended or the brown paper parcels of meat he delivered or pushed upon those who could not afford them. From all corners of Siedlce, neighbors delivered precious ingredients they'd put aside—chocolate, sugar, nuts, and fruit—to commemorate the special celebration. Laundered, pressed clothing was draped over every chair. Tatty drank a tea, with a cube of sugar, at the table and sampled the baked goods. The aroma of festivity was in the air.

"Tatty, Good morning! It feels like a holiday to see you home." Chana kissed her father on the cheek. She didn't remember a weekday morning that he wasn't at the meat market. "You will always be my pillar of strength and my fountain of wisdom." She snuggled beside him.

"My dear Chana, I am a truly rich man." He stood and hugged her, kissing the top of her head, and he lifted her off her feet and swung her in a strong bear hug. When he set her down, the world was spinning.

She slowly recovered, her stomach churning, and her tatty patted the chair next to him, inviting her to sit, and he held her hand.

"Tatty, you hold my hand for only a short time, but you'll hold my heart forever. What have you held back? Tell me before I marry and go to America."

"I cherish you. I'm with you now and forever. Make me proud and raise your children to be menschen. Give them a life based on the foundations of Torah."

"I promise."

He pressed an envelope into her hand, and she read

the printed stationery—*Nederlandsch-Amerikaansche Stoomvaart Maatschappij*. Wide-eyed, she clutched the Holland-America Line steamship tickets to her breast. She jumped to her feet, clapping her hands.

"Can it be true? We're going to America?" Chana clapped and jumped in place.

"You will go to America with Mordechai."

"But what about you and Mama and the children?" Chana stiffened and wrapped her arms around herself, suddenly overtaken with nausea.

"We'll come later." Tatty smiled, but his eyes were moist and sad.

For years she'd dreamed of nothing other than emigrating to the United States, and now she feared she'd made herself sick with nervous anxiety. She suppressed the urge to vomit, and her eyes watered. She knew the ticket she held in her hand represented nearly everything they had. She couldn't imagine leaving without her beloved family.

"Don't worry," Tatty reassured. "God has provided. The Siedlce Fellowship Foundation came through with funds to remunerate for our losses from the continued pilfering. I used some of the money to buy your steamship passage. The week after the Sheva Brachot, we'll leave for Warsaw, and from there we'll go to Rotterdam in Holland. You'll board the ship *Noordham* to the United States with Mordechai as husband and wife."

Chana's stomach reeled, and she couldn't suppress the spasms. She ran to the backyard as she began to retch.

****

Chana rested on the sofa and thought she would die. She had never felt so terrible for so long.

"The doctor will not come." Tatty had been gone for hours, and he looked exhausted.

Mama implored, "Why? Why won't he come?"

"He doesn't treat Jews." Tatty removed his hat and wiped the sweat and dust from his face and beard. Rather than celebrate at the vort, he'd spent the night seeking out doctors. Overnight, his dark hair had gone white. "Besides, he says, if it's cholera, she'll be gone before he can get here."

"It's the women's public wash house," Mama asserted, wringing her hands in distress as she collapsed in a chair at the table. "I've told the girls not to use the public wash house."

"We'll find a doctor," Tatty reassured Mama. "We have to give her fluids. The neighbors brought licorice root." Tatty wiped the sweat from his neck and put the samovar up for tea.

"It won't help," Mama persisted. "She's delirious. Nothing stays down. It's not just the vomiting—the diarrhea is worse. They say that this anti-Semitic doctor has medicine that can save her. Tell him she's a girl of fifteen." She wrung a cloth in cold water and wiped Chana's hot face.

"He claims there's no cure." Tatty shuddered.

"Perhaps no cure, but there's a remedy. You must go back!" Mama grasped her husband's strong forearm. "And there is certainly something he must want."

Despite the disorienting fever, Chana felt her parents were right. In hours her entire family could be infected. She had seen how quickly one moved from symptoms to death. She blinked away the salty tears, reached into her pocket, and withdrew her steamship passage to freedom, education, and hope.

"Give him this." She handed over the precious envelope and retched into the wooden pail.

****

The butler had retired for the night, and the doctor answered the door wearing his silk and velvet smoking jacket. Dovid forced entry into the elegant foyer.

"You again!" spat the doctor acridly. "How dare you trespass on my property."

He charged him like a bull and pinned the doctor against the bookshelf. Chopin's melodious "Nocturne in C-sharp minor" wafted from the phonograph in the sitting room. "I know you don't treat Jews, so I'll make this a very simple choice." He pressed his forearm into the doctor's throat. "I'll kill you now, and you'll never have to treat another Jew, or you give me the remedy for my daughter, and you'll live to see another day."

The doctor fought for his breath, choking, and his eyes bulged. His face registered understanding, and he nodded agreement. The remedy he provided was a simple solution—just a liter of water, six teaspoons of sugar, and half a teaspoon of salt.

Chapter Thirty-Nine—Reckoning

Loretto, Pennsylvania

Ira dressed in his familiar weekend wardrobe from life on the outside—a pair of brown corduroy, wide-leg slacks and matching knit mock turtleneck. The accommodations in the camp were tolerable. He had yet to see a rat in the showers, and the absence of barbed wire fences, locked doors, and stand-up middle-of-the-night counts created a sense of normalcy. At times, he would have felt safer with a higher staff-inmate ratio, but the screened selection of nonviolent inmates close to release allowed for the relaxed camp policies. Greater access to the library and sports facilities like the track, basketball court, gym, and cafeteria gave Ira a taste of freedom. It was like night and day compared to the restricted movement of the higher security facilities, and he had been relieved from his laundry responsibilities. His new role as primary physician for Nicky permitted him further access to the infirmary and all medical resources. He had yet to meet Dr. Williams, the part-time on-staff physician.

Ira rested on the edge of his cot, feeling tired despite an uninterrupted night's sleep, and rubbed his temples to alleviate a headache. He poured himself a drink from the pitcher of water he kept on the nightstand. Today he vowed to go to the library and act on Nanci's suggestion that he look into what he could do on the outside if his medical license was never reinstated. He chuckled at the irony that as long as he was in the camp at Loretto, he had a job as a doctor.

"Take a deep breath." Ira pressed the stethoscope against Nicky's back and listened for signs of fluid in the two lower lobes of his lungs. Then he wrapped a cuff around Nicky's arm, checked his blood pressure, and put two fingers on his wrist, checking his pulse. "How are you feeling?"

"I've got a headache, and I keep getting nosebleeds." Nicky spoke in a raspy, weary voice.

"Have you noticed any blood in your urine? Any difficulty breathing or chest pain?"

"Eh, a little from time to time. Did I mention leg cramps? And my hair, look at this." He combed his fingers through his jet-black hair and extended a hand, cupping clumps of hair. "Why am I suddenly losing my hair? This can't be normal. No one in my family is *bald*!" He spat out the word like it was a curse.

"I need a complete list of your medications. Your blood pressure is elevated. Are you taking medication for high blood pressure?"

"Nah, I've declined the prescription from the dispensary. It don't bother me, Doc." Nicky's caterpillar eyebrows knitted together.

"How about I make the medical decisions? We need to get you back on your blood pressure meds right away." Ira prodded Nicky's neck, feeling for swollen glands. He cupped his chin in both hands and checked the glands in front of and behind the ears. "Open your mouth and say ahh." Ira found no sign of redness or swelling. He shined a light into Nicky's eyes and held up his index finger. "Follow my finger with just your eyes." Ira watched Nicky's tracking, which was a bit delayed. His health had deteriorated in the last three weeks. Something beyond high blood pressure presented, but he couldn't yet say what. "I'll need a urine sample. Pee into this container for me."

Nicky placed the half-filled container on the top shelf of the rolling medical cart and sat in the metal chair beside the examination table, looking exhausted.

"Have you altered your diet or made any other recent changes?"

He shook his head. "None I can think of."

"Okay, I'll send this urine sample to the lab for analysis and have the dispensary resume your script." The words hit him like a ton of bricks. He shouldn't be ordering scripts. He *couldn't* be ordering scripts. The regret and shame came rushing over him like a wave, sounds and images of that last day at the pain clinic when the receptionist buzzed open the door and a swarm of FBI and DEA agents bypassed security guards and infiltrated the clinic, wielding guns and shouting.

The patients scattered, stampeding over one another, and escaped through any exit. The agents rounded up the medical team, read them their rights, and pushed them into black vans. They put him in handcuffs. At the police station they offered him a cigarette and a cup of coffee in the interrogation room at the beginning of a long night of questioning. He didn't feel like a physician. He felt like a fraud and a drug trafficker and took a plea bargain where he explained the details of how he recruited doctors, who were paid based on the number of patients they saw and agreed from the initial interview to prescribe a "cocktail" of controlled substances with only a cursory physical exam. Without a treatment plan in place, the prescription was not based on medical need.

The model was duplicated in six clinics across the state, each one allegedly examining close to five hundred patients a day. His testimony in court enabled the shutdown of the entire operation, including a wide network of pharmaceutical wholesalers who were required to report to the DEA suspicious orders of unusual size and frequency. The clinics prescribed more than thirteen million doses of opioids to addicts and traffickers and generated more than five hundred million dollars. While he knew how it operated, he never knew who was at the top. He'd made sure his hands were clean and distanced himself from actually writing prescriptions.

"What was I thinking?" He shook his head in disbelief as the picture clarified in his mind. *I thought the more money I had, the better life would be. I just didn't want to get caught.*

The FBI and DEA identified him as the ringleader recruiting a steady supply of young doctors drowning in medical school debt, often in excess of two hundred thousand dollars. It wasn't hard to find colleagues anxious to moonlight and alleviate the financial pressure. His assertions of impunity fell on deaf ears, and he quickly became one of the most culpable medical professionals contributing to opioid overdose, deaths, and addiction by converting doctors to drug dealers in exchange for cash. He broke into a cold sweat, trembling uncontrollably. The weight of what he had done and what he had become was more than he could bear.

"Doc, maybe you should sit down."

"Yeah." Ira spun around the metal chair at the desk

and sat across from Nicky, steadying his elbows on his knees. "You see, I've got a problem." He breathed the words. "On the outside, I've got a wife and a daughter, and someone is trying to kill them."

"I'm sorry about that." Nicky looked him straight in the eyes. "It was not personal."

"It is very personal." Ira gripped Nicky's brawny wrist.

"But that's all behind us." Nicky waved his free hand as though shooing away a mosquito.

"Behind us?" Ira's eyebrow shot up.

"I told you you're my family now. We take care of each other."

"Since when?"

"Since Feb 25th, the day you saved my life."

"Well, someone didn't get the memo." His heart beat fast with apprehension.

Nicky's eyes narrowed, and his face grew dark. "Angelo, Tony!" the don yelled to his boys standing outside the infirmary door.

"Yes, Don Vece." They stepped inside, their bodies tight like springs. Their loyalty to Nicky ran deep like the blood in their veins.

"You talked with Enzo. You told him to call off his dogs on the doctor's case?"

"Yes, Boss, but Fabio says Enzo has changed tack. He's turned, stopped following orders, working for himself. Fabio says Enzo has a drive-by planned and something else big that he can't figure out."

"Give Fabio backup, an army. Tell him to hold the turf, provide protection, and send the message Enzo is out. Fabio will rule the street, and Enzo will not go home tonight." Irritation and impatience shone in Nicky's eyes. As he left the infirmary, his face wore a sudden formidable look that Ira had not seen before.

****

Ira was alone in the library, immersed in thoughts of Nanci. She was his first love, his only love, that was until Rubie. Now his heart was truly ransomed. He did the assignment she asked of him while he prayed in the corner of his mind that she was protected. Three sheets of paper were arranged in a pyramid on the table in front of him. The top page was titled *Insurance Consultant*. The one on the bottom left said *Practice in Another Country* and the one on the bottom right was titled *Limited License*. He filled in the details for each, scanned the bullet points, and shuffled their positions like a magician with cups upside down on the table where only one included the red ball. For the first time, he asked himself which of the three unhappy choices he could live with.

He couldn't shake Nicky's words. *It was not personal.* The words caused his temper to flare, and he wanted to punch something. He pounded his fists on his head. It was what he told himself when he recruited physicians and explained their role to prescribe Schedule II narcotics with only a cursory medical exam, no treatment plan or medical need, without regard for addiction, overdose, or possible death. Each and every patient was a potential victim. He looked down on the ruined lives, broken marriages, teenage pregnancies, and lost hopes that came from the bad choices of others, but he was responsible.

He thought he was better, privileged, in a different class, but he was a ringleader of drug traffickers just like Nicky. They were more alike than they were different. It hadn't been hard to convince himself that he was acting responsibly to moonlight and pay off student debt, buy a bigger home for his family, and make it possible for Nanci to be a stay-at-home mom with a growing family. His greed masked itself in righteousness. He was in perpetual pursuit of the next thing to fill him up, and fulfillment was elusive. An inner battle raged within him, like two kings fighting for control of one country, one evil, greedy, and without a soul, and one good, loving, and grasping a rope to heaven. He could choose.

****

"Of course, you and Rubie will stay here." Anna buttered Rubie's toast and cut off the crust.

"We don't have to decide now. I haven't told Ira yet that we need to sell the house. The mortgage payments are too high, and without him, well…it's just a house. I don't know how long I'll be able to work. He's not going to like it, but we have to make changes."

"I'd just be rattling around in this house by myself. And I wouldn't have the joy of being with the two of you every day." Anna squeezed Nanci's hand. "Not to mention, you'll need help when the baby comes." A bittersweet smile turned the corners of her mouth.

"Can Rubie stay with you while I meet the realtor?" Nanci finished her coffee.

"I've nowhere to go today. I thought we'd bake chocolate chip cookies."

"Perfect!" Nanci dropped a kiss on Anna's cheek, and Rubie climbed onto her lap. "I won't be gone long."

It's just a house Nanci repeated to herself as she started Anna's Oldsmobile Cutlass, which was pretty much the same as the luxury coupe she'd driven to Loretto, except the rear end had not been rammed by a snowplow. Despite the trauma of that day, she felt tough when she relived the scene in her mind again and again. Something bigger and braver than she knew had taken over, and against all odds she'd delivered herself from danger. A smile was spreading over her face as she backed down the driveway.

When she pulled into the street where they lived, something felt amiss. Vehicles parked at odd angles formed a barrier in front of the house. She inched closer, not driving more than five miles per hour, assessing the scene, then stopped kitty-corner across the street and observed figures running across the lawn and sprawled below bushes. The realtor would breeze in for their appointment any moment, and the house was not ready to show, but she hesitated to move. A cold shiver ran down her spine. She checked the time. The realtor was late.

Suddenly, a motorcade of three black town cars squealed around the corner and sped down the block. They slowed as they approached the house. Bodies holding guns hung out the car windows, shooting automatic weapons, and immediately, a protective return fire showered from the lawn and perimeter of the house, flattening tires and piercing holes in metal. The town cars' side windows shattered, and two lithe young bodies hanging out the windows fell onto the street.

Figures from the lawn ran toward the motorcade, took cover behind the engines of the parked cars, and continued firing at closer proximity. When the gunfire from the convoy subsided, four men emerged from behind the parked cars, ran toward the motorcade, and fired point-blank directly into the driver and passenger seats. One of the town cars peeled out, and two remained crippled, inoperable, and driverless, splattered with the blood and flesh of its passengers. Like an army of ants, the men from the watchful perimeter loaded into the parked vehicles and made a swift getaway.

Nanci sprawled across the front seat, her arms still over her head, peering out the window. The ambush lasted not more than two minutes. A tremor shook her body. *Was I the intended target?* It was like a war had erupted on her lawn. Police would report at least one hundred fifty rounds fired into the craftsman-style home. Anyone inside would have likely been killed. The immobilized blood-splattered town cars remained at the scene, and Nanci heard sirens approaching. She took in the gruesome scene of the crippled, bloodied vehicles and limp mangled bodies and suddenly understood that her unknown protectors had defeated the enemy, given them the message to stay off their turf and not to come back. By the grace of God, she was a witness—she was alive. Her throat tightened. "We will make it." Her voice throbbed. She wiped the tears from her cheeks with the back of her hand.

A horn blasted and made her jump. The realtor banged on the driver's window, and Nanci rolled it down.

"Oh my God! Oh my God!" she shouted over the sound of the sirens as police cars and ambulances sped by. "We were supposed to be in there."

Chapter Forty—Meet

Southwood, Michigan

Ben was ecstatic to be back in the water with his original medley relay team reunited. The alternates filling in for Andy and Chris were just as happy to get back to diving. In black silicone swim caps and goggles, the relay team's heads bobbed above the water in a circle, their arms stretched around one another's broad swimmers' shoulders.

Andy, who swam the backstroke in the first leg of the relay, had been slowest to recover from his blow to the head, causing mild traumatic brain injury, that occurred in the bus accident. For the last six weeks, Ben had visited Andy every day and walked his dog, Luna, all the while uncertain Andy would ever swim again. Chris had bounced back quicker, gaining strength and endurance after suffering broken ribs, internal bleeding, pain, and chills when he was slammed against the dashboard of the bus, and Tom Peters had managed to escape the accident uninjured. Of course, Ben hadn't even been on the bus.

Tom swam breaststroke in the second leg, and Chris swam butterfly in the third leg. While Ben could swim any stroke, he liked swimming freestyle anchor best. When the team finally made a state qualifying time, they were euphoric. He admitted he'd had moments of serious doubt throughout the season, but against all odds, their hard work and determination had paid off. They were state bound.

Coach Walker's shrill whistle pierced the natatorium. "Everyone on deck!" he announced through the bullhorn. "Dry off and take a seat."

Ben tied a towel around his narrow waist over the wet black nylon suit and pulled on a sweatshirt before he hopped onto the bleachers in front of Coach Walker, joining the other nineteen swimmers wrapped in towels and sweatshirts.

"Pay attention! Swimmers with qualifying times will compete in the state meet. The bus leaves tomorrow, Friday morning at seven a.m. sharp. If you are late, we will leave without you. The swimming prelims begin at noon, and the diving prelims begin at two thirty. The fastest sixteen swimmers and two alternates will be determined and will return Saturday to swim in the finals. The schedules are on the bulletin board. Any questions?"

"Is the heat sheet available?" Tom Peters shouted out.

"Swimmers are pre-seeded for Friday's prelims based on your state qualifying time—you can check the heat sheet for your lane and heat assignments. Those qualifying to compete on Saturday, check the bulletin board in the ready room at the Oakland University Natatorium."

"Are dorm rooms assigned?" Ben asked, wondering how all this was going to work out.

"Dorm assignments will be handed out before you get off the bus tomorrow. Friedman, I want to see you before you leave." Walker scanned the group for any remaining questions. "Remember to drink to prevent dehydration—you won't know it, but you will be losing fluid, and it will cause swimmers' cramps and sick feelings." Coach looked into the eyes of each swimmer lined up on the bleachers, and the silence in the room echoed off the walls. "You have overcome a lot of setbacks this season, and you have come out of it stronger. Each one of you made every practice count. You moved through the pain and the disappointments. I know you will give this meet your all. I have never been prouder of this team."

The room exploded in cheers, howls, whistles, and foot stomping on the bleachers.

In his street clothes, Ben knocked on the glass window of the coach's office door, and Coach Walker motioned for him to enter.

"Ben, have a seat." Walker closed a file folder spread in front of him and focused on Ben. "I usually say opportunity never knocks twice at any man's door, but you've proven me wrong."

"Sir?" He could feel Coach's eyes boring through him.

"The point is, seize the opportunity when it comes. It rarely comes again." Ryan Walker leaned across his desk. "I assume we don't have to have this conversation again."

"I'm not sure what you mean, sir." Ben's mouth suddenly went dry. He couldn't tell if this was an ultimatum.

"You'll be on the bus at seven a.m.?" The coach's eyes narrowed.

"Yes, sir, I'll be there for the prelims." He did not think he needed to remind Coach Walker that he would not swim on Saturday. He felt confident that they had come to an arrangement back in January.

Coach Walker nodded, dismissing Ben.

****

"Who knew there was a kosher pizzeria less than a mile away?" Dad distributed a tower of pizza boxes, stamped with the words *Rami's Pizza,* across the length of the dining table. Grandma Libby, who accompanied him on the pickup, placed a stack of paper plates and napkins between the boxes.

"Smells fantastic." Ben opened the boxes to inspect the variety. "What's this one with spinach and feta cheese?" This was the closest to a restaurant experience he'd had since Alan's bar mitzvah.

"Must be the Greek." Aunt Nanci peered into the box, slid a slice onto her paper plate, and took a bite. "Yumm..."

"So there's no pepperoni?" Estie flipped open all the boxes. It was more of a complaint than a question, so no one bothered to answer.

"Will Ira be home for the bar mitzvah?" Grandma Ann helped herself to a slice of pizza.

"Sydney Blackwell thinks not and says it would take a miracle. Seems Ira still has too much time remaining to be considered for early release. Unlike funerals and medical issues, neither bar mitzvahs nor new babies are on the list of eligible reasons for furlough." Aunt Nanci cut up a slice of cheese pizza for Rubie.

"Son, what time do the prelims start tomorrow?" Dad passed around cans of cola, good-humoredly.

"Noon," Ben mumbled with a mouthful. "At Oakland University, Athletics Center." Ben instinctively got nervous when his father called him "son."

"And finals?" Dad grabbed a soda.

"I don't know—I may not even make the championship finals." Ben swallowed. "We'll leave tomorrow after the prelims around five p.m." He wondered exactly how much his father understood about the prelims, the qualifying process for the state finals, and the schedule this year. He wasn't sure his father knew that the state finals were *this* Saturday, but he figured it was just a matter of time before he found out.

Dad popped open a can, and the carbonated soda exploded. "Holy cow!" He grabbed a stack of napkins and mopped up the bubbles.

Amidst the chaos, Grandma tossed Dad a roll of paper towels. Ben had a flashback of the Friday night in January when Coach and Dad joined the Shabbat dinner at the rabbi's, uninvited. He expected his father to explode from excessive buildup of pressure, but the moment passed, and Aunt Nanci filled the airtime with her own pressing issues, for which he was grateful.

"So instead of having the realtor work up a CMA, comparative market analysis, on the house, which is now pummeled with gunshots, I'm working with the insurance company to see whether they will cover the damage. The homeowners' policy doesn't specifically exclude drive-by shootings." Aunt Nanci's face crinkled with concern. "I need to call Loretto and make certain that Ira got the message that we're staying with Mom."

"Kids, you can eat your pizza in front of the TV." Mom handed Joel a plate of pizza and directed him to the den. Rubie and Estie followed, but Ben remained in his seat at the table and tried to make himself small.

"What in the world happened over there?" Mom leaned in and lowered her voice.

"It was like a scene from an old gangster movie. This motorcade of black town cars came squealing around the corner. They slowed in front of the house with bodies hanging out the windows firing automatic weapons, an honest-to-goodness drive-by shooting. Then all this return fire flashed from figures on the lawn, like a sporadic fireworks display with each explosion equally loud. It looked like a war zone."

"Oh my God, Nanci, if you had arrived just a few minutes earlier, you could have been killed!" Mom broke into tears and buried her face in her hands.

"I got the feeling that was the idea, but this counteroffensive was in position, expecting the assault on the house and prepared to retaliate with a strike that would not just do away with the assailants, but send a message to all that they should never return. The town cars were targeted at point-blank range and left shot full of holes with flat tires and the blood of its passengers splattered on the broken windows, flowing into the street like a river. There were no survivors."

"Holy moly, and you watched this unfold?" Mom murmured, wiping the tears from her face.

"It happened so fast—in no more than two or three minutes, it was over, and the counteroffensive just vanished. I had this sense of *victory*. I can't explain it, but I felt like we had won."

"Does Ira know what's happened?"

"I don't know. I only told Sydney Blackwell this morning." She hugged herself.

Chapter Forty-One—Prelims

Rochester, Michigan

The Athletics Center doors opened to officials, competitors, and coaches at nine thirty a.m. Ben's heart gave a nervous jolt when he saw his father was the first into the spectator area on the third floor. The team gathered in the ready room adjacent to the natatorium and huddled around the bulletin board, reviewing the schedule. The warm-up period for swimmers and divers ran from ten a.m. to eleven forty-five—ending fifteen minutes before the start of the prelims.

"Titans, gather 'round!" Coach Walker trumpeted. "First rule is to stay well hydrated." He handed out bottles of orange, blue, and purple electrolyte-loaded sports beverages. "Take your time and warm up properly. Don't forget to eat small snacks to replenish your energy. You can step outside to get fresh air if you need a break. Prelims start at noon. Be happy, have fun, and stay positive!"

Ben's heartbeat quickened as he entered the massive and loud natatorium. The height of the ceiling and the size of the pool stunned him. Their blue-and-white titan banner was displayed on the wall. He suddenly felt small, humbled in the aquatic center that was the epicenter of state championships. Dozens of other team banners were also displayed, sporting their team logos and sponsors. Colossal and colorful flags, suspended high over the width of each end of the pool, extended about fifteen feet from the wall. His skin prickled with sparks of electricity. The energy of past events permeated the air, and the excitement was palpable. While swimmers of various levels and ages swam in "The Nat," it was dedicated to the best of the best. The wall behind the diving boards displayed the names of athletes and champions who had competed and set records there over the years. It was the most beautiful aquatic center he had ever seen.

Ben stretched and loosened his major muscle groups before jumping in the water to begin his pre-race warm-up. He stood behind the block of the lane he would swim in later and visualized the dive, the feel of the water, the kick tempo, and then his body slicing through the water. He entered the pool. It was crowded, and he tried to fit in between swimmers and avoid getting kicked. Arms, ankles, and capped heads bobbed in the water. Bodies were everywhere.

Coach had drilled into him how critical warming up was, and he refused to retreat. At first, he could barely hold his breath long enough to do more than a few dolphin kicks. He needed to wake up his body, fire up his nervous system, and warm up his lungs. He cranked out a general warm-up of 400 meters and a few twenty-five-meter sprints. He'd start a second warm-up about twenty minutes before his event since it would have been a while. He rotated through the strokes—butterfly, backstroke, breaststroke, and freestyle. The endorphins kicked in, and he felt satisfied and invincible.

The men's 200 medley relay was the last event of the preliminaries and absolutely the most critical relay.

Eight heats took their places. The Titans huddled in heat six at the edge of the pool, arms around one another's shoulders.

"Let's do this," Ben said. His heart pounded in his chest.

Andy jumped in the pool and hung backward on the edge in position for the first leg backstroke. The natatorium was dead silent. "Take your mark," a monotone voice announced. "Here we go." *Beep*.

The swimmers exploded backward. Shouting shattered the silence and echoed off the walls. Chris, Tom, and Ben fixed their gazes on Andy. They pumped their fists and yelled, "*Go, go, go.*" Andy stayed mostly underwater and led the heats with the fastest backstroke on the first half but fell way behind on the second. Poised for the second leg, Tom dove over Andy and glided underwater in a fabulous breaststroke.

"What a great turn by heat four!" the announcer said. "Heat six has time to make up. Can they do it?"

Ben's entire body was vibrating to the thump of his heart. He glanced from Tom to the clock and saw he was making up time, probably coming in at twenty flat. Chris was taut in position and sprang over Tom, cutting the water with a powerful butterfly stroke.

"Heat four has had the most amazing first two legs, but they are now behind at the second half of the third leg. It looks like heat three is pulling ahead," the announcer said.

Ben saw he was going to have a lot of room to make up. He put his goggles in place, stepped up on the block, crouched forward with his fingertips at the edge of the block, and dove as Chris touched the wall. He sliced the water and was half the length of the pool before he came up for air. *Pull. Pull. Pull.* He gave it everything he had, kicked off the wall, and surged underwater.

"Ben Friedman in lane six is the dark horse in this race. Friedman's record-setting freestyle earned a top spot in the individual 200 meter medley earlier today with a record time of 1:38.71. The two teams battling for this race are the Titans and the Cardinals. Oh my God, he's coming home in less than nineteen. Kiss nineteen good-bye, he's come home in eighteen six. The Titans have won the 200 meter relay! What a moment for the Titans!"

The quartet shouted, hugged, and threw their goggles into the air. The team's time of 1:22.11 was a pool record. Coach Walker walked into the pool in his clothes, doing a victory dance. Their medley relay time had earned them the number-one seed in the finals. And they had set a new state record, smashing the record that had been held for over ten years. Their time solidly placed them in the running for a state championship title, something Ben's school had never taken home before.

A sports reporter with a microphone corralled the team. "Congratulations, Titans. The story of today *is* the Titans. What did you say to one another before the race?" The reporter thrust the microphone in front of Ben.

"Let's do this." Ben thrust the trophy in the air.

"How did you pull off a personal best?"

"It's something we've been working for all year." Ben caught the eye of Andy, Tom, and Chris. "Working together, we got it done."

"What a great record-setting freestyle leg. Everybody wishes their Dad could be here to watch him. But yours actually is. Ben, what do you want to say to your father?"

285

"Just that I'm glad he's here." He broke off and searched for his father in the crowd. A wave of spectators moved toward him, and his arm shot up instinctively when he caught his father's gaze.

"Son, you've got what we call grit. The way you gave it your all was spectacular!" His father embraced him in a bear hug that was so tight he could barely breathe. He had never seen his father so excited.

"Yeah, I can't believe we set a new record."

"*You* set a new record," Dad corrected.

"Listen, I need to meet up with the team and gather my stuff. I'll meet you at the exit to the parking lot in twenty minutes."

The whole team squeezed into their small dorm room and pushed through to slap the relay swimmers on the back. Finally, it was just the four of them.

"To us!" Andy raised a bottle, cross-legged in a sweat suit on the bed.

"To us!" repeated Chris, Tom, and Ben as they clinked their plastic bottles together and drank their blue electrolyte drinks exuberantly.

Ben gathered his few personal belongings into his swim bag. He'd lost some time when the finals concluded twenty minutes early. It was four p.m. "You guys will go all the way now." He zipped his bag and slapped the backs of Chris and Tom.

"You're leaving?" Andy leaped up from the bed, his face wrinkled in confusion.

"Come on, buddy. Don't act like this is a surprise. I've already checked the 'intent to scratch' box, and Coach will put in the first alternate."

"No one scratches when they've set a state record time!" Andy raised his arms over his head, shaking his hands in punctuated astonishment.

"Yeah, who would have thought…" Ben raised an eyebrow, slung the duffle bag over his shoulder, and headed to the parking lot to meet up with his father.

Coach Walker stood with Dad outside the entrance to the natatorium in intense conversation. They got silent and shifted when Ben approached.

"You don't want to do this." Coach Walker put a hand on Ben's shoulder.

"Come on!" Ben backed away and shook it off. "We've been all through this. On a Friday night in January, I offered to quit the team if this was a problem, and you said, 'No, we'll work it out.' Well, now is the time to 'work it out.' Your team is positioned for victory. Put in the first alternate—done!"

"Seize this opportunity, Ben. A state-ranked swimmer can get college scholarships. It could change the course of your life," Coach Walker implored.

"You're right about that." Ben's eyes were fixed upon him. "But not in the direction I've chosen. We've got to get going, Dad."

"Ben, I can't allow you to walk away from your commitment. This is part of being a man and living up to your responsibilities to others." Steven's car keys chinked in his hand as he selected the key to the emerald town car and walked away.

"Dad, we had an agreement!" Ben ran after him.

"That was before I had the full picture." Steven kept walking.

Ben was left standing alone in the parking lot. He couldn't believe his father would leave him. His brain froze, and his heart seemed to turn over. He was on his own. It was as though his vision were impaired and everything was out of focus. He heard his father drive away. He couldn't think. He realized he was holding his breath, and he exhaled. Suddenly, it dawned on him, and he understood he had been a fool, wanting something from his father that his father could not give.

He pushed some coins into the pay phone in the lobby of the aquatic center and dialed. It rang once, twice, three times, and thank God she answered.

"Grandma, it's me, Ben. I'm stranded at the swim meet in Rochester."

****

The taxi arrived at Grandma Ann's house minutes before Shabbos, and she paid the exorbitant fare. Ben was agitated and had no appetite. Both his grandmas, Nanci, and Rubie gathered and lit Sabbath candles, and a calm descended over them as the sun sank below the horizon. He thought he wouldn't be able to eat, but the savory aromas stirred his hunger. He was ravenous from the physical exertion and stress of the last twenty-four hours, and devoured two plates of brisket and potato kugel, before they spoke of it.

"Thanks for saving me. With no transportation or money, the only thing I could think of was to call you. I'm lucky I even had change for the pay phone."

"One of us would have come to get you, but there wasn't time to go round trip, especially on a Friday in rush hour traffic. What happened to your ride?" Grandma Ann asked.

"It left without me." Ben spoke in a flat tone of voice.

"But I thought your dad was going to be there?" Nanci said.

"He *was* at the prelim competition. When it was

over, at the agreed-upon time for us to leave, he told me that I couldn't walk away from my responsibility to the team and left me in the lurch." Ben rolled his eyes and saw Aunt Nanci exchanging disbelieving looks with Grandma Ann.

"I think I'd better put Rubie to bed." Nanci avoided looking at Ben and scooped Rubie into her arms.

Both Grandma Ann and Grandma Libby were silent and averted their eyes. Ben knew they would never bad-mouth his father.

Ben awoke refreshed, having slept soundly, and to Rubie's delight, he played with his little cousin all morning. At noon when Grandma brought the steaming Shabbat stew with meat, potatoes, and beans to the table, Ben thought about his teammates preparing for the big finals. He felt confident they would win the State Medley Relay Championship. They were each proficient in their stroke technique and had the endurance and race strategy required. He hoped for their success.

After lunch, Ben remained at the dining room table, deeply engaged in his 3-D puzzle. He'd solved the bottom and middle layer, had the yellow cross on top, and concentrated on the yellow corners, which was the remaining step to solve the final layer. He'd memorized the algorithm and repeated it now twice to get the colors on the side to match. He rotated right side down, bottom to the left, right side up, bottom to the right, right side down, bottom to the left, right side up, bottom to the right.

In the background, his left brain processed the triumph, pride, and anger he experienced over the last couple of days. His heart soared as he relived the victory of their heat. He could feel the water like velvet surround him and the cool air on his skin when his teammates raised him on their shoulders. The sting of betrayal and the burn of anger consumed him when he realized the collaboration of his father and his coach in double-crossing him. How could he not have anticipated their deception and trickery?

He felt different, older and a little bit wiser. He knew Coach Walker. He knew his father. He frowned with the awareness that he was naive to have expected anything different. He rotated the cube in his hands and smiled as he observed the matching colors on all six sides. The puzzle was solved. He'd scrambled each layer repeatedly, moving one piece out of the way to put the right one in place. He'd persevered and wished he could show his grandpa that he had figured it out.

"Congratulations, Ben!" Grandma sat across from Ben with a book in her lap. "I see you solved your puzzle."

Aunt Nanci and Rubie played on the living room floor.

"Pretty cool." Ben admired the cube. "Next Shabbat is my bar mitzvah, Grandma, and I'm torn about what to do. Every time I think I know, a voice in my head says *maybe not*."

"What is your struggle?" Grandma Ann leaned back in her chair and wrapped an afghan around her.

"Which way to go." Ben sighed. "Dad 'fixed' things at the temple, and I can still be called to the Torah even though I quit Mitzvah Day. They'll be expecting me, the friends and family from out of town. I could show up and go along with the program, the hypocrisy, do what I am told. Or I could follow my heart and go to the shul where I belong and read the holy words with my teacher."

"That's a tough one."

"I'm angry at Dad for deserting me yesterday. Part of me says, 'He didn't keep his agreement. Why should I keep mine?' But even I know this is about more than getting even."

"What is it about, Ben?"

"It's about being true to my purpose, standing up for what I believe, but what about my family?"

"Your family will always be your family."

"Dad says I have to honor my commitments, and that is exactly what I am doing, but he will never see it that way." He wrung his hands.

"I won't tell you what to do, Ben, but I trust that whatever decision you make will be the right one." Her eyes brightened, and he could see she believed in him with her heart and soul.

****

Shortly after three stars appeared in the sky and the Sabbath was over, the doorbell rang, and Ben answered. Coach Walker stood on Grandma's porch with his hands in his pockets.

"Your father told me I would find you here." He shuffled his feet and said nothing further, studying Ben's face with an inquisitive gaze.

"What's going on?" Ben cracked the storm door open.

"May I come in?" Coach held the door, and Ben nodded in agreement. Coach Walker stepped into the foyer and stood, shifting from one foot to the other. "There was a power outage, and the state championship meet was postponed until tomorrow. You don't have a problem swimming on Sundays, do you?"

Chapter Forty-Two—Prussian Blue

Loretto, Pennsylvania

Dr. Williams left an interoffice mailer for Ira in the infirmary. Inside was confirmation of Nicky's blood pressure meds for the dispensary and the lab report for the urine analysis. Ira eagerly scanned the lab report, and the blood drained from his face. "Holy crap," he said, and a chill crawled down his spine. *He's being poisoned.* Ira sat at the metal desk, studying the lab report and processing what it meant. *Of course, the "poisoner's poison," fairly untraceable, colorless, odorless, and tasteless. Slow-acting, painful with a wide range of symptoms pointing to a multitude of other illnesses and conditions—thallium, commonly known as rat poison.*

That was why Ira couldn't make sense of Nicky's symptoms. He raked his fingers through his hair and shook the loose strands off his hands. He guessed that rat poison was easy enough to come by in Loretto, and given the nightly banquets, it wouldn't be difficult for anyone to slip the poison into Nicky's food. But who in the don's family would betray him and bite the hand that fed him? Ira pressed a hand to his forehead to alleviate a throbbing headache. Nicky needed to be told and treated, and the hitman needed to be stopped.

Nicky shuffled into the infirmary and plopped into a metal chair. Meanwhile, Tony and Angelo hovered in the

292

hall. Ira closed the door.

"Your lab work came back." Ira sat across from Nicky. "The good news is I know what's wrong with you."

"I knew you would take care of me, Doc. What is it? You've got a treatment?" A smile spread across Nicky's ashen face.

"The lab work revealed dangerously high levels of poison in your system—thallium. There is an antidote, Prussian blue, which is a solid ion exchange material, that absorbs the thallium and passes it through the digestive system and out through the stool. I don't have it. You need to go to the hospital, Nicky. I wanted to tell you before I notify Dr. Williams and the administration."

"Doc, will I die without this antidote?"

"Yes."

"Then this is the second time you've saved my life."

"I suppose it is." Ira put a hand on Nicky's shoulder. "I have to tell you that you're not safe here."

"Wha' d'ya mean? You think someone poisoned me on purpose?"

"I do. This is no accident. Someone is trying to kill you."

Ira scrutinized each agitated member of the don's family as Nicky was wheeled to the ambulance on a stretcher. Angelo and Tony were equally upset and stared down at the other members of the family with vengeance in their eyes. They took the attack on Don Vece as an act of war and were set on avenging his honor. Ira sensed the undercurrent of hostility about to erupt in violence. The crowd dispersed, and Ira went back to the infirmary to review the levels of thallium in Nicky's urine, obsessed with Nicky's condition and anxious to assess the dosage of Prussian blue that would be required for treatment, even though he would not be the physician administering therapy. When he went back to his room, dog tired and ready to drop, he collided head-on with Matteo who was rushing out.

"I'm sorry, so sorry, Doc, wrong room." The agile progeny moved ahead undaunted, meaning business.

Ira lit up his second cigarette, awaiting the chaplain, Rabbi Berk, and took a deep drag. The short, spirited man in black hat, jacket, and long scraggly beard cut across the lounge, wearing a warm smile. Ira rose and extended a hand. The rabbi met him with a vigorous and enthusiastic handshake.

"Thank you, for coming, Rabbi, and thank you for all you've done for me since I've been here. I was thinking about things, and I hoped we could talk for a few minutes?"

"Of course—Rabbi Silverstein asked me to look after you and do whatever I can to help. How do you like the kosher meal program?" Rabbi Berk took the chair across from Ira at the round wooden table.

"Fine, better than the standard menu. That was one of the things I wanted to ask you about. Aside from tasting better, what exactly is the benefit?"

"Ever hear 'you are what you eat'? The Torah tells us that some foods are 'fit for use' while others are not. The energy we get from food can be elevated only if it is kosher. There are many practical explanations focusing on health and ethics, but keeping kosher is one of the commandments for which we are not given an explanation. Keeping kosher, because God instructed you to do so, can connect you to the divine."

"Does it work if I don't think about it?"

"It works better if you do think about it." Rabbi Berk grinned. "Just like thinking about your wife when you do something for her connects you to her."

"That makes sense." Ira nodded in agreement. "There's something else I wanted to talk to you about. I've been thinking about what I did that landed me in prison. I've got a dark side, Rabbi. I was driven to make more money with no concern for the immense suffering, misery, and sorrow of countless people," he murmured, his eyes downcast.

"You're right, you do have a dark side. We call it the evil inclination. But don't think you're special. We've all got it." A sudden look of compassion crossed Rabbi Berk's face. "And you have an equally strong desire to do good. The sages tell us that our only free will is the ability to choose good or evil."

"How can I get rid of it?" Ira looked at him with slight surprise in his eyes.

"You can't get rid of your evil inclination. You can learn to resist it, and it will become less active, but you can never let down your guard," he replied, not a vestige of humor showing on his face.

Ira needed to talk to Nanci. The gaps and delays in communication were agonizing. He yearned to hear her voice and know that she and Rubie were safe. The monthly limits on talking time and the long lines at the bank of phones translated into unbearable communication blackouts. Dead tired, he returned to his room to rest with a vow to return later when the lines were shorter.

Elbows on his knees, he supported his forehead in the palms of his hands when he noticed bright-red droplets of blood dripping onto his slacks. His nose was bleeding. He sat upright, grabbed a tissue, pinched his nose, and leaned forward while breathing through his mouth, trying to prevent blood from draining down the back of his throat. He was already nauseous. His mind was racing repetitively through the symptoms that Nicky had reported, certain that nosebleeds were among them. Ira never in his life recalled having a nosebleed. *God, I'm a terrible doctor when it comes to taking care of myself. I smoke and drink too much coffee and don't remember the last time I had a physical exam. I should have been paying attention, if not for myself, for my family. My children should not have to grow up without a father. Where was I when Rubie took her first steps? What was her first word?* Why did he not remember these milestones?

He shuddered when he admitted that those events did not seem significant at the time. Such mundane developments were allocated no head space. And now, what was her favorite bedtime story, comfort object, video cartoon? What was her favorite color? He did not know. He made a vow to himself that he would be there, both in body and soul, for his family.

After twenty minutes of applying continuous pressure to his nose, when the bleeding had not stopped, he staggered to the infirmary, procured an ice pack, and placed it on the back of his neck to constrict the blood vessels and reduce the bleeding. The cold cleared his head. The bleeding was severe, not normal, and Ira was light-headed. The anticoagulant rodenticide effectively eliminated the rat population by causing the animal to bleed out internally and externally. He picked up the house phone, which rang to the switchboard. "This is Ira Rosen in the camp. I need an ambulance in the infirmary right away."

"Who is the patient, and what is the medical emergency?"

"I am the patient," he said, dropping his head. "I've been poisoned." He felt light-headed as the blood drained from his face.

****

"Knock, knock." Sydney Blackwell flashed the guards visitor passes for himself and Rabbi Berk and pushed open the door to Ira's hospital room. "Dr. Rosen, are you up to having visitors?" Sydney Blackwell was a large presence at six feet four inches tall, towering over the rabbi, even with his fedora hat.

"Sydney, Rabbi." Ira smiled, surprised. "Don't mind the blue teeth." He boosted himself up in the hospital bed and adjusted his gown carefully around the tubes in his body. An IV in his right arm was for hemoperfusion, and dangling from his neck was a tunneled permcath for daily hemodialysis, both processes to expedite removal of the thallium.

"How are you feeling?" The rabbi went to Ira's bedside, and Sydney Blackwell stood at the foot of the bed, assessing Ira's countenance.

"Glad to be on the top side of the grass." Ira smiled weakly. "How is Don Vece?"

"He's also recovering, but one of the inmates at the camp, Matteo, had a fatal accident. Did you know him?"

Ira had a flashback of running into Matteo on his last day at the camp. Matteo had been rushing furtively out of his room. "Yeah, I knew him." His voice shook, betraying his horror.

"I'm so sorry you've had to go through this." The rabbi's face crinkled in concern. "Your family is on their

297

way."

Sydney rested a hand on Ira's arm. "Ira, this never should have happened to you and reflects gross negligence. You clearly are in danger at this facility, and believe me, we will get to the bottom of this and find out who is responsible. The rabbi and I met with the state parole board this morning in a hearing concerning a motion for your early release. The rabbi served as your representative and provided testimony that was very influential in the decision of the parole board."

"That was today?" Ira raised an eyebrow questioningly.

"Given the circumstances, we made a case for an expedited hearing. The rabbi presented a persuasive case that you posed no threat to society, would successfully integrate into the community, and had demonstrated a deep remorse and unusual transformation of character." A smile tugged at the corners of Sydney Blackwell's mouth.

"Did they make a decision?" Ira's head was spinning. He could hardly think straight. This was the last thing he expected.

"The board agreed with the argument that you could make a far greater contribution to the public good outside of incarceration and granted the motion for your early release with six months of obligatory community service at a drug rehabilitation center. Further, Dr. Williams has volunteered to be the first of three MDs needed to recommend reinstatement of your medical license. While it is unlikely it will be reinstated without restrictions, there is a process, albeit it lengthy and rigorous, to have your license restored." Sydney's mouth stretched into a wide grin, and his eyes sparkled.

"Does this mean I'm not going back?" Heat rushed into Ira's cheeks. A lump and a sob caught in his throat.

"Do you have a suit for your nephew's bar mitzvah?" The rabbi winked and rested a hand on Ira's shoulder.

Chapter Forty-Three—Rite of Passage

Southwood, Michigan

Throughout the night Ben wrestled an invisible adversary. A succession of images, thoughts, and emotions swept over him, like wind and waves, as he struggled in the tangled sheets. The impressions weren't dreams, that would have required him to have been asleep, and he had never been more awake. When the light of dawn broke, he bolted upright in bed, his head pounding. He imagined himself in a pressure cooker, the increasing weight of an unseen object exerting force upon him, squeezing him from all directions.

He splashed water on his face, dressed in his new blue suit, and sat on the bed, holding and inspecting his newest trophy from the state championship meet. He flicked some of Luna's hair from his trousers; he missed walking her since Andy had assumed his regular routine again.

"Ben." His father knocked on the bedroom door. "We're leaving now. Are you sure you don't want a ride?"

"I'm good." Ben returned the trophy to its place and tried to get the knot right on his tie.

"Okay, then we'll see you at the temple."

He heard his father's footsteps recede down the staircase and the grinding of the electric garage door open and then close a few minutes later.

He drank a glass of orange juice and ate a cinnamon bun topped with white icing. He still couldn't shake his father's final words before leaving him in the parking lot at the swim meet last week. *Son, I can't allow you to walk away from your commitment.* He realized that they did not see eye to eye about Ben's commitments, and Ben knew now that his father couldn't support him. All his life his values had been defined through his father's eyes. Since he was a small boy, he'd looked to his father for approval and believed he was the strongest, smartest, and most trustworthy. At that moment the scales fell from Ben's eyes, and he accepted that he couldn't rely upon his father's judgment. He needed to trust himself and his own truth.

The doorbell startled him. *Who could that be?*

"Uncle Ira! Wow, I wasn't expecting you." Ben embraced his uncle in a bear hug.

"I dropped the others at the temple and thought you might want someone to walk with," he said supportively.

"I'd given up hope that you would be here today." Ben closed the front door to the house behind them, and they strode down the walk.

"So did I. I'm still not entirely sure how it came about, but I wanted to spend some time with you before things got crazy later. Nanci's been filling me in on everything that's been going on. Oh, and congrats on that state championship!" Uncle Ira slapped Ben on the back and stepped into sync with him, conforming to his nephew's cadence.

"Actually, I'm not entirely sure how that worked out. You probably heard that I don't swim on Saturday anymore—"

"Or drive," his uncle interrupted and flashed an acknowledging smile as they took synchronized steps.

"Well, yeah, that too. Suffice it to say, it was very unlikely I'd have been able to compete, but there was a snowstorm, a bus accident, and a power outage, and at the end of the day, the state meet was rescheduled for Sunday."

"Million-to-one chance."

"Sometimes, though, odds come through."

"I know what you mean. What I want to say is I think I understand what you're going through, and I just wanted to offer my help if there's anything I can do."

Ben stopped on the pavement in front of the shul. "Uncle Ira, you don't know how much that means to me. I really appreciate your support, because I'm truly going to need it." He looked up at the red-brick house that Rabbi Silverstein had converted to a shul. "This is my stop."

"Isn't the temple down the next block?" Ira raised an inquisitive eyebrow.

"That's right, you can't miss it." Ben extended his right hand halfway toward Ira, their hands locked, and he firmly shook up and down several times before loosening his hold.

Ira was slow to release Ben. His eyes flicked over him, and he placed his left hand on top of Ben's, gripping him warmly with a two-handed handshake. He gazed at him intently for a moment before turning away.

Fear gripped Ben's heart, its fingers reaching into his blood and his nervous system releasing cortisol and adrenaline, increasing his blood pressure and heart rate. His senses heightened, preparing to respond to a threat. Panic rose up, spreading in a mission to dominate and prevent his ability to think. He got ahold of himself, looked around, saw no danger, and suppressed the panic. He could do this. He would do this. *Grandpa, I understand now. Please be with me today.* He pulled open the door to the shul and prepared to honor his commitment.

****

"What do you mean he's not coming?" Steven's whisper developed into a loud hiss like a bobcat scaring off a predator.

Anna motioned for Steven to follow her out of the sanctuary into the large lobby with tall stained-glass windows that reached the height of the thirty-foot ceiling. They settled into a pair of upholstered armchairs in the newly furnished sitting area.

"Ira says he knows where he is." She smoothed the front of her dress.

"What the hell is going on?" Steven rocketed out of his chair. Irritation and impatience shone in his eyes.

"Your son is becoming a man, Steven. This is his day. Let's go to him, all of us."

"I'll be damned if I'm going to capitulate to this madness." He paced wildly.

"Sit down and let's talk about it." Anna's voice was soothing. "This isn't like you, Steven. How about you tell me what's going on? Why have you gotten into this power struggle with Ben over his bar mitzvah?"

Steven paced a couple more laps across the lobby before he sat, elbows on his knees, and cleared his throat. "When I was growing up, we lived down the block from Precious Blood School. Every Monday and Wednesday afternoon, the Hebrew school bus dropped me off at the corner. I'd run home as fast as I could while the neighborhood kids chased me, threw rocks, and called me names I didn't even comprehend. The Polish woman down the street turned her garden hose on me and called me a 'kite' when I came to play with her son. I asked my father why she would call me a 'kite.' And he explained she was calling me a 'kike' not a 'kite,' basically a dirty Jew. When my father put a *Happy Hanukkah* sign in our picture window, I begged him to take it down and told him he was marking me for death."

Anna swallowed the bitter taste in her mouth and listened to Steven as he continued.

"I chose this neighborhood so we could safely practice our Judaism in a normal way and be free from persecution and prejudice. Now my son wants to be more Jewish? If Ben starts walking around looking and acting like an orthodox rabbi, I won't be able to protect him. He'll stand out like a sore thumb and draw attention to his Jewishness. He doesn't know the repercussions because I have protected him from all of that. It's my obligation to protect him, to teach him how to blend in."

Anna felt his wounds of trauma imprinted upon his soul, a deep laceration surrounded by lesions of insult and anguish. "I understand. I guarantee you, Steven, that the Nazis did not differentiate which synagogue a Jew belonged to. Someone has always been trying to kill us, and hiding has never been the answer," she said.

Without warning the well-guarded scars within her awakened and opened the floodgates of torment and persecution that she'd kept tightly sealed. She was in Weisman's Meat on Piekna Strasse, preparing for the rescheduled vort and the pre-Shabbat rush of customers, when she heard the jingle of the bell on the front door, the bang of the shop door closing, and the distinct tromp of Cossacks' boots on the scarred floor. Her emotions were running high with the anticipation of the engagement ceremony and celebration at the shul Saturday evening. By the grace of God, and a bit of sugar and salt mixed in water, Chana had fully recovered from cholera. At the sound of the bell, she peeked out of the smokehouse where she was selecting choice meats for the celebration. She caught a glimpse of Cossacks with rifles standing on either side of her tatty at the chopping block.

"Weisman, you never disappoint me. Despite your woes and tribulations, again you have meat when there is none to be found." Commandant Aleksandrov pressed a filthy finger into the red meat on Tatty's butcher block. He smiled when it quickly sprang back, a sign of freshness. He caught Chana's gaze as she peered into the shop, and his smile broadened. "How fortunate, the finest delicacy of all is available today!"

A hand of fear clutched Chana's heart as she remembered the night Aleksandrov had taken Sora. The tentacles of panic rose within her, and a wave of dread flooded and consumed her. Where to hide? Where to be safe? She froze, not knowing.

"You'll wrap up those cuts of meat for my comrades who will load them into the wagon." He strutted behind the counter and prodded at lamb and chicken hanging from wooden pegs in the wall. "Load all this meat into the wagon," Aleksandrov directed his men, who jumped to attention and responded instantly to the command.

As the comrades carried lamb and chickens to the wagon, Aleksandrov strode to the smokehouse where Chana had taken shelter. He kicked in the door, searched the corners, and slid his gaze up and down her form, stopping his gaze at her breasts. He was on her in a flash, breathing the stench of alcohol and tobacco in her face, forcing her back against the wall. He ripped off her white butcher's apron, tore open her dress, and groped her. "While this is not the proper venue, this will have to do." He forced his mouth on hers.

She squeezed her eyes closed, shocked and willing herself to disappear, inhaling the smell of sweat and gunpowder that enveloped her. *Make him stop, please God, make him stop. Keep me for Mo*, she prayed.

Suddenly, his head snapped back. Her father restrained Aleksandrov in a full-body hold, stretching and twisting his neck with wild strength. Aleksandrov's muscle and fury flared as they struggled and shuffled across the floorboards, each one holding the other in a headlock. Her father rotated to loosen Aleksandrov's grip, and they were positioned back to back, each attempting to trip the other with his footwork. With one hand on the top of Aleksandrov's head and the other on his chin for leverage, her father pushed against the floor and used the violent might of his torso, pressing until the torque fractured Aleksandrov's neck. Chana heard the crack, saw Aleksandrov's eyes bulge, and witnessed the howl of pain before he went limp in near instant death.

Tears rose up in her eyes. She reached out for her tatty, near hysteria, her heart beating wildly. A sob strangled in her throat. She threw herself into her tatty's arms and held fast to his love and protection. He kissed the top of her head repeatedly, then she heard the shop door bang closed as the bell rang again.

Her father released her from his embrace and dragged Aleksandrov's body into the slaughterhouse. "Stay here until I come for you," he had instructed Chana in a hushed tone, wrapping her in a wool blanket, securely closing the latch on the smokehouse door.

"I know how you feel, Steven. I felt the same way. When I came to America, I set my mind that I would *not* be a greenhorn. I changed my name, the way I dressed, whatever I needed to do to blend in. It was the only thing Mo and I argued about. I thought that the answer was to quickly assimilate and be American first. Slowly, we moved further away from our authentic Jewish way of life, and we became comfortable. I hoped to protect my children and assure their survival and success in America, and we almost succeeded. What I didn't expect, and I've only really become aware of since Mo's passing, are the sacrifices we made and the realization that we lost out and deprived our children of the richness that Judaism brought to our life.

"Then your son, my grandson, awakened with a fire for something more than the watered-down Judaism he was offered. He wanted something deeper. While this synagogue gave Ben a foundation, he is seeking a traditional authentic interpretation and practice. For Ben, this is not enough. Ben is strong. He stands up for what he knows to be right and true, despite the consequences. Steven, how many of us are willing to do that? He has an old, wise soul. Protect him, support him, don't punish him and try to destroy him. I promise you he will make you proud."

Steven put his face in his hands and sobbed. "I am already proud."

****

Chana sat in the front row of the modest women's section of the shul, her daughter Aliza next to her on one side and her sister Sora and machutaneste, Libby, settled

next to her on the other. Nanci slid in beside Aliza, they
held one another's hands, and suddenly, Nanci placed a
hand on her rounded abdomen. *Did she feel the flutter of
life within her?* Estie withdrew to the back of the shul,
pouting. Chana was not blind to her increased irritability
and tendency to get annoyed over small things. *She did
not inherit those qualities from her namesake.*

On the men's side, Steven, Ira, and Aaron filed in
and took empty seats in the row where Ben sat waiting
to be called to the Torah. Rabbi Silverstein greeted them
warmly when they arrived and shook each of their hands.
Howard trailed behind, smiling broadly, and Ben's jaw
dropped at the sight of them all. Though the men had
little time for greetings, they nodded with the glint of
surprise in their wide eyes. At that moment Ben was
called to the Torah by his full Hebrew name. He covered
his head with his prayer shawl, kissed the scroll, and
recited the blessing.

Chana recollected the beit midrash in Siedlce the
night of the vort. Mo had dressed in fine woolen
garments, strikingly handsome with a shadow of concern
creasing his forehead. She'd worn a satin forest-green
ball gown, courtesy of the Pruss sisters. What was
originally intended only as an engagement ceremony
was transformed with the help of the community over the
course of the afternoon into a full marriage ceremony
under a chuppah, under the stars. She recalled the tight
hold of her parents' hands as they led her, while she was
veiled, seven times around her bridegroom. The goblet
of sweet red wine she and Mo drank from was broken,
and wild shouts of *mazal tov* rang into the darkness. The
following morning, with unprecedented urgency and
euphoria, children, parents, and in-laws packed their

most cherished worldly possessions, loaded wagons, and departed for the Holland-America steamship docks in Rotterdam, Holland. Chana's heart had soared. They were going to America!

Anna watched Ben roll the Torah scrolls apart and touch the fringes of his prayer shawl to the place where the reading began. He chanted the holy words with precise enunciation and the proper tunes just as she remembered her tatty had done in their beit midrash in Siedlce.

"It is customary to honor the relatives of the bar mitzvah boy by calling them to the Torah," Rabbi Silverstein addressed the small congregation. He spoke directly to Ben's family. "Due to Ben's tremendous dedication and hard work over the past months, he has the skills to read the text straight from the Torah parchment, an extraordinary accomplishment. He will have the honor of being our Torah Reader today. Family members, please come to the pulpit when you are called by your Hebrew name and the name of your father to recite the blessings. Steven Friedman, Melech ben Binyomin." The rabbi extended a hand to Steven, whose face was somber. "Let us remember for a moment the grandfather Binyomin for whom our bar mitzvah boy was named. Without doubt, he is with us today."

Libby shed tears when the rabbi pronounced the Hebrew names of her son and her late husband, which had not been uttered for decades. Aliza reached for her mother-in-law's hand. One after another the men were called and gathered around Ben at the Torah.

When Rabbi Silverstein called, "Eera ben Mordechai," and extended a hand to Ira, a stillness fell over the room. Chana felt a breeze pass over her and a lump at the back of her throat. She wiped the tears from her face with a tissue. Mo had named their son Eera, meaning watchful one, after one of King David's mighty warriors. A shiver ran like a ghostly touch over her skin. She felt that Mo was there.

They'd reached the docks in Rotterdam after two days of travel, only slightly worse for wear. Still exuberant from the joy of the wedding and anticipating their journey to America, Chana had to pinch herself to make sure she wasn't dreaming. Tatty brought the wagon to the checkpoint on the pier where luggage was hoisted to the deck. On May 29, 1915, her father presented the family's steamship passage tickets for the *TSS Nieuw Amsterdam*, crossing from Rotterdam to New York, to the steward. It would be one of the last Holland America ships sailing to America until the end of the war. That was when Chana learned they were clear to board, all of them, except Tatty. He'd been called to report for a third draft, and he could not obtain papers. She was blindsided by this development. Perhaps, if she were not so absorbed in her wedding, she would have recalled the many warnings of this very eventuality.

"Tatty, I cannot go without you," Chana cried.

"Of course you must." Tatty wrapped her in his arms. "You are my future. Promise me you will raise your children on the foundations of Torah." She kissed his face, he wiped her tears, she promised, and she'd never seen him again.

"Mazal tov, mazal tov! *L'chaim* to the Friedman and Rosen families!" Rabbi Silverstein recited a blessing, drank a goblet of wine, and passed a tray of shot-size cups filled with wine around the small, homey shul. They gathered around a long table with marble cake, seven-layer cake, and herring. Aliza and Steven stood next to Ben, Chana hugged him from behind, and Libby, Nanci, and the others huddled close.

Ben leaned in and said, "Dad, I just want you and Mom to know that I'll go to the party tomorrow." He spoke under the din of the room.

"That's not necessary now." His father draped an arm around him.

"I know you and Mom went to a lot of expense and planning…"

"It's not all-important, Ben. It's your day. If *you* want to go, we'll all go to the party. If you don't, we'll celebrate the way you choose."

Ben was radiant. Aliza and Steven wrapped their arms around his waist, and a wild pink color washed into their faces. Howard grinned and called, "*Mazal tov*," as he downed a cup of wine and helped himself to a second piece of seven-layer cake. He put a piece on a napkin and took it to Estie, who had drifted nearer and accepted with a smile.

Ben cleared his throat and got everyone's attention. The room was dauntingly quiet.

"I want to especially thank my mother and father for being here today. Actually, I didn't expect any of you were going to be here when I read from the Torah for the first time. It means a lot to me." He looked at the expectant faces of his family gazing at him and paused.

"We are told that the day the Torah was given, our people were one. The fact that all of you are here today proves that is still true. I know now that whatever happens, however difficult or disappointing or painful, it will never change the fact that we will always be connected and here for each other.

"I owe a special thanks to every person here today, mainly my grandma Ann who is always in my corner. I am also grateful to those who could not be here physically, like my grandpa Mo and my great-grandpa Dovid from Siedlce, who are also here in spirit."

Chana's eyes misted with tears. She stepped forward, dropped a kiss on Ben's cheek, and whispered, "I am the one who is grateful for you."

Glossary

Beit midrash—House of Learning. While distinct from a synagogue, the two are often the same place

Bar mitzvah—religious initiation ceremony of a Jewish boy who has reached the age of thirteen and is regarded as ready to observe religious precepts and take part in a quorum for worship

Baruch dayan ha'emet—Blessed is the True Judge. Traditional phrase recited upon hearing of the death of an immediate relative to express grief

Chassidus—movement founded in 1734 by Rabbi Yisroel (Israel) Baal Shem Tov incorporating mystical concepts of the Kabala, teaching everyone at their level how to understand these concepts and use them to build a personal, loving relationship with God, approaching the study and observance of Judaism with greater depth and vibrant enthusiasm

Cheder—a school for Jewish children in which Hebrew and religious knowledge are taught

Chuppah—a marriage canopy under which the couple stands during the ceremony representing the new home they will build together

Kippah—another term for yarmulke or skullcap, a brimless cap for men, usually made of cloth, to fulfill the customary requirement that the head be covered out of respect for God

Naches—pleasure, delight, pride, and gratification, especially at the achievements of one's children and grandchildren

Machatunim—co-mothers-in-law, co-grandmothers, two women who are mothers-in-law to each other's children

Mama—mother

Mensch—person of integrity and honor

Shochet—one trained in ritual kosher slaughter

Tatty—father

Tzitzit—fringes or tassels on garments worn by Jewish males as a reminder of the commandments

Upshern/Upshernish—a haircutting ceremony held when a Jewish boy turns three years old

Anna's Promise
Reading Group Questions

What leads Ben to the path he chooses?

Anna's Promise portrays a core-to-core culture confrontation. What are the differences between Chassidic and Reformed Jewish thought responsible for the conflict?

One of the central themes of the book is assimilation. Can you point to areas in your life where you have chosen to assimilate? Why or why not?

Looking at your family over several generations, has assimilation influenced who your family is today? How?

Do you think assimilation makes for a better society?

Ben and his father have different opinions about Ben's responsibilities and obligations when it comes to participating in the swim meets and competition on Saturday. Can you explain why and how they differ?

Do you believe Ben met his obligations? Why or why not?

How does Ira's journey echo Ben's journey? What do Ben and Ira learn from one another?

Why do you think the book is called *Anna's Promise?* Should the title be *Chana's Promise*?

A word about the author…

D.G. Schulman is a publishing executive who married the boy next door and lives in the Midwest where she and her husband raised their two daughters. She is a night owl who loves to write fiction into the wee hours of the morning. When she's not in front of a keyboard, she enjoys making chocolate, growing herbs, cooking, reading, and spending time with her married children and growing brood of grandkids.

~*~

Find D.G. online at:
https://dgschulman.com/
dgschulman@gmail.com
https://twitter.com/DGSchulman
https://www.facebook.com/dvora.schulman
https://www.instagram.com/DGSchulmanAuthor

Printed in the USA
CPSIA information can be obtained
at www.ICGtesting.com
LVHW050908151023
761140LV00008B/338

9 781509 247011